Designing Brand Identity

Published by John Wiley & Sons, Inc., Hoboken, New Jersey
Published simultaneously in Canada

For general information on our other products and services or for technical support, please contact our Customer Care Department within the United States at (800) 762-2974, outside the United States at (317) 572-3993 or fax (317) 572-4002.

Wiley also publishes its books in a variety of electronic formats. Some content that appears in print may not be available in electronic books. For more information about Wiley products, visit our web site at www.wiley.com.

Library of Congress Cataloging-in-Publication Data:

Wheeler, Alina
   Designing brand identity: a complete guide to creating, building and maintaining
        strong brands / by Alina Wheeler.—2nd ed.

   p. cm.
   Includes bibliographical references and index.
   ISBN 13: 978-0-471-74684-3 (cloth)
   ISBN 10: 0-471-74684-3 (cloth)

   1. Brand name products. 2. Brand name products—Marketing—Management. 3.
   Trademarks—Design. 4. Advertising—Brand name products. I. Title.
HD69.B7W44 2006
658.8'27—dc22   2005056961

Printed in the United States of America

10 9 8 7 6 5 4 3 2

Alina Wheeler

Designing
Brand
Identity

A complete guide to creating, building,
and maintaining strong brands

WILEY

John Wiley & Sons, Inc.

Because it didn't exist. Fascination.

On my bookshelf are brilliant books about brand strategy and exquisite books about the history of trademarks. I believe that a different kind of resource is needed to guide people through the process of creating a sustainable, differentiated brand identity. Fascination was another driving force—I am fascinated by how organizations and individuals express their identity and aspirations.

This book is dedicated to the individuals and teams behind the brand, and to the brand champions who go unnoticed as they define and express brands that astonish and delight.

Cingular Wireless: VSA Partners

No one does it alone.

To my husband who kept me laughing, and to my daughters who kept me smiling.

Thank you to my colleagues who shared their time + wisdom and who believed in this book.

Meejoo Kwon
Bart Crosby
Joel Katz
Steff Geissbuhler
Chris Pullman
Per Mollerup
Davis Masten
Susan Avarde
Paula Scher
Alan Siegel
Michael Cronan
Sylvia Harris
Marty Neumeier
Joel Grear
Ronnie Lipton
Ken Carbone
Nancye Greene
Chris Hacker
Hilary Jay
Michael Bierut
Kit Hinrichs
Laura DesEnfants
Joe Duffy
Dana Arnett
Hans-U. Allemann
Stephen Shackleford
Heidi Cody
Howard Fish
Ian Stephens
Pamela Thompson
Jack Cassidy
Sean Adams
Jack Summerford
Becky Wingate
Erich Sippel
Gael Towey
Phil Gatto
Geoff Verney
Clay Timon
Colin Drummond
Carla Hall
Richard Felton

Al Ries
Brian Tierney
John Coyne
John Hildenbiddle
Alan Brew
Jessica Berwind
Larry Keeley
Sean Haggerty
Joe Pine
Donna MacFarland
Dean Crutchfield
Steve Frykholm
Fo Wilson
Marius Ursache
Parag Murudkar
Sally Hudson
Louise Fili
Moira Cullen
Jamie Koval
DK Holland
Jody Friedman
Karin Hibma
Nate Eimer
Woody Pirtle
Richard Saul Wurman
Andrew Welsh
Mike Reinhardt
Linda Wingate
Stephen Doyle
Milton Glaser
Mindy Romero
Deborah Perloe
Meredith Nierman
Rob Wallace
Monica Little
Stephen Sapka
Sagi Haviv
J.T. Miller
Cathy Feierstein
Andrew Cutler
Ned Drew
Tom Geismar
Lori Kapner
Kurt Monigle
Malcolm Grear
Mike Reinhardt
Alan Jacobson

Dr. Delyte Frost
Dr. Barbara Riley
Rich Bacher
Colleen Newquist
Dr. Dennis Dunn
John Klotnia
Dr. Ginny Vanderslice
Marilyn Sifford
Dr. Karol Wasylyshyn
Ed Williamson
Q Cassetti
Ivan Chermayeff
Dick Ritter
Robbin Phillips
Kathleen Hatfield
Joan Carlson
Bob Warkulwiz
Gillian Wallis
Amanda Neville
Jaeho Ko
Pat Baldridge
Rosemary Murphy
Jenie De'Ath
Le Roux Jooste
Linda Matthhiesen
Lisa Kovitz
Marc Mikulich
Margie Gorman
Betty Nelson
Richard Kauffman
Mike Schacherer
Brad Kear
David Kendall
Jayoung Jaylee
Roger Whitehouse
Cortney Cannon
Albert Cassorla
Anne Moses
Steve Storti
Emily Cohen
Sunny Hong
Tom Watson
Trish Thompson
Bob Mueller
Arnold Miller
Scott Tattar
Tom Birk
R. Jacobs-Meadway

Peter Emery
Peggy Calabrese
Bonita Albertson
Jeffrey Gorder
Matthew Bartholomew
Kate Fitzgibbon
Steve Perry
Steve Sandstrom
Mary Sauers
Russ Napolitano
Stefan Liute
Charlene O'Grady
Cherise Davis
Lee Soonmee
Nancy Donner
Trisha Davidson
Michael Hirschhorn
Sarah Brinkman
Katie Wharton
Pat Duci
Dan Marcolina
Brian Fingeret
Ginnie Gehshan
Jerry Selber
Katie Caldwell
John Kerr
Melinda Lawson
Jim Bittetto
Kate Dautrich
Gerry Stankus
Jen Jagielski
Kent Hunter
Bruce Berkowitz
Melissa Lapid
Michael Donovan
Joanne Chan
Peter Wise
Aubrey Balkind
Maribel Nix
Marie Morrison
Mark Selikson
David Rose
Janice Fudyma
Craig Bernhardt
Helen Keyes
Jinal Shah
Kurt Koepfle
Ellen Shapiro
Michael Grillo
Heather Guidice

Dream team

Thank you for your creativity + brilliance

Lissa Reidel,
strategic advisor

Stella Gassaway,
visionary + creative principal
Stellarvisions

Margaret Anderson,
managing principal
Stellarvisions

Amy Grove Bigham,
thinker + designer

Jessica Robles Worch,
research

Tomasz Fryzel,
cover design +
grid + color bars

Mary Storm-Baranyai +
Gretchen Dykstra,
precision

Blake Deutsch,
consultant

Perpetual gratitude

Suzanne Young,
editor first edition
Mark Wills,
designer of my identity
Heather Norcini
Marc Goldberg
Liz Merrill
Chris Marshall
My favorite cousin
Uncle Stanley
All of the Wheelers
Cathy Jooste
Richard Cress
Dave Luck, Mac Daddy
My brother who asked when the film is coming out
Marie Taylor

My publishing team at Wiley:
Amanda Miller, VP + publisher
Margaret Cummins, senior editor
Justin Mayhew, senior marketing manager
Diana Cisek, production director

Contents

All subject matter is organized
by spread for easy accessibility.

Designing Brand Identity is an essential reference book. It describes a disciplined process to create and implement an effective brand identity. Its goals are to establish a common process and shared vocabulary for the entire branding team, and to support best practices.

Part 1 illuminates the difference between brand and brand identity, and what it takes to be the best. It's easy to bypass the fundamentals in the speed of a new project, and critical to establish a shared vocabulary for the entire branding team.

Process

Part 2 presents a universal identity process that underlies all successful brand identity initiatives, regardless of the project's scope and nature. This section answers the question "Why does it take so long?" and addresses collaboration and decision making.

Practice

Part 3 showcases best practices. Local and global, public and private, these highly successful projects, created by branding firms, design consultancies and in-house creative teams, inspire and exemplify original, flexible, lasting solutions.

1 Perception

Part 1 illuminates the difference between brand and brand identity, and what it takes to be the best. It's easy to bypass the fundamentals in the speed of a new project, and critical to establish a shared vocabulary for the entire branding team.

Image and perception help drive value; without an image there is no perception.

Scott M. Davis
Brand Asset Management

Since the beginning of time, the need to communicate has emerged from a set of universal questions: Who am I? Who needs to know? Why do they need to know? How will they find out? How do I want them to respond? Individuals, communities, and organizations express their individuality through their identity. On the continuum from the cave paintings at Lascaux to digital messages transmitted via satellite, humanity continues to create an infinite sensory palette of visual and verbal expression.

Humanity has always used symbols to express fierce individuality, pride, loyalty, and ownership. The power of symbols remains elusive and mysterious—a simple form can instantaneously trigger recall and arouse emotion, whether it is emblazoned on a flag, etched in stone, or on the screen of your cell phone. The velocity of life in the future will demand that brands leverage the power of symbols.

Competition for recognition is as ancient as the heraldic banners on a medieval battlefield. No longer limited by physical terrain, managing perception now extends to the airwaves, cyberspace, and beyond. As feudal domains became economic enterprises, what was once heraldry is now branding. The battle for physical territory has evolved into the competition for share of mind.

Battle for territory has evolved into competition for share of mind.

We have smaller spaces and less time to tell our stories.

Who are you?
Who needs to know?
How will they find out?
Why should they care?

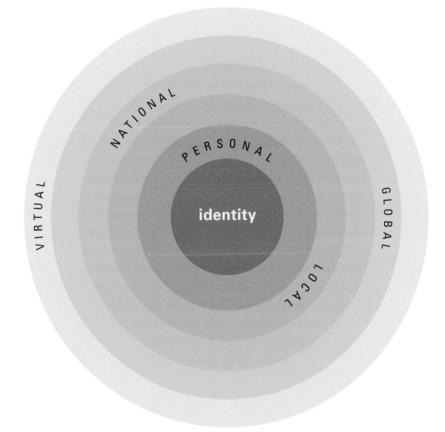

**It is never too late to be
what you could have been.**
George Eliot

Brand is the promise, the big idea, and the expectations that reside in each customer's mind about a product, service, or company. People fall in love with brands, trust them, develop strong loyalties to them, buy them, and believe in their superiority. The brand is shorthand. It stands for something.

Branding used to be the exclusive purview of big consumer products. Now every business talks about the brand imperative, and even individuals are challenged by Tom Peters, management guru, to become walking brands. Why have brands become so important? Bottom line: good brands build companies. Ineffective brands undermine success. As products and services become indistinguishable, as competition creates infinite choices, as companies merge into faceless monoliths, differentiation is imperative.

While being remembered is essential, it is becoming harder every day. A strong brand stands out in a densely crowded marketplace. Translating the brand into action has become an employee mantra. There is substantial evidence that companies whose employees understand and embrace the brand are more successful. What began as corporate culture under the auspices of human resources is fast becoming branding, and the marketing department runs the show.

Products are created in the factory. Brands are created in the mind.

Walter Landor, Founder
Landor Associates

**Brand is not what you say it is.
It is what they say it is.**

Marty Neumeier
The Brand Gap

Brand has entered everyone's lexicon. The term is a chameleon: meaning can change with context. Sometimes it is a noun, as in "That's my brand of choice," and sometimes a verb, as in "Let's brand this campaign." Brand has become synonymous with the name of the company and its reputation.

Brands are embedded in our daily lives, as in "Let's FedEx it to Chattanooga" or "Just do it." The work of Andy Warhol and Heidi Cody reminds us of the omnipresent power of brands as cultural symbols. Even those who do not precisely know what a brand is want one.

Brand touchpoints

Each touchpoint is an opportunity to strengthen a brand and to communicate its essence.

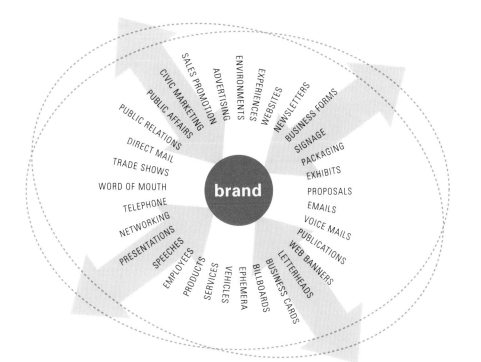

In a world that is bewildering in terms of competitive clamour, in which rational choice has become almost impossible, brands represent clarity, reassurance, consistency, status, membership— everything that enables human beings to help define themselves. Brands represent identity.

Wally Olins
On Brand

Brand is the nucleus of sales and marketing activities, generating increased awareness and loyalty when managed strategically.

A brand is a "trust mark." It's shorthand. It's a sorting device.

Tom Peters
Brand You

While brands speak to the mind and heart, brand identity is tangible and appeals to the senses. Brand identity is the visual and verbal expression of a brand. Identity supports, expresses, communicates, synthesizes, and visualizes the brand. You can see it, touch it, hold it, hear it, watch it move. It begins with a brand name and a brandmark and evolves into a matrix of tools and communications. Brand identity increases awareness and builds businesses.

The need for effective brand identity cuts across public and private sectors, from new companies, to merged organizations, to businesses that need repositioning.

The best brand identity systems are memorable, authentic, meaningful, differentiated, sustainable, flexible, and add value. Recognition becomes immediate across cultures and customs.

On an average day consumers are exposed to six thousand advertisements and, each year, to more than twenty-five thousand new products...Brands help consumers cut through the proliferation of choices available in every product and service category.

Scott M. Davis
Brand Asset Management

A logo is the point of entry to the brand.

Milton Glaser
Designer

Trademarks are the shortest, fastest, most ubiquitous form of communication available.

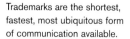

Design plays an essential role in creating and building brands. Design differentiates and embodies the intangibles—emotion, context and essence that matter most to consumers.

Moira Cullen
Design Director
Coca-Cola

Motorola RAZR

From left to right
Dosirak: Kbrand Associates
Eimer Stahl: Crosby Associates
Westside Organics: Grapefruit
PowerBook G4: Apple Computer
Late July Organic: Louise Fili Ltd.
The Franklin Institute: Allemann, Almquist & Jones
TiVo: Cronan
Time Warner: Chermayeff & Geismar
Alina Wheeler: Rev Group
Chambers Group: Stellarvisions
Cingular Wireless: VSA Partners
Aveda Uruku: Harry Allen and Associates
Kort & Godt: Kontrapunkt
Stem Cell Conference: Cronan
Amazon.com: Turner Duckworth
BP: Landor Associates

Brand identity implies an asset. Corporate identity sounds too much like an expense. This is an important distinction.

Chambers Group

Brand awareness and recognition are facilitated by a visual identity that is easy to remember and immediately recognizable. Visual identity triggers perceptions and unlocks associations of the brand. Sight, more than any other sense, provides information about the world. Through repeated exposure, symbols become so recognizable that companies, such as Target, Apple, Nike, and Merrill Lynch, have actually dropped the logotype from their corporate signatures in national advertising. Color becomes a mnemonic device—when you see a brown truck out of the corner of your eye, you know it is a UPS truck.

Identity designers are in the business of managing perception through the integration of meaning and distinctive visual form. Understanding the sequence of visual perception and cognition provides valuable insight into what will work best.

Artist and cultural anthropologist Heidi Cody demonstrates how we can recognize a consumer brand just by seeing one of the letters through her artwork "American Alphabet."

Heidi Cody © 2000

a. All
b. Bubblicious
c. Campbell's
d. Dawn
e. Eggo
f. Fritos
g. Gatorade
h. Hebrew National
i. Icee
j. Jell-o
k. Kool-Aid
l. Lysol
m. M&M's
n. Nilla Wafers
o. Oreo
p. Pez
q. Q-tips
r. Reese's
s. Starburst
t. Tide
u. Uncle Ben's
v. V-8
w. Wisk
x. Xtra
y. York
z. Zest

The sequence of cognition

The science of perception examines how individuals recognize and interpret sensory stimuli. The brain acknowledges and remembers shapes first. Visual images can be remembered and recognized directly, while words have to be decoded into meaning. Reading is not necessary to identify shapes, but identifying shapes is necessary to read. The brain acknowledges distinctive shapes which make a faster imprint on memory.

Color is second in the sequence. Color can trigger an emotion and evoke a brand association. Distinctive colors need to be chosen carefully, not only to build brand awareness but to express differentiation. Companies, such as Kodak and Tiffany, have trademarked their core brand colors.

The brain takes more time to process language, so content is third in the sequence behind shape and color.

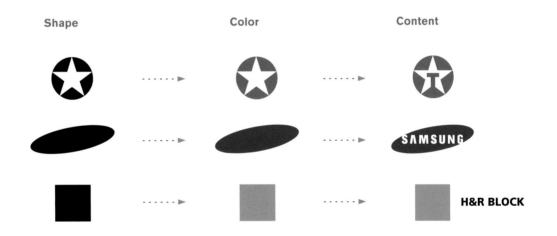

Shape	Color	Content

Think about how IBM triggers an immediate response with its horizontal banded television ads. Before the ad even runs, you know it's IBM, and you know it's going to be intelligent and engaging.

Marjorie Gorman
SVP
Tierney Communications

From the moment we wake up to the time we go to sleep, we experience 6,000 marketing messages. Opening the medicine chest, reaching into the closet, peering into the refrigerator, checking the mail, we are surrounded by the familiar brands that are part of our lives. In every case, a creative professional has considered how to generate recognition for the company and desire for the brand.

Every company needs to differentiate itself from its competitors and gain greater market share. Every company also has a compelling need to be distinctive. The same goal drives the approach of an internet café in the Scottish Highlands, a global information broker in cyberspace, or a Manhattan museum showing outsider art. Survival of the fittest requires a brand strategy and a medium to express it.

Businesses have an evolving need for brand identity. Think of the entrepreneurs who started out in a garage and have grown their firms into successful publicly owned companies. For a designer it is important to listen to the dreams of even the smallest entrepreneurs. Think about their need to communicate: first with their earliest customers and, as they create success, with their distributors and vendors, and on through the growth cycle to venture capital firms and shareholders.

When brand identity experts are needed

New company, new product

I'm starting a new business. I need a business card and a website.

We've developed a new product and it needs a name and a logo yesterday.

We need to raise millions of dollars. The campaign needs to have its own identity.

We're going public in the fall. We need to launch a world-class brand.

We need to raise venture capital, even though we do not have our first customer.

Name change

Our name no longer fits who we are and the businesses we are in.

We need to change our name because of a trademark conflict and then we need to revise all of our materials.

Our name has negative connotations in the new markets we are serving.

Our name misleads customers.

Revitalize a brand

We want to reposition and renew the corporate brand.

We're no longer in the business we were in when we founded our company.

We need to communicate more clearly about who we are.

We're going global—we need help to enter new world markets.

No one knows who we are.

Our stock is devalued.

We want to appeal to a new and more affluent market.

Identity aspirations

Developed by Sylvia Harris, information design strategist

What a new identity can do

Express the kind of organization you are

Reassure the public that you are who you say you are

Connect your organization to images and ideas

Serve as the thread for equity building over time

Provide consistency over communication channels

What a new identity can't do

Make people act

Change people's minds

Make new friends

Embody every message for everybody

Respond to current events

Revitalize a brand identity

We are a great company with cutting-edge products. We look behind the times.

Will our identity work on the web?

Our identity does not position us shoulder to shoulder with our competitors.

We have 80 divisions and inconsistent nomenclature. We are all over the place.

I am embarrassed when I give out my business card. We are a big business and the card sends the wrong signal.

Everyone in the world recognizes our icon, but admit it—she needs a face lift. She needs to look like she lives in the twenty-first century.

We love our symbol—it is known by our market. The problem is you cannot read our logotype.

Create an integrated system

We do not present a consistent face to our customers.

We lack visual consistency and we need a new brand architecture to deal with acquisitions.

Our packaging is not distinctive. Our competitors look better than we do, and their sales are going up.

All of our product literature looks like it comes from different companies.

We need to look strong and communicate that we are one global company.

Every division does its own thing when marketing. This is inefficient, frustrating, and not cost-effective. Everyone is reinventing the wheel.

When companies merge

We want to send a clear message to our stakeholders that this is a merger of equals.

We want to communicate that $1 + 1 = 4$.

We want to build on the brand equity of the merging companies.

We need to send a strong signal to the world that we are the new industry leader.

We need a new name.

How do we evaluate our acquisition's brand and fold it into our brand architecture?

Two industry leaders are merging. How do we manage our new identity?

11

Branding is big business. The sheer breadth of consulting firms that *do branding* is multiplying daily. From global brand and design consultancies to interactive specialists, individual experts in design, marketing, and public relations, the choice for any client may be daunting. In the old days the difference between a branding consultancy, a design firm, and an advertising agency were obvious. Convergence has come to branding. Virtual teams abound. And everyone wants the business.

There are no absolute criteria for what type of firm is the right fit for a company. An agency qualified to deliver a vast media campaign may not have the core competencies to create a brand identity. Developing a world-class brandmark, an integrated identity system, and sustainable brand architecture is a rigorous design discipline that requires experience.

Some companies need a firm that can deliver all the components—from advising on a global brand strategy to brand asset management. Others have a strategy in place and need a world-class designer to reposition the brand. Some need a firm that knows how to create the look and feel, across divisions, products or cultures. Package and environmental designers, communication architects, and naming experts also support the process.

Work with talented people to create something that will be of compelling benefit to the customer.

Susan Avarde, Managing Director, Global Branding
Citigroup Consumer Businesses

Time, money, quality. There is an old adage—if you cannot afford all three, pick two.

Selecting an expert

The selection process is similar to the process that companies use to select a consulting firm. Clearly establishing the project objectives, budget, and deliverables is key.

Establish the brand identity project team that will make the final decision.

Agree upon project objectives, budget, and deliverables.

Have senior management sign off on the project objectives, budget, and deliverables.

Prepare a Request for Proposal (RFP).

Identify three firms, and send them the RFP.

Have the brand identity project team review the RFP and agree on a short list.

Bring in firms on the short list for a presentation to the project team.

Make selection or narrow list further.

Carefully check references.

Meet with firm(s) for final presentation to senior management.

Frequently a client does not know whom to call or where to start. Companies will call different firms to educate themselves and identify the right fit. This is not the most efficient way to identify experts. Companies should hire firms with demonstrated experience and strategic imagination. Unlike advertising, which launches a new campaign each year, brand identity needs to endure. Brands, which are created and built over time, represent a major investment.

When Paul Rand designed IBM's brand identity, he was a sole practitioner. Today success frequently depends on bringing a team to the table. Clients often want to work with firms with experience in their industry sector. Is this necessary? Although it initially builds confidence, it is not a requirement. Unconventional thinking could help a company build a distinctive brand.

Citi works with a team of creative partners to express the Citi brand. The advertising campaign and tagline were developed by Fallon Worldwide. The look and feel of the campaign was inspired by the core brand identity designed by Pentagram in partnership with Michael Wolff, an independent brand strategist.

The best identity programs embody and advance the company's brand by supporting desired perceptions. Identity expresses itself in every touchpoint of the brand and becomes intrinsic to a company's culture—a constant reminder of its core values and its heritage. The mark is the pinnacle of a branding pyramid; recognition fuels comfort and loyalty and sets the stage for a sale. A stellar identity demonstrates rather than declares a unique point of view, from the interface of a website to the design of a product to the retail sales experience.

Brands are ranked regularly in the media. Business magazines feature such articles as "America's Ten Best Brands," citing market share and other economic indicators. Practically every book on brand strategy will remind you of the present value of the Coca-Cola brand, which seems to increase even when the economy falters. It is more challenging, however, to measure the impact and value of brand identity. If the Coke brand is worth $83.8 billion, we can assume that the Coca-Cola logotype and its packaging design are brand assets that have intrinsic value.

Brands help consumers cut through the proliferation of choices available in every product and service category.

Scott M. Davis
Brand Asset Management

perception ▶ behavior ▶ performance

Reasons to invest in brand identity

Make it easy for the customer to buy

Compelling brand identity presents any company, any size, anywhere with an immediately recognizable, distinctive, professional image that positions it for success. An identity helps manage the perception of a company and differentiates it from its competitors. A smart system conveys respect for the customer and makes it easy to understand features and benefits. A new product design or a better environment can delight a customer and create loyalty. An effective identity encompasses such elements as a name that is easy to remember or a distinctive package design for a product.

Make it easy for the sales force to sell

Whether it is the CEO of a global conglomerate communicating a new vision to the board, a first-time entrepreneur pitching to venture capital firms, a financial advisor creating a need for investment products, everyone is selling. Nonprofits, whether fundraising or soliciting new volunteers, are continually selling. Strategic brand identity works across diverse audiences and cultures to build an awareness and understanding of a company and its strengths. By making intelligence visible, effective identity seeks to clearly communicate a company's unique value proposition. The coherence of communications across various media sends a strong signal to the customer about the laserlike focus of a company.

Make it easy to build brand equity

The goal of all public companies is to increase shareholder value. A brand, or a company's reputation, is considered to be one of the most valuable company assets. Small companies and nonprofits also need to build brand equity. Their future success is dependent on building public awareness, preserving their reputations, and upholding their value. A strong brand identity will help build brand equity through increased recognition, awareness, and customer loyalty, which in turn helps make a company more successful. Managers who seize every opportunity to communicate their company's brand value and what the brand stands for sleep better at night. They are building a precious asset.

In *Brand Leadership* by David A. Aaker and Erich Joachimsthaler, the authors build a case that "when a high level of perceived quality has been (or can be) created, raising the price not only provides margin dollars but also aids perceptions." Their basic premise is that "strong brands command a price premium." A cup of Starbucks coffee is a case in point.

Aaker has also done research suggesting that "firms experiencing the largest gains in brand equity saw their stock return average 30%; conversely, those firms with the largest losses in brand equity saw stock return average a negative 10%."

Regardless of the size of a company or the nature of a business, certain ideals characterize the best brand identities. These ideals hold true whether the brand identity engagement is launching an entrepreneurial venture, creating a new product or service, repositioning a brand, working on a merger, or creating a retail presence. In every case these ideals are essential to a responsible creative process. It is vital for a company to understand the larger aspirations of a brand identity.

Functional criteria do not get to the heart of brand identity. There are 1,063,164 trademarks registered with the U.S. Patent and Trademark Office. The basic question is what makes one better than another and why. What are the essential characteristics of the best identities? How do we define the best identities? These characteristics, or ideals, are not about a certain aesthetic. Design excellence is a given. The best identities are most effective when they help advance the company's brand.

The best identities advance a brand.

Blake Deutsch

Functional criteria

Bold, memorable, and appropriate

Immediately recognizable

Provides a clear and consistent image of the company

Communicates the company's persona

Legally protectable

Has enduring value

Works well across media and scale

Works both in black and white and in color

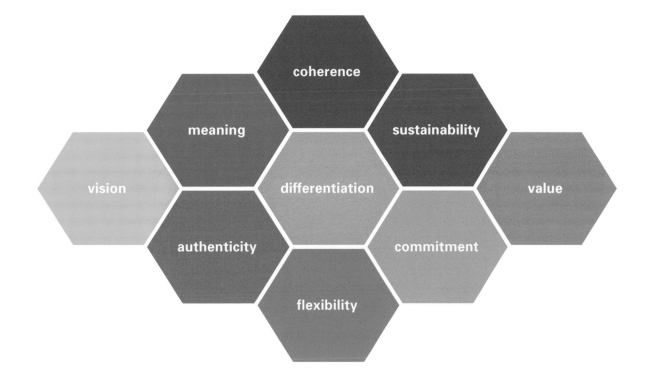

Vision

A compelling vision by an effective, articulate, and passionate leader is the foundation and the inspiration for the best brands.

Meaning

The best brands stand for something—a big idea, a strategic position, a defined set of values, a voice that stands apart.

Authenticity

Authenticity is not possible without an organization having clarity about its market, positioning, value proposition, and competitive difference.

Differentiation

Brands always compete with each other within their business category, and at some level, compete with all brands that want our attention, our loyalty, and our money.

Sustainability

Sustainability is the ability to have longevity in an environment in constant flux, characterized by future permutations that no one can predict.

Coherence

Whenever a customer experiences a brand, it must feel familiar and have the desired effect. Consistency does not need to be rigid or limiting in order to feel like one company.

Flexibility

An effective brand identity positions a company for change and growth in the future. It supports an evolving marketing strategy.

Commitment

Organizations need to actively manage their assets, including the brand name, the trademarks, the integrated sales and marketing systems, and the standards.

Value

Building awareness, increasing recognition, communicating uniqueness and quality, and expressing a competitive difference create measurable results.

A compelling vision by an effective, articulate, and passionate leader is the foundation and inspiration for the best brands. New ideas, enterprises, products, and services are created by individuals who have the ability to imagine what others cannot see and the tenacity to deliver what they believe is possible.

Behind every new initiative is a dynamic individual who has the intelligence, foresight, and imagination to perceive the future in a new way and to inspire others. A vision may be expressed by a first-time entrepreneur, a museum director, or a scientist breaking new ground. It is not the exclusive province of the CEO of a global company.

The challenge to the designer is to translate that vision into a tangible expression and a visual language that resonates with all stakeholders. As the designer becomes immersed in the company—its markets, its strengths and weaknesses, its value proposition, a new picture of the future begins to emerge. Great designers demonstrate an uncanny ability to visualize and, in effect, play back what the CEO is envisioning in his or her wildest dreams of the future.

The best way to predict the future is to create it.

Alan Kay
Computer scientist

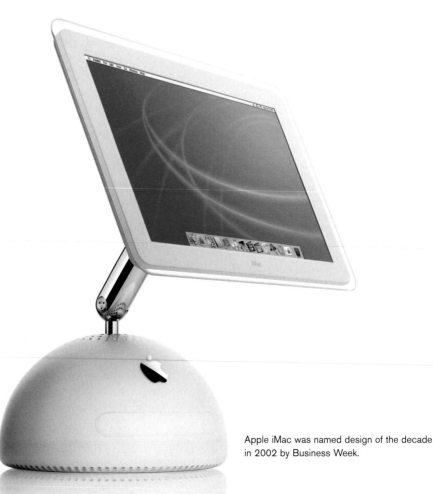

Apple iMac was named design of the decade in 2002 by Business Week.

Vision requires leadership

The best identities emerge in organizations with effective leaders, who make it a priority to articulate their vision clearly and to make it accessible. These leaders take the time to map out a strategy for the future and to motivate the people around them, whether they are customers or employees.

Brand identity needs to be a top-down initiative

Effective leaders invariably understand how to leverage symbols, prioritizing communication about the meaning of their brand. Not surprisingly, the brand identity projects that are successful are top-down initiatives, which means that a CEO has endorsed the project. This endorsement is critical because it sends a strong message to everyone involved that the project is a priority that will affect future success. Brand identity projects that do not have CEO endorsement tend to fail.

Designers need access to the vision

Designers must have access to senior leadership and to the key strategic issues. Brand identity cannot be created in a vacuum. The best identities result from designers who engage in an open dialogue with leadership. Respect must go both ways. Brand consultants are viewed as peers and team members. Designers who are denied access to senior leadership cannot do their work responsibly.

Design anticipates and visualizes the future

The designer's goal is to create an identity that positions a company for growth, change, and success. That identity needs to be future-oriented and anticipate what is not yet envisioned. Good designers bring their own vision to developing an identity for something that may not yet exist.

Steve Jobs, CEO, co-founded Apple in 1976. Under his visionary leadership and passion, Apple seizes every opportunity from innovative product design to smart advertising and sleek packaging to convey to its customers that it understands their digital lifestyles, their needs and their aspirations. By January 2006, 40 million iPods have been sold, a pipeline of new products have inspired the marketplace, and stock had soared. The Apple logo was designed in 1976 by Rob Janoff. It is an apple with a bite out of it—a friendly symbol of knowledge and anarchy from the PC world.

Great leaders see the future, set a course, and pursue it relentlessly. They conquer the present despite criticism, ambiguity, adversity. They reflect on, learn from, and weave patterns from the past. Great leaders possess the humility, optimism, passion, and wisdom to inspire others and evoke their full commitment.

Dr. Karol Wasylyshyn
President
Leadership Development Forum

The best brands stand for something: a big idea, a strategic position, a defined set of values, a voice that stands apart. Meaning inspires the creative process as it is conveyed through a symbol, a word, or an action. It is the DNA of brand identity, where form is imbued with rationale and assigned deeper resonance. Understanding what a mark represents accelerates recognition. A mark with relevant and aspirational meaning fosters employee pride.

Symbols engage intelligence, imagination, emotion, in a way that no other learning does.

Georgetown University Identity Standards Manual

Nike was the goddess of victory. The logo, an abstraction of a wing, designed by Carolyn Davidson, was an appropriate and meaningful symbol for a company that marketed running shoes. The "Just do it" campaign communicated such a strong point of view to the target market that the meaning of the symbol evolved into a battle cry and a way of life for an entire generation.

Time Warner's trademark was designed by Steff Geissbuhler, Partner, Chermayeff & Geismar for the Time Warner merger in 1995. No longer in use by corporate, it is now used solely for Time Warner Cable. The media frequently uses this mark as symbol of convergence.

Cingular's brandmark, designed by VSA Partners, is nicknamed "Jack." He stands for freedom of human expression. In an industry characterized by technological innovations and rate wars, "Jack" reminds us that our wireless needs come from our desire to communicate and express ourselves.

Meaning is distilled

Meaning emerges from insight into the essence of an organization: what it stands for now and in the future. The designer's challenge is to absorb and understand an enormous amount of information and then distill it into its purest and simplest form—a meaningful idea.

Meaning is assigned

Grasping the meaning of a brandmark is rarely immediate. Meaning needs to be explained, communicated, and nurtured. The American flag did not become an immediately recognizable and universal symbol of freedom and democracy until it was communicated over and over again. Designers need to articulate the big idea behind a mark. Then the company needs to seize every opportunity to share the larger meaning as a way of building the culture and the brand.

Meaning builds consensus

Meaning is like a campfire. It is a rallying point used to build consensus with a group of decision makers. Agreement on brand essence and attributes builds critical synergy and precedes any presentation of visual solutions. Once a new identity is launched, it becomes integrated into the corporate culture as a visible reminder of the meaning of the brand.

Meaning evolves over time

As companies grow, the nature of their businesses may change significantly. Similarly, the meaning assigned to a brandmark may evolve from its original intention. Meaning becomes amplified over time as the company and its culture become stronger. Meaning may also be redefined by customer experience, adding a new dimension.

Mitsubishi stands for quality and reliability and embodies a 130-year-old commitment to earning the trust and confidence of people worldwide. Protecting the trademark, designed by Yataro Iwasaki, is a top corporate priority. Each diamond represents a core principle: corporate responsibility to society, integrity and fairness, and international understanding through trade.

The CBS eye has been the television network's symbol for over a half century. It has remained unchanged, and has retained its original powerful, all-seeing iconic quality. Originally inspired by the human eye paintings on the side of Shaker barns to ward off evil, it is a highly recognized symbol around the world. Designed by William Golden, it was one of the first symbols designed to function primarily on the screen.

In psychology authenticity refers to self-knowledge and to making decisions and choices that are congruent with that self-knowledge. Similarly, an organization's identity needs to be aligned with its brand and its vision. Authentic identities emerge from a process that is both investigative and intuitive. Authenticity is not possible without an organization having clarity about its reason for being, its value proposition, and competitive difference.

Brand identity must be an authentic expression of an organization: its unique vision, goals, values, voice, and personality. The design must be appropriate to the company, its culture and values, its target market, and the business sector in which it operates.

Know thyself.

Plato
First Alcibiades

logo

look and feel

targeted messages

core messages

we know who we are

This pyramid illustrates that organizations cannot support the identity process without understanding what they stand for. Companies with this self-knowledge start the process from a position of strength and create solutions that are sustainable.

American Folk Art Museum:
Pentagram

The American Folk Art Museum's identity program designed by Pentagram honors both constituencies within folk art: the traditionalists and "outsider" artists, who are self-taught and contemporary. Patterns and pieced techniques that characterize folk art are used in the logotype design and a multitude of applications from banners and brochures, to mugs and shopping bags. Objects from the collection have become elements of the identity and appear in a range of eclectic treatments from silhouettes to mezzotints. The identity also reflects the architecture of the new museum building by Tod Williams Billie Tsien & Associates, which has a façade of cast-metal panels. The environmental graphics were designed to harmonize with the new building and to reveal a "sense of the hand."

An identity needs to embrace an organization's history and incorporate enough flexibility to evolve as that organization anticipates the future.

Woody Pirtle
Partner, Pentagram

We live at a time when we are bombarded by brands. They reveal themselves in every aspect of our personal and professional spaces. Brands always compete with each other within their business category, and at some level compete with all brands for our attention, our loyalty, and our money. When a designer creates a brandmark, it is his or her responsibility to create a unique symbol that is differentiated, has the power to communicate within a split second, and in many cases is reproduced smaller than a wild blueberry.

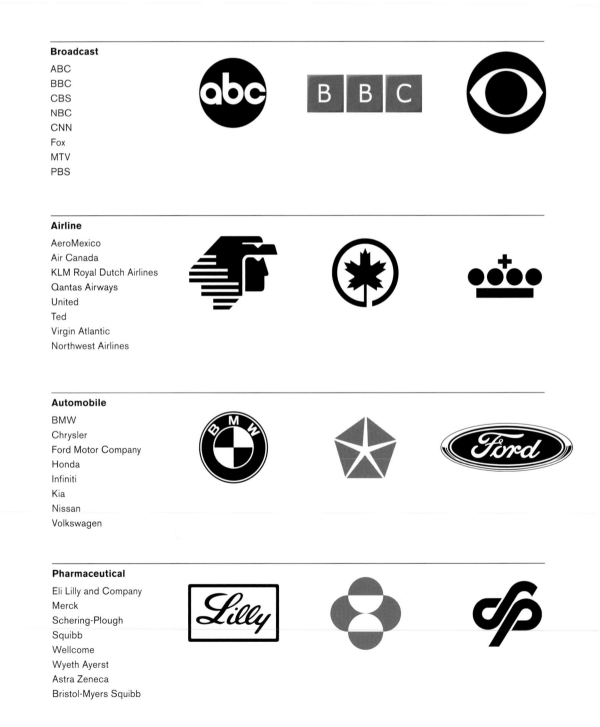

Broadcast
ABC
BBC
CBS
NBC
CNN
Fox
MTV
PBS

Airline
AeroMexico
Air Canada
KLM Royal Dutch Airlines
Qantas Airways
United
Ted
Virgin Atlantic
Northwest Airlines

Automobile
BMW
Chrysler
Ford Motor Company
Honda
Infiniti
Kia
Nissan
Volkswagen

Pharmaceutical
Eli Lilly and Company
Merck
Schering-Plough
Squibb
Wellcome
Wyeth Ayerst
Astra Zeneca
Bristol-Myers Squibb

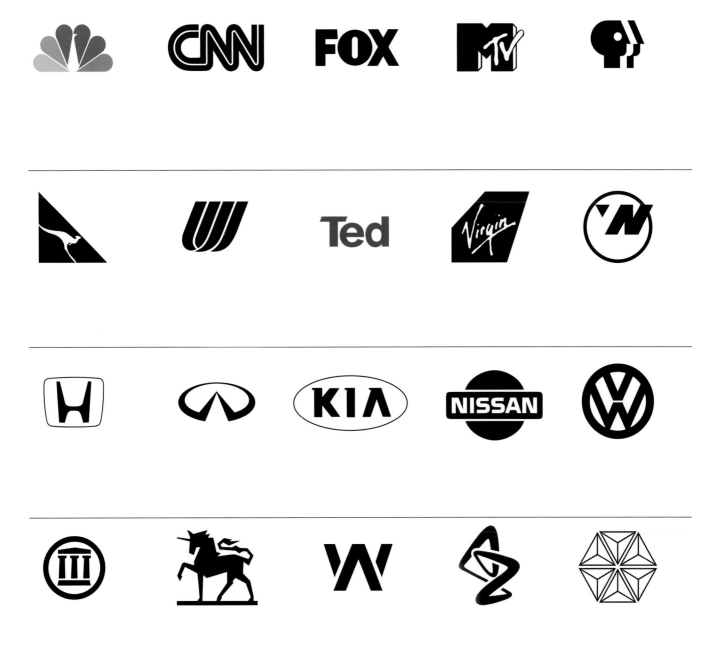

In the twenty-first century, the only constant is ongoing change. Our institutions, technology, science, style, and vocabulary are in continuous flux, and the rate of change is accelerating. And yet designers, who are the arbiters of style, need to design identities that have sustainability. Sustainability is the capacity of an identity to last in a changing environment, characterized by permutations no one can predict.

Brands are messengers of trust. Credibility is communicated in part by a trademark that does not fluctuate with the economy or changing business trends. Consumers depend on trademarks to be constant, and are reassured by what they represent in a changing world.

Media and modes of communication are always changing. When Saul Bass designed the AT&T globe in 1984, the ability of a symbol to spin and morph through space was not a technological possibility. However, during the 2000 Olympic Games, the AT&T globe became an acrobat spinning through space in an advertising campaign that captivated viewers around the world.

Trademarks, by definition, must last well beyond the fashion of the moment.

Chermayeff & Geismar

Three years after the car was born (1896), Bibendum, the name of the Michelin Man, became the company's unique symbol. Redrawn numerous times, the "tire man" is immediately recognizable around the world.

The Chase trademark, designed by Chermayeff & Geismar in 1960 for the Chase Manhattan Bank, has survived sweeping change in the financial services industry, including the Chemical Bank merger in 1996 and the J. P. Morgan merger in 2000.

Trademarks and their date of origination

Löwenbräu	1383		London Underground	1933		Exxon	1966
Guinness	1862		Volkswagen	1938		Metropolitan Life	1967
Olympics	1865		IKEA	1943		L'Eggs	1971
Mitsubishi	1870		CBS	1951		Eastman Kodak	1971
Nestlé	1875		NBC	1956		Nike	1971
Bass Ale	1875		IBM	1956		Quaker Oats	1972
John Deere	1876		Chase Manhattan	1960		Atari	1973
Johnson & Johnson	1886		International Paper	1960		Merrill Lynch	1973
Coca-Cola	1887		Motorola	1960		United Way	1974
General Electric	1892		Westinghouse	1960		Dunkin' Donuts	1974
Prudential	1896		UPS	1961		I Love NY	1975
Michelin	1896		Weyerhaeuser	1961		Citicorp	1976
Shell	1900		McDonald's	1962		PBS	1976
Nabisco	1900		General Foods	1962		United	1976
Ford	1903		Wool Bureau	1964		Apple	1977
Rolls-Royce	1905		Rohm & Haas	1964		Transamerica	1979
Mercedes-Benz	1911		Mobil	1965		Texaco	1981
Greyhound	1926		Diners Club	1966		AT&T	1984

Since John Deere's founding, the leaping deer has been the core identity element. A history of the company's trademarks can be found on its website.

1878

1912

1936

1937

1950

1956

1968

2000

Whenever a customer experiences a brand, whether by using a product, talking to a service representative, or making a purchase on a website, the brand must feel familiar and have the desired effect. Coherence is the quality that ensures that all the pieces hold together in a way that feels seamless to the customer.

An effective identity consistently applied over time is one of the most powerful marketing tools that a company can deploy. Consistency does not need to be rigid and limiting—rather, it is a baseline that is designed to build brand equity through repetition, persistence, and frequency. It is made possible by a commitment to brand identity standards, and is supported by a culture that values the brand and its expressions.

The goal in creating a brand identity is not just surface consistency but inner coherence.

Aubrey Balkind

Identity does not mean identical.

Steff Geissbuhler, Partner
C&G Partners

Although no longer in use, the Gymboree brand identity system designed by Pentagram partner Kit Hinrichs is a model for future generations. The visual vocabulary of colors, shapes, and patterns were imaginatively integrated across customer touchpoints, allowing the brand to stay fresh and relevant.

How is coherence achieved?

The brand experience feels the same, whether the customer is online, in his car, at her desk, or watching television. This is a result of understanding the needs and preferences of the target customer and designing a brand experience that produces a desired perception. Every touchpoint is considered a brand experience.

Look and feel

A brand identity system is unified visually and structurally. It builds on cohesive brand architecture and utilizes specially designed colors, typeface families, and formats. The identity system advances immediate recognition of the company and supports brand attributes across various media.

A unified voice

The company is clear about how it wants to be perceived, and every communication supports that goal. Consistent messages appear in sales presentations, advertising campaigns, speeches, and a myriad of other strategic marketing tools. The messages are aligned with the positioning strategy, and the tone is consistent as well.

One company strategy

The company looks the same around the world. As companies become more complex and have numerous business lines selling different products, a unified global image reinforces the message that "we are one company." As companies diversify into new areas of business, consistency jumpstarts acceptance and awareness of new initiatives.

Uniform quality

A high and uniform level of quality imparts a degree of care which is given to each of the company's products and services. This is a sustainable advantage. The company identity is a critical asset. Anything less than superior quality reduces the value of the asset on both a conscious and unconscious level.

Clarity and simplicity

Using clear language consistently to communicate about products and services helps the customer navigate choices. Naming that is logical and consistent within the brand architecture also makes it easier for the customer to understand and decide. Communicative names are established when legal names are too cumbersome for marketing purposes.

Gymboree: Pentagram

29

Identity systems must continuously demonstrate an inherent flexibility. Stellar programs easily adapt to a broad range of marketing and communications applications over time to achieve sustainability. Flexibility ensures that communications stay fresh and relevant.

Designers examine how flexibility can be achieved within the brand architecture. Will the new identity facilitate brand extensions in the future? Does it have long legs? No one can say with absolute certainty which new products and services a company may offer in five or ten years. The designer, however, needs to anticipate and create a flexible infrastructure to accommodate the future.

We wanted to simplify Nickelodeon's toolkit, and focus internal creative on the core messages of the brand, with a system that was flexible and encouraged creative thinking and execution.

Sean Adams
Partner
Adams Morioka

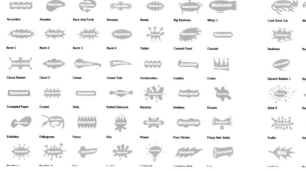

Marketing flexibility

An effective identity positions a company for change and growth in the future. It needs to be equally effective in a range of marketing and sales applications from the website, to direct mail, to a news release, to sales promotions and products. It also supports an evolving marketing strategy.

Brand architecture flexibility

A flexible identity system does not lock a company into the current list of products and services. It has long legs, which means that the marketing of new businesses, products, and initiatives is facilitated by a durable and flexible system.

Standards flexibility

An effective identity system takes into consideration the multitude of professionals who will use the identity in the future, from the internal design department to the company's advertising agency. A carefully designed balance between control and creative latitude makes it possible for professionals to adhere to the identity standards while achieving specific marketing objectives.

Performance flexibility

In the design development of a logo and logotype, the designer conducts an intensive testing and design adjustment process to ensure the functionality of the signature. The designer examines:

Various scales, from smaller than a dime to as large as a billboard

Color, from full-color, to two-color, to one-color

Color, from Pantone, through process, through web-friendly

Variations of color combinations

Black and white, from a fax through a newspaper ad

Positive and negative

Electronic and print media

New media

Uniform standards

From Nick @ Nite to Noggin, the Nickelodeon brand grew organically and had become wildly successful, and after 15 years, disjointed. Adams Morioka's goals were to bring together Nickelodeon's world of brand extensions on the same playing field and to unify the messages and the visual vocabulary across media. The brand needed to be more accessible and less mysterious to anyone involved with Nickelodeon.

Nickelodeon, Viacom International: Adams Morioka Design

A good identity does not guarantee success. An effective brand identity is tied inextricably to management's desire to nurture it. The bottom line is that identity systems need to be enforced, tweaked, monitored, and occasionally revitalized. A new brand identity program signifies the beginning of an investment of time and capital, not the end.

Perhaps the most important characteristic of a sustainable identity is taking responsibility for actively managing the asset, which includes the brand name, the trademarks, the system, and the standards. A common mistake is assuming that once a company has a new brand identity, the hardest work has been accomplished. In reality the whole process is just beginning, and the hard work is ahead.

Managing a brand identity system is not exclusive to large global corporations. Small companies and nonprofits also need an individual who has the responsibility of overseeing the brand assets and who reports directly to the president. The mantra is to keep moving—with ongoing management, dynamic adherence to the central idea, the monitoring of standards which help preserve the asset, and the tools the organization needs to build its brand.

We recognize the value of a disciplined approach to building, protecting and enhancing our brand.

Dave Reyes Guerra, Brand Management Director
Ernst & Young

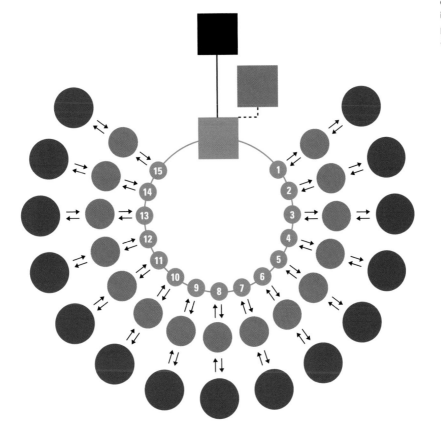

■ Chairman of the Board
■ Corporate Design Manager
■ Design Consultants
● Graphic Design Advisory Group
● Staff Coordinators
● Field Coordinators

Mobil diagram: Chermayeff & Geismar

Accountability

Chermayeff & Geismar worked with Mobil for more
than 30 years to develop and maintain a strong
identity program. This diagram, featured in the Mobil
Graphic Standards, demonstrates how each of the
major functions of Mobil's worldwide operations is
charged with the responsibility for coordinating the
Mobil identity program within each of its respective
areas. All staff and field coordinators report to
the corporate design manager, who reports to the
chairman of the board. The organization also includes
an ongoing relationship with the design consultants.

Creating value is the indisputable goal of most organizations. The best companies consistently demonstrate their value through the superior quality of their products and services and their unswerving dedication to meeting their customers' needs. The best brand identities are the most public and widely communicated symbols of that value.

Within a company, big or small, a brand identity has value when it is viewed as an important asset by senior management. It is valued by the organization through dedication to uniform standards and the highest-quality communications. Its value is further ensured through legal protection.

Consumer brands are often financially valued and measured. Although a brand is more than a brandmark, the logo is almost indistinguishable from the brand in the mind of the consumer. Effective identity is valued because it builds awareness, increases recognition, communicates uniqueness and quality, and expresses a competitive difference.

A strong brand commands a premium.

David A. Aaker and Erich Joachimsthaler
Brand Leadership

Establishing a new brand identity was the catalyst to transforming our organization. The unified identity was reflected in our new name and logo and was the foundation to see ourselves in a world class light.

Rebecca G. Wingate
President
LifeMark Partners

We made the decision to adopt a new, unified identity system that would enable all of our lines of business to benefit from one another's recognition and leadership in the marketplace.

Joseph Neubauer
Chairman and CEO
ARAMARK

The foundation of the CIGNA brand identity system is our trademark. It is one of CIGNA's most valuable assets and is legally protected only if it is used properly and consistently.

CIGNA Brand Identity Guidelines

The Safe & Ready identity inspired a pride of ownership for public health on our team. When we're working on an emergency, people come together and their identity becomes 'Safe & Ready,' symbolizing the immense responsibility to protect the public.

Tres Schnell
Director
Office of Health Emergency Management
New Mexico Department of Health

Value as a symbol

As a symbol of the corporate culture, an identity engenders pride. As a symbol of the future, an identity engenders trust. It extends customer loyalty through familiarity and can build synergies across business lines.

Valued as an asset

The brand identity is viewed as a strategic business tool that actively builds trust and promotes awareness. It is valued as a competitive advantage that has measurable results.

Commitment to value is ongoing

Adherence to the brand identity standards and the relentless pursuit of the quality of communications is priority throughout the organization.

Value is preserved through legal protection

The identity is trademarked, registered, owned, and defended. It can be protected in the range of markets that are served, both local and global. The best identity standards educate employees and vendors about compliance.

Valued by marketing

Through consistent, smart, and clear messages, value is reinforced by strategic brand identity.

Good design is good business.

Tom Watson, former Chairman
IBM

The thoughtful creation of a symbol can serve as the foundation for an entire branding initiative.

John Coyne
President
Brinker Capital

Our literature was a mishmash of styles. Now we have a vibrant image that reflects the diversity of our constituency. Our look mirrors who we are, and puts us in a much stronger position to take on an ambitious fundraising campaign.

Margaret Fraser
Executive Secretary
Friends World Committee for
Consultation Section of the
Americas

Logos act as flags for employees and supply chain partners to rally around. And in a merger or a takeover situation, the unveiling of the new logo can be used to represent a psychological break from the past.

Helen Keyes
Former Creative Director
Enterprise IG

35

Brand strategy is like the corpus callosum. It connects the left brain with the right brain and makes the brand work. Effective brand strategy provides a central unifying idea around which all behavior, actions, and communications are aligned. It works across products and services, and is effective over time. The best brand strategies are so differentiated and powerful that they deflect the competition. They are easy to talk about, whether you are the CEO or an employee.

Brand strategy builds on a vision, is aligned with business strategy, emerges from a company's values and culture, and reflects an in-depth understanding of the customer's needs and perceptions. Brand strategy defines positioning, differentiation, the competitive advantage, and a unique value proposition.

Brand strategy needs to resonate with all stakeholders: external customers, the media, and internal customers (including employees, the board, and core suppliers). Brand strategy is a road map that guides marketing, makes it easier for the sales force to sell more, and provides clarity, context, and inspiration to employees.

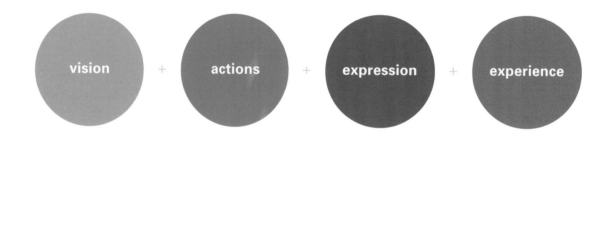

vision + actions + expression + experience

The role of the consultant in developing brand strategy is to facilitate the process: asking the right questions, providing relevant input and ideas, getting key issues to surface, and achieving resolution.

Erich Sippel
President
Erich Sippel & Company

Every senior leader in an organization must be focused and accountable for translating the brand strategy.

Betty Nelson
Group Director, Global Communications
IMS Health

The importance of brand strategy and the cost of building brand identity should be understood at the highest levels of an organization and across functional areas—not just sales and marketing—but in legal, finance, operations and human resources as well.

Sally Hudson
Marketing Consultant

Who develops brand strategy?

It is usually a team of people; no one does it alone. It is a result of an extended dialogue among the CEO, marketing, sales, advertising, public relations, operations, and distribution. Global companies frequently bring in brand strategists: independent thinkers and authorities, strategic marketing firms, and brand consultants. It often takes someone from the outside who is an experienced strategic and creative thinker to help a company articulate what is already there.

Sometimes a brand strategy is born at the inception of a company by a visionary, such as Anita Roddick, Steve Jobs, Martha Stewart, or Jeff Bezos. Sometimes it takes a visionary leader, such as Lou Gerstner, former CEO, IBM, to redefine brand strategy. Companies frequently survive and prosper because they have a clear brand strategy. Companies falter because they do not have one.

Branding imperatives

Acknowledge that we live in a branded world.

Seize every opportunity to position your company in your customers' minds.

Communicate a strong brand idea over and over again.

Go beyond declaring a competitive advantage. Demonstrate it!

Understand the customers. Build on their perceptions, preferences, dreams, values, and lifestyles.

Identify touchpoints—places in which customers interface with the product or service.

Use brand identity to create sensory magnets to attract and retain customers.

IKEA offers good design and quality at a low price. IKEA's strategy resonates across cultures in 29 countries. IKEA's values and company soul are aligned with its origin in a small village in Sweden where it was founded in 1943. Low prices are maintained by asking the customer to work as a partner to assemble the furniture. IKEA's mission is to "make it easy and affordable for people to live better and attain the home of their dreams." IKEA's positioning is unboring.

Supporting every effective brand is a positioning strategy that drives planning, marketing, and sales. Positioning evolves to create openings in a market that is continually changing, a market in which consumers are saturated with products and messages. Positioning takes advantage of changes in demographics, technology, marketing cycles, consumer trends, and gaps in the market to find new ways of appealing to the public. Positioning enables companies to turn obstacles into opportunities.

Distinguishing a product or service becomes more and more challenging. Developed by Al Ries and Jack Trout in 1981, positioning becomes the scaffolding on which companies build their brands, strategize their planning, and extend their relationships with customers. Positioning takes into account the mix of price, product, promotion, and place (distribution), which are the four dimensions that affect sales.

Ries and Trout were convinced that each company must determine its position in the customer's mind, considering the needs of the customer, the strengths and weaknesses of that company, and the world of competition. This concept continues to be a fundamental precept in all marketing communications, branding, and advertising.

Positioning breaks through barriers of oversaturated markets to create new opportunities.

Lissa Reidel
FolioOne Ltd.

Henry Ford said customers could have any color they wanted as long as it was black. General Motors came along with five colors and stole the show.

What are positioning statements?

Positioning statements are short, pithy, powerful drivers in brand strategy. They are more than marketing slogans since they summarize a promise to the customers. They also represent the company's vision of the future: the big dream, the ultimate goal, the long-term possibilities.

The difference between sales and marketing

Sales and marketing use similar approaches: publications, advertising, and direct mail. But in a sales campaign the focus is the product. A company that is market-driven focuses on consumers. The product is defined and finite, but in the minds of clients there are infinite possibilities. Marketing penetrates into the psyches of customers. The company that markets has its fingers on the pulse of consumers.

Sneakers

In the 1950s, everyone had one pair of white tennis sneakers. They were the most mundane necessities. Then sneakers were redesigned and repositioned in consumers' minds. They became endowed with celebrity status and were transformed into symbols of empowerment in the mid-1970s, when Nike and Reebok picked up on the increased interest in health, changed the perception, and raised the price. Today, sneakers have brand status, and everyone needs more than one pair.

Water

Until the 1980s, tap water tasted good. If consumers thought about water at all, it was only that they should have eight glasses a day. Health trends coincided with the water supply becoming less than the dependable utility it had always been. The three-martini lunch was no longer hip, yet people still wanted something with cachet to drink. Presto: bottled water reassured people that they were drinking something healthy and ordering something trendy. It is slimming, it is nonalcoholic, it is pure, celebrities buy it. . . and it is affordable for everyone. How could it miss?

Big-box stores

Target created a new position for itself as a big-box store with products that were designed by some of the best designers in the world. Target's positioning is dramatically different from that of Wal-Mart, the biggest store on earth. While Wal-Mart is about the lowest price, Target's positioning is created around appeal (design), as well as necessity and price. Target has built recognition of its brand to the degree that some ad campaigns feature the Target logo in audacious applications, including fabric patterns and spots on a dog, without mentioning the company name.

The next disciplinary seismic shift in branding is customer experience: building loyalty and lifelong relationships at each point of contact. The vast amount of purchasing choices is inspiring companies to enhance the brand experience to lure and keep customers. Every customer contact provides an opportunity to enhance an emotional connection. A good experience generates positive buzz. A bad experience becomes a lost opportunity sabotaging the brand.

It is essential for the branding team to look up from the desktop and see the world through the eyes of the customer. Shopping has become a subset to being engaged and entertained. The customer goes to the Genius Bar at the Apple Store for education, the American Girl Place for afternoon tea, and the Sushi Bar at Whole Foods for a free taste of something new.

Even the most mundane transactions can be turned into memorable experiences.

B. Joseph Pine II and James H. Gilmore
The Experience Economy

Sip, surf, and save is the hip wireless café's value proposition. The coffee is good and the shopping for cool orange stuff is fun. Since 2000, the company has signed more than 3.2 million customers. Cafés are in key urban locations.

Donovan/Green identified moments of truth for a hotel guest that ranged from sighting the hotel from the highway, walking into the front lobby, and glimpsing into the room. The firm viewed each touchpoint as an opportunity to create a memorable and positive experience to support the brand culture.

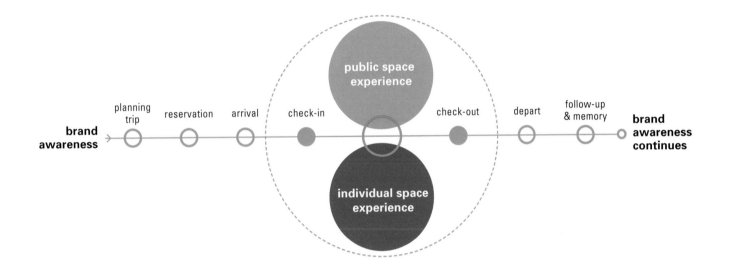

Our orange ING DIRECT Cafés welcome the public to buy a cup of coffee, experience our brand, and learn about the great deals we offer to anyone who wants to save money, simply and easily.

Arkadi Kuhlmann
President and CEO
ING DIRECT

Those businesses that relegate themselves to the diminishing world of goods and services will be rendered irrelevant. To avoid this fate, you must learn to stage a rich, compelling experience.

B. Joseph Pine II and James H. Gilmore
The Experience Economy

Shopping at Trader Joe's gives me a sense of discovery. There is always something new to try.

Blake Deutsch

The art of being a great retailer is to preserve the core while enhancing the experience. It is very hard to do and many people have lost their way. We need to push for reinvention and renewal and to extend things without diluting ourselves.

Howard Schultz
Founder and CEO
Starbucks

Brand architecture refers to the hierarchy of brands within a single company. It is the interrelationship of the parent company, subsidiary companies, products, and services, and should mirror the marketing strategy. Brand identity design brings consistency, visual and verbal order, thought, and intention to disparate elements to help a company grow and market more effectively.

As companies merge with others and acquire new companies and products, the branding, nomenclature, and marketing decisions become exceedingly complex. Decision makers examine marketing, cost, time, and legal implications.

The need for brand architecture is not limited to Fortune 100 companies or for-profit companies. Any company or institution that is growing needs to evaluate which brand architecture strategy will support future growth. Most large companies that sell products and services have a mixture of strategies. A number of different types of brand architecture have been identified over the years by various marketing strategists. There is no universal agreement on the types of brand architecture terms.

Consider

Visible
Invisible

Endorsed
Branded
Co-branded

Generic
Premium

Primary
Secondary
Tertiary

One identity
Many identities

Big type
Tiny type

Bold type
Light type

Strategic questions

What are the benefits of leveraging the name of the parent company?

Does the positioning of our new entity require that we distance it from the parent?

Will co-branding confuse consumers?

How do we brand this new acquisition?

Do we change the name or build on existing equity even though it was owned by a competitor?

Should we ensure that the parent company is always visible in a secondary position?

Monolithic brand architecture

In this scenario there is a strong, single master brand around which everything is unified. Customers have a clear picture of this company—its persona, its ethos, and its values—and make purchasing decisions based on loyalty. The features and benefits of the product are less important than the brand promise because the consumer trusts the brand. The visual identity and the brand name are consistent across products and services, and in global locations. In both the corporate and consumer sectors, brand extensions are built by using generic descriptions.

Starbucks

Vanguard

FedEx

Hewlett-Packard

The Body Shop

Virgin

Mercedes-Benz

Martha Stewart

Subbrand or subsidiary brand architecture

In this scenario a branded subsidiary, product, or service is combined with the core brand. Either the master brand dominates, or the two brands serve as co-drivers.

Subaru Outback

Sony Walkman

Adobe Acrobat

Nike Air Jordan

Endorsed brand architecture

In this scenario there is marketing synergy between the product or division name and the parent name. The product or division has a clearly defined market presence, but it benefits from the association and visibility of the parent. The parent, in essence, endorses the product, service, or division.

iPod and Apple Computer

Polo and Ralph Lauren

Oreo and Nabisco

PowerPoint and Microsoft

Navy Seals and the U.S. Navy

Sesame Street and PBS

Residence Inn and Marriott

Pluralistic brand architecture

In this scenario a parent has a series of products that are well-known consumer brands. All marketing resources are focused on selling these brands to their specific target markets. The name of the parent may be either invisible or inconsequential to the consumer. Many parent companies develop a system for corporate endorsement that is tertiary. The parent name is primarily recognized by the investment community.

Wharton (University of Pennsylvania)

Tang (Kraft Foods)

Godiva Chocolate (Campbell Soup)

Jeep Cherokee (DaimlerChrysler)

Prozac (Lilly)

The Ritz-Carlton (Marriott)

Hellman's Mayonnaise (Unilever)

When we hear the term "global brand," we instantly picture the world's largest conglomerates. In cyberspace, on our desktops, and on satellite cell phones, geography has become irrelevant. The internet has made every organization and every brand global. While globalization has blurred the distinctions among cultures, the best brands pay attention to cultural differences.

Cultural insight is critical to anyone who is building a brand. Naming, logo design, image development, color, key messages, and retail spaces require the creative team to pay attention to connotation and the complexity of subtle cultural differences. The history of marketing is filled with too many stories about companies offending the very market that they were trying to impress. Assumptions and stereotypes stand in the way of building brands that understand customers and celebrate their uniqueness.

Cultures are intensely complex. Customs, attitudes and preferences are often too subtle for the visitor to notice.

Ronnie Lipton
Designing Across Cultures

Photography: Ed Wheeler

Pay attention

Diversity

America is diverse. The twenty-first century is diverse. Names, symbols, and brand attributes need to have no strong negative connotations in ethnic and religious communities.

Market niche

The process should always begin with an understanding of the target market. For example, American Hispanic populations include people from many countries who speak Spanish differently, have different accents and slang, and have different physical characteristics.

Change and contradictions

A negative association in one culture might mean a positive association in another. Thoughtful analysis facilitates responsible creative solutions.

Naming

Certain names in English may have unintended connotations in different languages. For example, according to naming lore, Chevy named one of its models, "Nova," discovering after it was launched that it means "won't go" in Spanish.

Color

Each culture has its own unique heritage. In China the color white was historically a color associated with mourning. In Korea the color yellow is associated with the center of life.

Symbols

Visual iconography has the ability to transcend language barriers. However, a symbol with positive or sacred connotations in one culture may have exactly the opposite connotation in another.

Fundamental principles

Inspired by Ronnie Lipton

Assume nothing. "Hispanic," "Asian," or "Chinese" is not "a" market.

Identify and eliminate stereotypes and assumptions.

Submerge your team in the culture(s) of your customers with native experts. Explore perceptions, values, behaviors, and trends.

Research everything. Test everything. Observe everything. Test it again.

Identify experts to trust. Subtle cultural differences and trends are often invisible to outsiders and understood by the native inhabitant.

Be sensitive to nuance.

Not every culture has a nationality.
HSBC advertisement

Setting up shop in Japan meant learning about the way of life, attitudes and needs of our future customers. Aveda salons are designed with local materials and architects. We modified our products to better serve our new customers, where needed.
Chris Hacker
SVP, Global Marketing and Design
Aveda

Stay on message is the brand mantra. The best brands speak with one distinctive voice. On the web, in an advertisement, in conversations by a salesperson, in a speech given by the president, the company needs to project the same unified message. It must be memorable, identifiable, and centered on the customer. Voice and tone work harmoniously with clarity and personality to engage customers, whether they are listening, scanning or reading. Each word offers an opportunity to inform, inspire and fuel word of mouth.

Whether it is a call to action or a product description, language must be vital, straightforward, eloquent and substantive. Be sure the meaning is accessible to all customers. When developing key messages and company descriptions, preserve the impact by cutting through hype and clutter. Brand messages work well if they distill the essence of the product or service. A memorable message grows with repetition, taking on a life of its own.

Language and communications are intrinsic to all brand expressions. Unified, consistent high-level messages demand buy-in at all levels: the commitment must be long-term. Integrated communications require that content and design work together to differentiate the brand.

Let's give them something to talk about.

Bonnie Raitt

Consider the following possibilities:

Nomenclature	Brand esssence	Communications	Information	Touchpoints
Company name formal	Mission statements	Voice	Content	Websites + blogs
Company name informal	Vision statements	Tone	Call to action	News releases
Taglines	Value propositions	Headline style	Phone numbers	FAQs
Descriptors	Key messages	Punctuation	URLs	Press kits
Product names	Guiding principles	Capitalization	Email signatures	Annual reports
Process names	Customer pledges	Emphasis	Voice mail messages	Brochures
Service names	Vocabulary	Accuracy	Abbreviations	Shareholder communications
Division names	History	Clarity	Titles	Call center scripts
	Boilerplate	Consistency	Addresses	Sales scripts
	Elevator speak		Directions	Presentations
				Announcements
				Blast emails
				Advertising campaigns
				Direct mail
				Product directions
				Signage

Fundamental principles

Developed by Lissa Reidel, FolioOne

Use language that resonates with meaning. Readers will complete the message with layers of their own experience.

Aim for clarity, brevity, and precision. A busy executive with only minutes to spare can glean what she needs to know.

Polish and cut as if you were a jeweler. Every sentence will reveal new, intriguing facets to the customer.

Cut through the clutter to produce soundbites that acquire a vibrant identity when they are heard again and again. Consistency is built on repetition.

Edit out modifying phrases, adverbs, and extraneous conversational text and what remains is the distillation, the essence. Eliminate distracting references and the text will have impact. Less is more.

Powers of three

In brand communications, the unified big idea is ideally supported by three key messages.

Originally developed by Dr. Vincent Covello as a risk communications strategy, message mapping was developed because people at risk can only comprehend three messages. This thinking is helpful in brand communications and press relations.

Vigorous writing is concise. A sentence should contain no unnecessary words, a paragraph no unnecessary sentences, for the same reason that a drawing should have no unnecessary lines and a machine no unnecessary parts.
William Strunk Jr. and E.B. White
The Elements of Style

Establishing our key messages for the holding company helps protect our assets and conveys to our operating companies that we value clarity and strategic communications.
Jessica Berwind
Director of Communications
Berwind Corporation

We had our client team take each word in the long scientific name, and put it into different parts of speech (verb, adjective, adverb, noun). It was a starting point to exploring meaning, understanding nuance, participating in discovery, and coming together as a team to discuss key messages.
Margaret Anderson
Managing Principal
Stellarvisions

The right name is timeless, is tireless, is easy to say and remember, stands for something, and facilitates brand extensions. Its sound has rhythm. It looks great in the text of an email and in the logo. A well-chosen name is an essential brand asset, as well as a 24/7 workhorse. A name is transmitted day in and day out, in conversations, emails, voice mails, websites, on the product, on business cards, and in presentations.

The wrong name for a company, product, or service can hinder marketing efforts, through miscommunication or because people cannot pronounce it or remember it. It can subject a company to unnecessary legal risks or alienate a market segment. Finding the right name that is legally available is a gargantuan challenge. Naming requires a creative, disciplined, strategic approach.

In today's competitive world, a name must function as a total messenger.

Naseem Javed
Naming for Power

Just by naming a process, a level of service, or a new service feature, you are creating a valuable asset that can add to the worth of your business.

Jim Bitetto
Partner
Keusey Tutunjian & Bitetto, PC

Companies miss a huge opportunity when they fail to communicate the meaning of a new name. Audiences will better remember a name if they understand its rationale.

Lori Kapner
Principal
Kapner Consulting

Naming myths

Naming a company is easy, like naming a baby.

Naming is a rigorous and exhaustive process. Frequently hundreds of names are reviewed prior to finding one that is legally available and works.

I will know it when I hear it.

People often indicate that they will be able to make a decision after hearing a name once. In fact, good names are strategies and need to be examined, tested, sold, and proven.

We will just do the search ourselves.

Intellectual property lawyers need to conduct extensive searches to ensure that there are no conflicting names and to make record of similar names. It is too large a risk—names need to last over time.

We cannot afford to test the name.

Various thoughtful techniques must be utilized to analyze the effectiveness of a name to ensure that its connotations are positive in the markets served.

Qualities of an effective name

Meaningful
It communicates something about the essence of the brand. It supports the image that the company wants to convey.

Distinctive
It is unique, as well as easy to remember, pronounce, and spell. It is differentiated from the competition.

Future-Oriented
It positions the company for growth, change, and success. It has sustainability and preserves possibilities.

Modular
It enables a company to build brand extensions with ease.

Protectable
It can be owned and trademarked. A domain is available.

Positive
It has positive connotations in the markets served. It has no strong negative connotations.

Visual
It lends itself well to graphic presentation in a logo, in text, and in brand architecture.

The right name has the potential to become a self-propelling publicity campaign, motivating word of mouth, reputation, recommendations, and press coverage.

Lissa Reidel
Folio One

Zoom, the PBS show, has a name with "long legs."

Zoom brand extensions:

Zoomers

Zoomerang

ZoomNooz

Zoomzones

Zoomphenom

CafeZoom

ZoomNoodle

Types of names

Founder
Many companies are named after founders: Ben & Jerry's, Martha Stewart, Ralph Lauren, Mrs. Fields. It might be easier to protect. It satisfies an ego. The downside is that it is inextricably tied to a real human being.

Descriptive
These names convey the nature of the business, such as Toys "R" Us, Find Great People, or E*TRADE. The benefit of a descriptive name is that it clearly communicates the intent of the company. The potential disadvantage is that as a company grows and diversifies, the name may become limiting. Some descriptive names are difficult to protect since they are so generic.

Fabricated
A made-up name, like Kodak, Xerox, or TiVo, is distinctive and might be easier to copyright. However, a company must invest a significant amount of capital into educating its market as to the nature of the business, service, or product. Häagen-Dazs is a fabricated foreign name that has been extremely effective in the consumer market.

Metaphor
Things, places, people, animals, processes, mythological names, or foreign words are used in this type of name to allude to a quality of a company. Names like Nike and Patagonia are interesting to visualize and often can tell a good story.

Acronym
These names are difficult to remember and difficult to copyright. IBM and GE became well known only after the companies established themselves with the full spelling of their names. There are so many acronyms that new ones are increasingly more difficult to learn and require a substantial investment in advertising. Other examples: USAA, AARP, DKNY, and CNN.

Magic spell
Some names alter a word's spelling in order to create a distinctive, protectable name, like Cingular and Netflix.

Combinations of the above
Some of the best names combine name types. Some good examples are Cingular Wireless, Citibank, and Hope's Cookies. Customers and investors like names that they can understand.

Taglines influence consumers' buying behavior by evoking an emotional response. A tagline is a short phrase that captures a company's brand essence, personality, and positioning, and distinguishes the company from its competitors. A tagline's frequent and consistent exposure in the media and in popular culture reinforces its message. Traditionally used in advertising, taglines are also applied on marketing collateral as the centerpiece of a positioning strategy.

Taglines have a shorter life span than logos. Like advertising campaigns, they are susceptible to marketplace and lifestyle changes. Deceptively simple, taglines are not arbitrary. They grow out of an intensive strategic and creative process.

A tagline is a slogan, clarifier, mantra, company statement or guiding principle that describes, synopsizes or helps create an interest.

Debra Koontz Traverso
Outsmarting Goliath

Taglines change

GE's "We bring good things to life" was in place for decades. Viagra's tagline "Let the dance begin" had a relatively short run and was followed by "Keep the spark alive."

"Be the Change," Mercy Corps' new tagline, was developed by Foote Cone Belding and inspired by the Gandhi quote: "You must be the change you wish to see in the world."

The origin of the word *slogan* came from the Gaelic *slaughgaiirm,* used by Scottish clans to mean "war cry."

The advertising tagline "Live Richly," developed by Fallon Worldwide, positions Citi as an advocate for a healthy approach to money.

Brad Jakeman
Managing Director
Global Advertising
Citigroup Consumer Businesses

Taglines sum up the sell, and the best of them evoke an emotional response.

Jerry Selber
LevLane

Essential characteristics

Short

Differentiated from its competitors

Unique

Captures the brand essence and positioning

Easy to say and remember

No negative connotations

Displayed in a small font

Can be protected and trademarked

Evokes an emotional response

Difficult to create

A cross-section of taglines

Company	Tagline
Imperative	
Commands action and usually starts with a verb	
Nike	Just do it
MINI Cooper	Let's motor
Hewlett-Packard	Invent
Apple Computer	Think different
Toshiba	Don't copy. Lead.
Mutual of Omaha	Begin today
Virgin Mobile	Live without a plan
Outward Bound	Live bigger
Descriptive	
Describes the service, product, or brand promise	
Philips	Sense and sensibility
PNC	The thinking behind the money
Target	Expect more. Pay less.
Concentrics	People. Process. Results.
Bank of America	Embracing ingenuity
MSNBC	The whole picture
Ernst & Young	From thought to finish
Allstate	You're in good hands
GE	Imagination at work
Superlative	
Positions the company as best in class	
DeBeers	A diamond is forever
BMW	The ultimate driving machine
Lufthansa	There's no better way to fly
National Guard	Americans at their best
Hoechst	Future in life sciences
Provocative	
Thought-provoking; frequently a question	
Cingular Wireless	What do you have to say?
Sears	Where else?
Microsoft	Where are you going today?
Mercedes-Benz	What makes a symbol endure?
Dairy Council	Got milk?
Specific	
Reveals the business category	
HSBC	The world's local bank
The New York Times	All the News That's Fit to Print
Olay	Love the skin you're in
Volkswagen	Drivers wanted
eBay	Happy hunting
Minolta	The essentials of imaging

From literal through symbolic, from word-driven to image-driven, the world of brandmarks expands each day. Designed with an almost infinite variety of shapes and personalities, brandmarks can be assigned to a number of general categories. The boundaries among these categories are pliant, and many marks may combine elements of more than one category.

Is there a compelling practical reason to categorize them? Although there are no hard-and-fast rules to determine the best type of visual identifier for a particular type of company, the designer's process is to examine a range of solutions based on both aspirational and functional criteria. The designer will determine a design approach that best serves the needs of the client and create a rationale for each distinct approach.

Topology of marks

Wordmarks

A freestanding acronym, company name, or product name that has been designed to convey a brand attribute or positioning

Letterforms

A unique design using one or more letterforms that act as a mnemonic device for a company name.

These marks were designed by Joel Katz Design Associates and his precedent firms over the course of more than 20 years. The range of these marks (which represent only a portion of his firms' identity work) reveals how the best marks are not genre- or style-specific but respond to the nature of the client and its audience.

The Wharton School of the University of Pennsylvania

Verge Restaurant

AGS

Toby Lerner

Qualicon, a DuPont subsidiary

The designer is the medium
between the client and the
audience. A mark should
embody and imply the
client's business goals and
positioning, and address the
end user's needs and wants.

Joel Katz
Joel Katz Design Associates

Synonyms

Brandmark
Trademark
Symbol
Mark
Logo
Identity

Emblems

A mark in which the company
name is inextricably connected to a
pictorial element.

Pictorial marks

An immediately recognizable literal
image that has been simplified and
stylized.

Abstract/symbolic marks

A symbol that conveys a big idea,
and often embodies strategic
ambiguity.

Center City District

Rittenhouse Square District

Joel Katz Design

Energy Department Store

Compass Rose

Penn's Landing

Arx Financial Services

Urban icon, Rome

Most brand identity initiatives entail redesign. As organizations grow, their purpose becomes more lucid, their positioning is refined, and the stakes may shift as new markets open. The creative team is challenged by three crucial questions: What is the business imperative for the change? What elements need to be maintained to preserve brand equity? Should the change be evolutionary or revolutionary?

Before   **After**

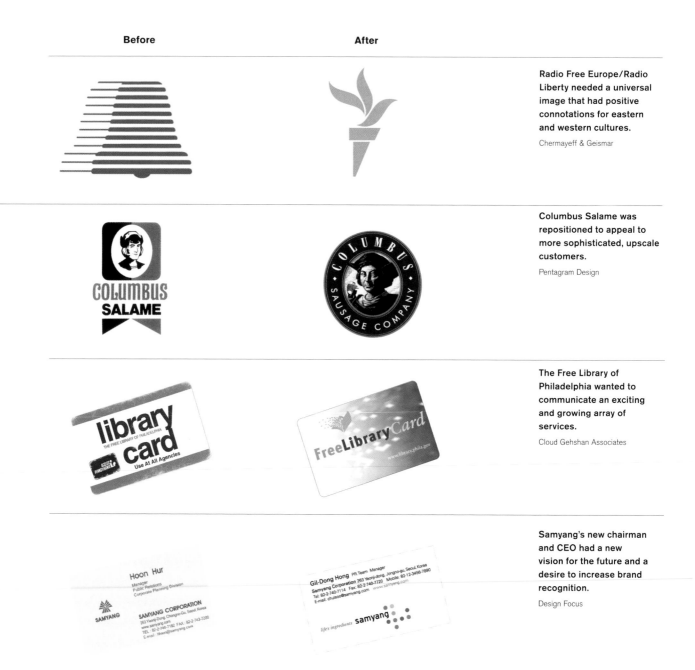

Radio Free Europe/Radio Liberty needed a universal image that had positive connotations for eastern and western cultures.

Chermayeff & Geismar

Columbus Salame was repositioned to appeal to more sophisticated, upscale customers.

Pentagram Design

The Free Library of Philadelphia wanted to communicate an exciting and growing array of services.

Cloud Gehshan Associates

Samyang's new chairman and CEO had a new vision for the future and a desire to increase brand recognition.

Design Focus

Before	After

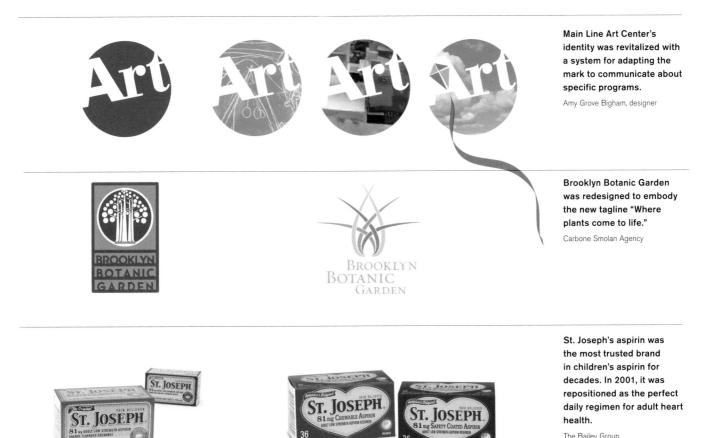

Unilever's new brand identity expressed a core brand idea aligned with the mission, "Adding Vitality to Life."

Wolff Olins

Main Line Art Center's identity was revitalized with a system for adapting the mark to communicate about specific programs.

Amy Grove Bigham, designer

Brooklyn Botanic Garden was redesigned to embody the new tagline "Where plants come to life."

Carbone Smolan Agency

St. Joseph's aspirin was the most trusted brand in children's aspirin for decades. In 2001, it was repositioned as the perfect daily regimen for adult heart health.

The Bailey Group

2001

2005

A wordmark is a freestanding word or words.
It may be a company name or an acronym.
The best wordmarks imbue a legible word(s)
with distinctive font characteristics, and may
integrate abstract elements or pictorial elements.
The distinctive tilted "E" in "Dell" activates
and strengthens the one-syllable name. The
IBM acronym has transcended enormous
technological change in its industry.

Alvin Ailey: Chermayeff & Geismar

Mr. and Mrs. Aubrey Hair: Woody Pirtle

foodsource BY CLEMENS

Kubota

IBM

truth®

CTW

Mobil

OSLO

DELL™

BRAUN

+ TAZO +

foodsource:
Bonita Albertson Design
Kubota: Pentagram
IBM: Paul Rand
truth:
Crispin Porter + Bogusky
Children's Television Workshop:
Milton Glaser
Mobil:
Chermayeff & Geismar
Oslo Airport: Mollerup Design Lab
Dell:
Siegel & Gale
Braun:
Wolfgang Schmittel redesign
Tazo: Sandstrom Design

The single letter is frequently used by designers as a distinctive graphic focal point for a brandmark. The letter is always a unique and proprietary design that is infused with significant personality and meaning. The letterform acts as a mnemonic device, e.g., the "M" for Motorola, the "Q" for Quest Diagnostics. The Westinghouse mark by Paul Rand represents the ideal marriage of letterform and symbolism.

Opposite page A to Z:

Arvin Industries: Bart Crosby

Brokers Insurance: Rev Group

Champion International: Crosby Associates

Dominion: Lizette Gecel

Energy Department Store: Joel Katz Design Associates

Fine Line Features: Woody Pirtle

Goertz Fashion House: Allemann Almquist + Jones

Hammerschön: Britt Funderburk

Irwin Financial Corporation: Chermayeff & Geismar

JoongAng Ilbo: Infinite

Joel Katz: Joel Katz Design Associates

Lifemark Partners: Rev Group

Motorola: Morton Goldsholl

NEPTCO: Malcolm Grear Designers

Owens Illinois: Chermayeff & Geismar

Providence Journals: Malcolm Grear Designers

Quest Diagnostics: Q Cassetti

Rogers Ford: Summerford Design

Seatrain Lines: Chermayeff & Geismar

Telemundo: Chermayeff & Geismar

Univision: Chermayeff & Geismar

Vanderbilt University: Malcolm Grear Designers

Westinghouse: Paul Rand

Royal Caribbean SeaXpress: Greteman Group

YMCA: unknown

Zeek's Pizzeria: Nick Glenn Design

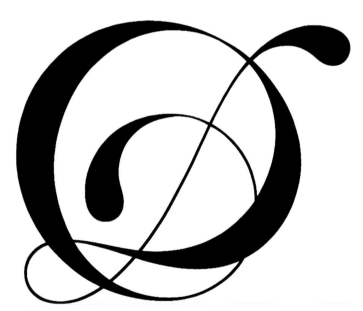

Dallas Opera: Woody Pirtle

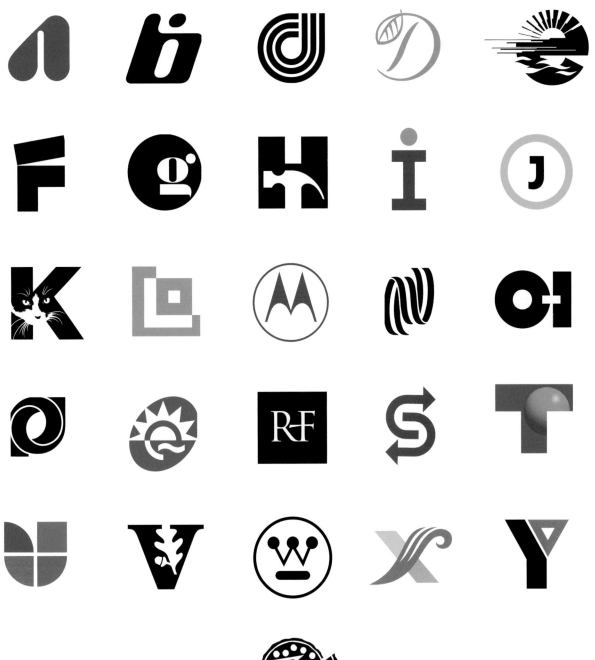

A pictorial mark uses a literal and recognizable image. The image itself may allude to the name of the company or its mission, or it may be symbolic of a brand attribute. The eagle of the U.S. Postal Service is both a symbol of America and a symbol of speed and dependability.

The Fancy Pants Press brand was designed with a balance of wit and elegance. The publisher's name arose from their particular method of "undercover" research. The figure of the traveling journalist is designed to be an ever-morphing model of consistency (professional attire) and audacity (the fancy pants), depending on where it appears.

Richard Cress
Alusiv

Fancy Pants Press: Alusiv

This page from left to right:

CIGNA: Landor Associates

Greyhound USA:
Raymond Loewy

British Telecom:
Wolff Olins

Lacoste: Robert George

March of Dimes:
Pentagram

Merrill Lynch: King-Casey

Flab Bat 25/a division of
the Swiss Army: Allemann
Almquist + Jones

NBC: Chermayeff & Geismar

PBS: Chermayeff & Geismar

Tusk: Milton Glaser

World Wildlife Foundation:
Landor Associates redesign

Angels in America:
Milton Glaser

Great American Fish:
Warkulwiz Design
Associates

An abstract mark uses visual form to convey a big idea or a brand attribute. These marks, by their nature, can provide strategic ambiguity, and work effectively for large companies with numerous and unrelated divisions. Marks, such as Chase's, have survived a series of mergers easily. Abstract marks are especially effective for service-based and technology companies; however, they are extremely difficult to design well.

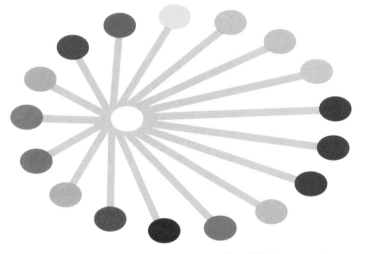

Stem Cell Conference: Cronan

The Stem Cell Conference symbol represents both an undifferentiated stem cell represented by the white dot in the center and a mature cell represented by the whole form. I wanted to suggest the possibilities of scientific discovery, as well as the creative aspect symbolized by an artist's palette.

Michael Cronan
Cronan

This page from left to right:

Sprint: Lippincott Mercer

Hyatt Place: Lippincott Mercer

Penns Landing:
Joel Katz Design Associates

Screen Gems:
Chermayeff & Geismar

Concentrics: Rev Group

Ilona Financial Group:
Rev Group

Alina Wheeler: Rev Group

JDM Partners: Rev Group

The Field Museum:
Crosby Associates

Merck: Chermayeff & Geismar

Pan American World Congress of Architects:
Chermayeff & Geismar

Sacred Heart Hospital: Infinite

Brinker Capital: Rev Group

Emblems are trademarks featuring a pictorial element inextricably connected to the name of the organization. The elements are never isolated. The sea nymph that dwells inside the green and black Starbucks Coffee trademark will never swim away from her green circular band. Emblems look terrific on a package, as a sign, or as an embroidered patch on a uniform.

As mobile devices continue to shrink and multi-branding ads with one-sixth inch logos increase, the emblem presents the biggest legibility challenge when miniaturized.

Bruegger's Bagels: Milton Glaser

Milton Glaser created a linkage between the idea of freshly baked bagels and time. The logo began with an actual clock – as the central disks rotate, animated bagels begin to dance. In addition, Glaser also designed a proprietary typeface, "Bruggers," that is used in interior signage and wall menus.

Harry's Road House:
Anthony D'Agostino

Itza Pizza:
Warkulwiz Design Associates

333 Belrose Bar & Grill:
Anne Pagliarulo

Columbus Salame:
Pentagram

Zao Noodle Bar:
Cronan

Bella Cucina:
Louise Fili Ltd.

John Templeton Foundation:
Rev Group

TiVo:
Cronan

Polly-o:
Wallace Church

Studio 360:
Opto Design

Brooklyn Brewery:
Milton Glaser

92:
Louise Fili Ltd.

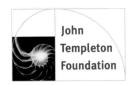

It's alive! A character trademark is created to embody brand attributes or values, and is usually tied to a product-based brand. Characters quickly become central to advertising campaigns and trade shows. The best ones become cultural icons cherished by children and customers alike. Along with their distinctive appearance and personality, many characters have recognizable voices and jingles, enabling them to leap off the silent shelf space into your television and onto your desktop.

While the ideas that drive the personification may be timeless and universal, characters rarely age well and usually need to be redrawn and dragged into contemporary culture. The Michelin man, well over 100 years old, has been modified numerous times. As moms became working women, Betty Crocker was caught between generations. The Columbia Pictures goddess received a major facelift, but she has never looked happy and satisfied holding that torch. Each Olympics creates a mascot that will be animated and deanimated in thousands of stuffed animals. Who knew a gecko could sell car insurance?

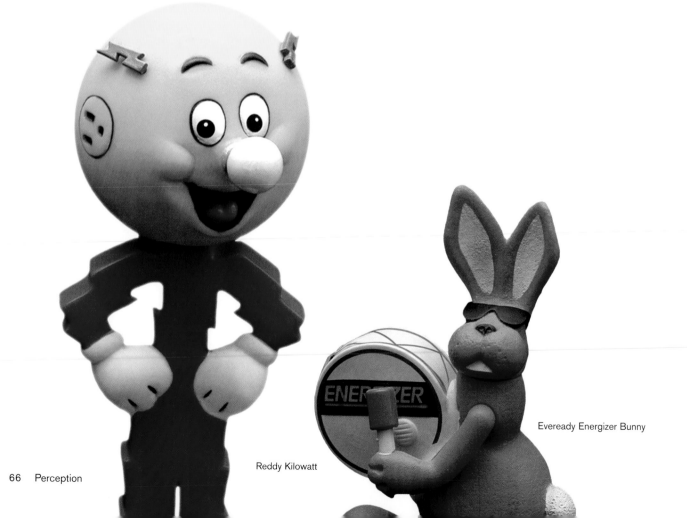

Reddy Kilowatt

Eveready Energizer Bunny

Character	Company	Year created
Uncle Sam	Government war bonds	1838
Aunt Jemima	Pancake mix and syrup	1893
Michelin Man	Michelin tires	1898
Mr. Peanut	Planters	1916
Betty Crocker	Food products	1921
Reddy Kilowatt	Electric company	1926
Jolly Green Giant	Green Giant vegetables	1928
Leo the Lion	MGM Pictures	1928
Mickey Mouse	Walt Disney Co.	1928
Windy	Zippo lighter	1937
Elsie the Cow	Borden dairy products	1939
Rosie the Riveter	Illustration for working woman, WWII	1943
Smokey the Bear	USDA forest service	1944
Elmer the Bull	Elmer's Glue-All	1947
Tony the Tiger	Kellogg's Frosted Flakes	1951
Trix the Bunny	General Mills cereal	1960
Charlie the Tuna	Starkist tuna	1960
Columbia Goddess	Columbia Pictures Corporation	1961
Ronald McDonald	McDonald's restaurants	1963
Exxon Tiger	Exxon Oil Company	1964
Pillsbury Doughboy	Assorted Pillsbury foods	1969
Ernie Keebler & the elves	Kellogg's crackers	1969
Nesquik Bunny	Nesquik	1970s
Energizer Bunny	Eveready Energizer batteries	1989
Jeeves	Ask Jeeves	1996
Aflac duck	Aflac Insurance	2000
Gecko	Geico	2002

Elsie the Cow was created in 1939 by Stuart Peabody, Director of Advertising for Borden Dairy Products.

In 1948 on the eve of the presidential election, 88 percent of the American public knew who Elsie was, compared to 84 percent for the Republican candidate, Thomas Dewey.

In 1957, in Borden's centennial year, Elsie had twins. A name-the-calves contest drew 3 million entries via mail.

Elmer the Bull was originally created to be Elsie's husband. Since 1947 Elmer has been the mascot of America's best-known consumer adhesive brand, Elmer's Glue, and has appeared on hundreds of products.

Look and feel is the visual language that makes a system proprietary and immediately recognizable. It also expresses a point of view. This support system of color, imagery, typography, and composition is what makes an entire program cohesive and differentiated.

In the best programs designers create an overall look that resonates in the mind of the customer and rises above the clutter of a visual environment. All elements of a visual language should be intentionally designed to advance the brand strategy, each doing its part and working together as a whole to unify and distinguish.

You should be able to cover up the logo and still identify the company because the look and feel is so distinctive.

Michael Bierut, Partner
Pentagram

The identity for the Brooklyn Academy of Music (BAM), designed by Pentagram, hinges on an unrelenting commitment to a bold visual language that takes the identity to a place no logo could venture alone. Every piece of communication is instantly recognizable from across the room because it is built with the same visual vocabulary: horizontal bars interrupting large News Gothic type. These repeating bars merging with overscaled type create a dramatic, rhythmic structure for event-specific imagery and information.

Brooklyn Academy of Music:
Pentagram

Design

Design is intelligence made visible. The marriage of design and content is the only marriage that lasts.

Color palettes

Systems may have two color systems: primary and secondary. Business lines or products may have their own colors. A color system may have a pastel range and a primary range.

Imagery

Within the category of content, style, focus and color, all need to be considered whether the imagery is photography, illustration, or iconography.

Typography

Systems incorporate typeface families: one or sometimes two. It is not unusual for a special typeface to be designed for a high visibility brand.

Sensory

There are also material qualities (how something feels in your hand—texture and weight), interactive qualities (how something opens or moves), and auditory and olfactory qualities (how something sounds and smells, respectively).

BAM identity mantra

An identity is not a logo.

Start from the inside out.

Use simple, easy-to-understand rules.

Don't get bored.

Be talented.

Have fun.

Everyone involved on the marketing committee loved it but said, "Harvey is going to want to know why." In response I said, "It's about showing that BAM is transgressive—it crosses boundaries and it's over the horizon."

Michael Bierut
Partner
Pentagram

69

2 Process

Part 2 presents a universal brand identity process that underlies all successful brand identity initiatives, regardless of the project's scope and nature. This section answers the question "Why does it take so long?" and addresses collaboration and decision making.

The process is the process, but then you need a spark of genius.

Brian P. Tierney, Esq., Founder
Tierney Communications

The brand identity process is a proven and disciplined method for creating and implementing an identity. It is a rigorous process demanding a combination of investigation, strategic thinking, design excellence, and project management skills. It requires an extraordinary amount of patience, an obsession for getting it right, and an ability to synthesize vast amounts of information.

Regardless of the nature of the client and the complexity of the engagement, the process remains the same. What changes is the depth with which each phase is conducted, the length of time and the number of resources allocated, and the size of the team, on both the identity firm and client sides.

The process is defined by distinct phases with logical beginning and ending points, which facilitate decision making at the appropriate intervals. Eliminating steps or reorganizing the process might present an appealing way to cut costs and time, but doing so can pose substantial risks and impede long-term benefits. The process, when done right, can produce remarkable results.

Navigating through the political process–building trust–building relationships–it's everything.

Paula Scher, Partner
Pentagram

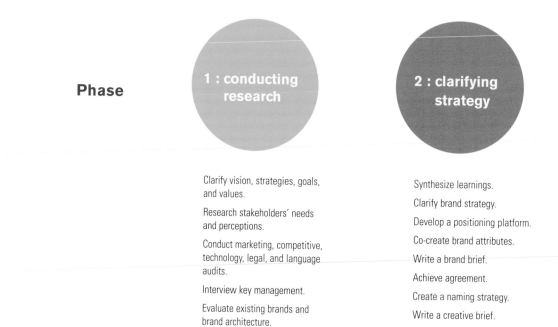

Phase

1 : conducting research

Clarify vision, strategies, goals, and values.

Research stakeholders' needs and perceptions.

Conduct marketing, competitive, technology, legal, and language audits.

Interview key management.

Evaluate existing brands and brand architecture.

Present audit readout.

2 : clarifying strategy

Synthesize learnings.

Clarify brand strategy.

Develop a positioning platform.

Co-create brand attributes.

Write a brand brief.

Achieve agreement.

Create a naming strategy.

Write a creative brief.

Process is a competitive advantage

Assures the client that a proven method is being used to achieve business results

Accelerates understanding and acceptance of the investment of necessary time and resources

Engenders trust and confidence in the identity firm

Positions project management as smart, efficient, and cost-effective

Builds credibility and strengthens identity solutions

Sets expectations for the complexity of the process

Most processes leave out the stuff that no one wants to talk about: magic, intuition and leaps of faith.

Michael Bierut
Partner
Pentagram

3 : designing identity

Visualize the future.

Brainstorm big idea.

Design brand identity.

Explore applications.

Finalize brand architecture.

Present visual strategy.

Achieve agreement.

4 : creating touchpoints

Finalize identity design.

Develop look and feel.

Initiate trademark protection.

Prioritize and design applications.

Design program.

Apply brand architecture.

5 : managing assets

Build synergy around new brand.

Develop launch strategy and plan.

Launch internally first.

Launch externally.

Develop standards and guidelines.

Nurture brand champions.

Astute project management is critical to achieving the long-term goals of a brand identity project. Responsible project management is the foundation for mutual respect, confidence, and long-term success. The identity process demands a range of skills on both the client side and the identity firm side. It demands leadership and creativity working hand in hand with planning, coordinating, analyzing, understanding, and managing time, resources, and money. In addition to organization and discipline, the process requires patience, enthusiasm, and a laser-like focus on achieving the end goal.

How long will it take?

All clients have a sense of urgency, regardless of the size and nature of the company. There are no shortcuts to the process, and eliminating steps may be detrimental to achieving long-term goals. Developing an effective and sustainable identity takes time. There are no instant answers, and a commitment to a responsible process is imperative.

Time factors

The length of a brand identity project is affected by the following factors:

Size of organization

Complexity of business

Number of markets served

Type of market: global, national, regional, local

Nature of problem

Research required

Legal requirements (merger or public offering)

Decision-making process

Number of decision makers

Number of applications

Pay as much attention to the process as to the content.

Michael Hirshhorn
Organizational dynamics expert

Process : project management

Team protocol	> Team commitment	> Benchmarks and schedule	> Decision-making protocol	> Communications protocol
Identify client project manager + team.	Team must commit to:	Identify deliverables.	Establish process.	Establish document flow.
Identify firm contact + team. Clearly define team goals.	Robust debate	Identify key dates.	Determine decision makers.	Decide who gets copied how.
Establish roles and responsibilities.	Open communications	Develop project schedule.	Clarify benefits and disadvantages.	Put everything in writing.
Understand policies and procedures.	Confidentiality	Update schedules as necessary.	Put all decisions in writing.	Create agendas.
Circulate pertinent contact data.	Dedication to brand	Develop task matrix.		Circulate meeting notes.
	Mutual respect			Develop Internet project site if appropriate to scale of project.

Who manages the project?

Client side

For a small business, the founder or owner is invariably the project leader, the key decision maker, and the visionary. In a larger company, the project manager is whomever the CEO designates: the director of marketing and communications, the brand manager, the public relations firm on retainer, or maybe the CFO.

The project manager must be someone with authority who can make things happen, given the enormous amount of coordination, scheduling, and information gathering. He or she must also have direct access to the CEO and other decision makers. In a large company, the CEO usually forms a brand team, which may include representatives from different divisions or business lines. Although this team may not be the ultimate decision-making group, they must have access to the key decision makers.

Identity firm side

In a large brand consultancy, a dedicated project manager is the key client contact. Various tasks are handled by specialists, from market researchers and business analysts, to naming specialists and designers. In a small to midsize firm, the principal may be the main client contact, senior creative director, and senior designer. A firm may bring on specialists as needed, from market research firms, to naming experts, to create a virtual team that meets the unique needs of the client.

Characteristics of the best project managers

Developed by Dr. Ginny Vanderslice, Praxis Consulting Group

Focus
Ability to see and maintain the big picture and at the same time to break it down into smaller ordered pieces; ability to keep moving despite challenges and constraints

Discipline
Ability to plan, track numerous tasks, and balance time and cost factors

Strong communication skills
Ability to communicate clearly, respectfully, and in a timely fashion to keep all team members fully informed

Empathy
Ability to understand and respond to the needs, viewpoints, and perspectives of all players in the project

Effective management skills
Ability to define needs, priorities, and tasks; ability to make decisions; ability to flag problems; ability to hold people accountable

Flexibility (adaptability)
Ability to stay focused and in control when things go wrong or change in midstream

Creative problem-solving ability
Willingness to see problems as challenges to address rather than as obstacles

Insight
Understanding of policies, procedures, corporate culture, key people, and politics

---

> **Documentation**

Date all documents.

Date each sketch process.

Assign version numbers to key documents.

> **Information gathering**

Determine responsibilities.

Determine dates.

Identify proprietary information.

Develop task matrix.

Develop audit.

Determine how you will collect audit materials.

> **Legal protocol**

Identify intellectual property resource.

Understand compliance issues.

Gather confidentiality statements.

> **Presentation protocol**

Circulate goals in advance.

Hand out agenda at meeting.

Determine presentation medium.

Develop uniform presentation system.

Obtain approvals and sign-offs.

Identify next steps.

Great outcomes require vision, commitment, and collaboration. Collaboration is not consensus or compromise. It evolves from a thoughtful and genuine focus on problem solving, generating an interdependent, connected approach. It also acknowledges the tension between different viewpoints and different disciplines.

Most brand identity projects involve individuals from various departments with different agendas. Even small organizations have silos that stand in the way of achievement. Collaboration requires the ability to suspend judgment, listen carefully, and transcend politics.

It was an amazing collaborative experience. There is so much complexity in making something so simple. Each one of us had a piece of soul in this Centennial Olympic project.
Malcolm Grear
CEO
Malcolm Grear Designers

Let go of stereotypes. Intellectual property lawyers do have creative thoughts, investment bankers can feel compassion, and designers can do math.
Blake Deutsch

When I work with a writer, we shed our own passionate and personal viewpoints, listen deeply, and allow a third person to emerge with a new vision.
Ed Williamson
Art Director

You may have the greatest bunch of individual stars in the world, but if they don't play together, the club won't be worth a dime.

Babe Ruth

Fundamental principles

Developed by Linda Wingate, Wingate Consulting

Leadership must believe in collaboration and its organizational benefits.

Listen to all perspectives; share your viewpoint honestly; put all issues on the table.

Promote participation.

Everyone's contribution is important.

Develop strong professional relationships, building high levels of trust and rapport; suspend titles and organizational roles.

Engage in dialogue; find a common purpose and language for learning and communicating; construct guiding principles for decision making.

Provide equal access to information; create a common work process; examine assumptions and data objectively.

Guarantee cooperation, engagement, and ownership; recognize that rewards are earned for the group, not for individuals; shed any competitive "win–lose" mentality.

Create team protocols.

Like King Arthur's Round Table, effective teams acknowledge and respect diverse expertise, share power, actively debate, unite around a common purpose and use their collective intelligence to achieve ambitious goals.

Moira Cullen
Design Director
Coca-Cola Company

To be on a team, you have to let go of your ego, and strive for the endpoint.

Cathy Feierstein
Vice President
Organizational Learning
Assurant

The integrated marketing team sees branding as a continuous network activity that needs to be controlled from within the company, where best-in-breed specialists work side by side with internal marketing people. The advantage of this model is the ability to unify the message across media.

Marty Neumeier
The Brand Gap

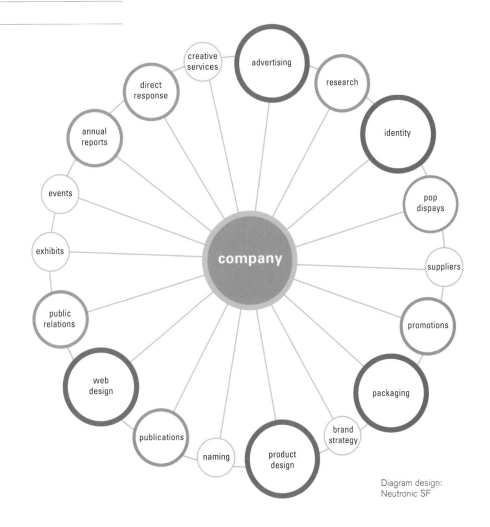

Diagram design:
Neutronic SF

Decision making can be designed to be an intelligent, engaging process that builds trust and helps organizations make the right choices to build their brand. Most people can recall a scenario in which the wrong decision was made because of either politics or too many decision makers. Experts in the social sciences believe that decisions made by large groups tend to be more conservative and less inspired than decisions made by small groups. Yet organizational development experts may tell you that decision by consensus has the potential to result in higher-quality decisions because the organization uses the resources of its members.

The path to reconciling these seemingly conflicting points of view leads to a brand champion or CEO with strong leadership skills—someone who can elicit ideas and opinions from a wider group without succumbing to group-think. In an ideal situation, the final decision makers, regardless of the size of the organization, should be kept to a very small group led by the CEO. The group makes informed choices that are aligned with the vision of the organization, and is involved throughout the process at key decision points, e.g., agreement on goals, brand strategy, names, taglines, and brandmarks.

Smart organizations often use the branding process to refocus stakeholders in the vision and mission of the organization. When it is done well, people throughout the organization feel valued and begin to "own" the new brand.

Decision making requires trusting yourself, your process and your team.

Dr. Barbara Riley, Managing Partner
Chambers Group LLC

A lot of decisions are made in quiet conference rooms where new work can look radical or intimidating. But the work—the branded experience—needs to work OUT THERE. It's a noisy and busy world. You can spend a lot of money and discover that the customer doesn't know the difference. When you build things by consensus, you can lose your distinctiveness.

Susan Avarde
Managing Director
Global Branding
Citigroup Consumer Businesses

Red flags

The CEO (or global brand manager) does not have time to meet with you.

I will know it when I see it.

We are going to show all the partners to see if they like it.

We are going to use focus groups to help us make the right decision.

We know that is the better design, but the CEO's husband does not like it.

We want to show the entire list of 573 names to the CEO and let her decide what she likes best.

Let's vote on our favorites.

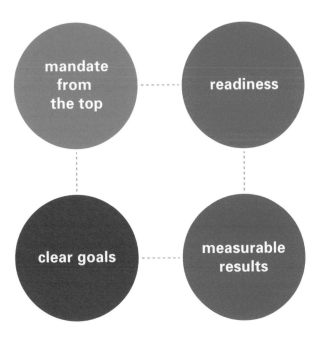

Essential characteristics

The CEO leads a small group that includes marketing brand champions.

The entire process is clearly communicated to key stakeholders.

Decisions are aligned with vision and goals.

All members are trusted and respected.

Agreement on goals and positioning strategy precedes creative strategy.

All relevant information and concerns are voiced and tracked.

Pros and cons are always fully discussed.

A commitment is made to communicate about the brand through all levels of the organization.

Focus groups are used as a tool, not as a thought leader.

Decisions are communicated internally first.

Confidentiality is honored.

Challenging scenarios

When the CEO is not involved.

When new decision makers get involved in the middle of the process.

When team members' opinions are not respected.

When critical steps are eliminated in the process to save money and time.

When personal aesthetics get confused with functional criteria.

Mergers and acquisitions

Financial stakes are high.

Difficult to gather input when confidentiality is critical.

Time frame is compressed and atmosphere is tense.

Names and marks used in a symbolic chess match.

Everyone needs attention of leadership.

Critical to maintain focus on customer benefit.

Critical success factors

The CEO supports this initiative.

The company is ready to invest time, resources, and brainpower.

There is an endpoint that everyone understands and agrees on.

Everyone agrees on how success will be measured. There is value to the outcome.

If you have gone through a process with people you respect, a decision is not a leap of faith. It's planning.

Dr. Barbara Riley
Managing Partner
Chambers Group LLC

Designing an identity is a dance between the intuitive and intentional. The greatest challenge of the brand identity process is to realize that you cannot control anything other than your focus and attention. Trusting the process and keeping the ball in the air will always deliver extraordinary outcomes. Just breathe.

Although research is the business discipline for gathering and interpreting data, insight comes from a more personal and intuitive place. Observing the world and listening nonjudgmentally to ideas of others opens up possibilities. The work itself becomes the hero.

listening

One-on-one interviews
Focus groups
SWOTs
Visioning

Insight leads to compelling new customer experiences.

Michael Dunn, CEO
Prophet

collecting data

Market sizing
Awareness
Attitudes
Recognition
Reputation
Statistics
Demographics

Corpus callosum

Left brain	Right brain
Logical	Random
Sequential	Intuitive
Rational	Holistic
Analytic	Synthesizing
Objective	Subjective
Looks at parts	Looks at wholes

The future belongs to a very different kind of person with a very different kind of mind—creators and empathizers, pattern recognizers and meaning makers. These people (are) artists, inventors, designers, storytellers, caregivers, consolers, big picture thinkers. We are moving from an economy and a society built on the logical, linear, computer-like capabilities of the Information Age to an economy and a society built on the inventive, empathic, big picture capabilities of what's rising in its place, the Conceptual Age.

Dan Pink
A Whole New Mind

Analytics are important, providing the data that allows marketers to stay focused and pragmatic, while also serving to set boundaries and provide the underlying rationale for marketing decisions. But analytics shouldn't be allowed to overwhelm the intuition that characterizes great marketers. It's the insights that the data leads to that result in breakthrough products and compelling new customer experiences.

Michael Dunn
CEO
Prophet

Insights appear when we stop thinking and let go. Answers to an intractable problem can come on a walk, in a dream, or in the shower. When we least expect it, fragmented thinking falls away and the whole appears, with the solution in bold type.

Lissa Reidel
Folio One

observing

Customer experience
Ethnography
Digital ethnography
Usability studies
Mystery shopping
Eye tracking

weaving

History and future
Competitive analysis
Trend analysis
Benchmarking
Perceptual mapping
Audit readout

dreaming

Visioning
Mood board

focusing

Goals
Segmentation
Mind map
Positioning

Hold that thought!

Timing is everything. "Parking lots" are documents that capture insights as they happen. At various points in the process, revisit them. Powerful and creative thoughts are preserved through the swirl of deadlines and politics.

risk-taking

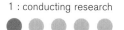

The best identities have business acumen, as well as aesthetic value. The first priority is to understand the organization: its mission, vision, target markets, corporate culture, competitive advantage, strengths and weaknesses, marketing strategies, and challenges for the future. Learning must be focused and accelerated. Clients hire firms with the intellectual capacity to understand the business as a way of ensuring that the solutions are linked to business strategies and goals.

Understanding comes from various sources— from reading strategic documents and business plans, to interviewing key stakeholders. Requesting the appropriate information from a client is the first step, it should precede interviewing of any key management or stakeholders.

Listening to the organization's vision and strategies for the future forms the nucleus of the creative process for a new identity. Interviewing key people face-to-face provides invaluable insight into the voice, cadence, and personality of an organization. Frequently, ideas and strategies that may never have been recorded before emerge during an interview.

Understanding may also be achieved by experiencing the organization from a customer's perspective, gaining insight from navigating the website, and seeing how easy it is to understand the product offerings, receive a sales pitch, or use the products. The goals are to uncover the essence of this company and to understand how the organization fits into the larger competitive environment.

Answering questions is relatively easy. Asking the right question is more difficult.

Michael Cronan
Cronan

Baseline information to request

Request these business background materials to learn more about the organization prior to any interviews. If it is a public company, examine what financial analysts say about the company's performance and future prospects.

Mission	Existing marketing research
Vision	Cultural assessments
Values statement	Employee surveys
Value proposition	CEO speeches
Organization chart	Press releases
Strategic planning documents	News clippings
Business plans	History
Marketing plans	Domains
Annual reports	Intranet access

Interviewing key stakeholders

Interviewing key management is routinely done face-to-face. Frequently, the identity firm principal will tape the interview and transcribe it rather than taking notes. This facilitates eye contact and a better interview. If necessary, interviewing can be done over the telephone. Building trust is another agenda. The quality of the questions and the rapport established in the interview set the tone for an important relationship. Encourage individuals to be brief and succinct. Do not provide questions in advance, if possible, since spontaneous answers may be more insightful. It is absolutely critical for you to read through the baseline information about the company before conducting any interview.

The following questions should be customized before the interview. It is important to convey that you have already examined the documents provided. The list of who is interviewed is co-created with a client. It is best to keep interviews under one hour in length.

Core interview questions

What business are you in?

What is your mission? What are your three most important goals?

Why was this company created?

Describe your products or services.

Who is your target market?

Prioritize your stakeholders in order of importance. How do you want to be perceived by each audience?

What is your competitive advantage? Why do your customers choose your product or service? What do you do better than anyone else?

Who is your competition? Is there a competitor that you admire most? If so, why?

How do you market your product and services?

What are the trends and changes that affect your industry?

Where will you be in five years? In ten years?

How do you measure success?

What values and beliefs unify your employees and drive their performance?

What are the potential barriers to the success of your product or service?

Place yourself in the future. If your company could do anything or be anything, what would it be?

If you could communicate a single message about your company, what would it be?

Market research is the gathering, evaluation, and interpretation of data affecting customer preferences for products, services, and brands. This tool is used to understand attitudes, awareness, and behavior of potential and existing customers in various market segments. Results often indicate opportunities for future growth.

From brand image studies, to online surveys examining customer satisfaction and web usability, market research takes many forms. Traditionally research is classified as qualitative or quantitative, and primary or secondary. Research is not a black box that automatically provides an answer. Rather, it is a tool that seeks to probe and reveal new insights about customer preferences and behavior. Believers hold that it is a necessary foundation for meaningful brand strategy—and the only way to validate preconceived impressions. Smart research can be a catalyst for change; useless research can stand in the way of innovation.

Large brand consultancies have developed proprietary research tools and client intelligence competencies to help global corporations develop brand strategy. Smaller branding firms may partner with market research firms and, in many cases, are provided with existing research reports about customer preferences or marketing segments. Interpretating data is a skill in itself. The web has enabled almost anyone to become a market researcher, which means that even the smallest business can gain new insights. All you have to do is Google or "Ask Jeeves."

Not everything that counts can be counted, and not everything that can be counted counts.

Albert Einstein

Search engines have empowered a new generation of sleuths as they quietly surf across mountains of data and links to the unknown.

Researchers use information to quantify, qualify, define, benchmark, and cast a critical eye on a company and its brand, the markets they serve, and the opportunities they seek.

Dennis Dunn, Ph.D.
Principal
B2BPulse

Ethnography is the holistic study of experience, meaning-making, and behavior in the context of daily life.

Davis Masten
Chairman and Catalyst
Cheskin

Primary research
The collection of new information designed to fit specific needs.

Secondary research
The interpretation and application of existing statistical, demographic, or qualitative data.

Qualitative research
Qualitative research can reveal customers' concepts, beliefs, feelings, and motives. Findings are often rich in context and may offer new insights and perspectives about the brand. Qualitative research, e.g. listening and observing, is intrinsic to the brand identity process, and a prelude for success.

One-on-one interviews
Individual in-depth interviews with senior management, important customers, and thought leaders are ideally conducted face-to-face, but may be conducted on the phone. The information and anecdotes that this method yields are rich and are particularly valuable to the brand identity process.

Focus groups
A fast-paced group discussion about predetermined topics led by a moderator with participants who are carefully selected because they share common characteristics. Focus groups are best used to uncover attitudes, perceptions, needs, prejudices, ways of using products, and viewpoints on pricing and distribution. The value of focus groups is frequently debated.

Competitive intelligence
Many business information database services on the web provide data and information about industries, private and public companies, and their stock activity and management. Some of this information is free and easy to access, while a good deal of it is through subscription. Brokers are also a good source of industry and stock reports, as are press archives.

Quantitative research
Quantitative research creates statistically valid market information. The aim is to provide enough data from enough different people to enable companies to predict—with an acceptable range of confidence—what might happen. A large group of people is asked exactly the same questions in precisely the same way. The sample is a microcosm that has the same characteristics of the overall target market. Researchers attempt to project the opinions of a relatively small number of people (the sample) to model the opinions of the entire population.

Online surveys
An online survey is one of several ways to gather primary research data. This approach uses the Internet to gather information from respondents as they sit at their own computers. Typically, potential respondents receive an e-mail inviting them to take a survey, with a link to the survey itself.

Usability testing
This type of testing examines how easily users navigate a website. Teams of designers and human-factor engineers observe a user through a two-way mirror in a formal laboratory testing environment. Users are selected carefully, and results are analyzed in depth. Informal usability testing takes place in an individual's work environment and may not include human-factor engineers. This type of testing is also used for products.

Eye tracking
Eye movement recorders examine how an individual views packaging, advertisements, signs, shelf displays, or computer screens by tracking eye movements. These devices show when the subject starts to view a picture, the order in which the elements of the image were examined and reexamined, and the amount of viewing time given each element.

Mystery shopping
Trained mystery shoppers anonymously visit stores, branch banks, and other locations where they pose as customers. They evaluate the shopping experience, salesmanship, professionalism, closing skills, follow-up, and overall satisfaction. Mystery shoppers follow a list of predefined steps, make mental notes, observe conditions and performance, and produce audit reports that provide objective feedback.

Segmentation
Consumers and businesses are divided into clustered groups, each with its own special interests, lifestyles, and affinity for particular goods and services. Consumer segments are usually defined by demographic and psychographic information. Demographics are vital statistics, such as age, sex, marital status, ethnicity, family size and composition, education, income, occupation, and housing. Psychographics refer to psychological attributes that describe an individual's lifestyle or attitudes. Business segments are often described in terms of the nature or size of the business. Such variables as industry, geographic scope, number of employees, dollar volume, and types of customers served are important.

Global segmentation
Geography, culture, and language are segmentation variables just as industry, occupation, sex, income, education, and marital status are. As companies become global, the desire to understand customer needs, desires, expectations and behaviors becomes more complex. Language, cultural perspectives, and value systems differ dramatically. Concepts and approaches that work well in the United States may be destined to fail in Saudi Arabia, France, or Japan.

Brand equity research
Surveys and interviews are combined with market analysis to track the reach of the brand, the degree of recognition by consumers, and the brand's ability to capture market share. This research is a frequent tool used to gauge the impact of mergers and acquisitions and name changes.

Name awareness research
Surveys of users and non-users seek to determine name recognition, gaps, brand strengths and weaknesses, and opportunities for extending the brand to new market segments.

Reputation research
Reputation research investigates how the brand, company, and product are viewed, and identifies the various stakeholders and audiences and their perceptions and expectations.

Repositioning an organization, revitalizing and redesigning an existing identity system, or developing a new identity for a merger requires an examination of the communications and marketing tools an organization has used in the past. Identifying what has worked and what has been successful or even dysfunctional provides valuable learning in the creation of a new identity. Mergers present the most challenging audit scenarios because two companies that were competitors are now becoming aligned.

Marketing audits are used to methodically examine and analyze all marketing, communications, and identity systems, both existing systems and those out of circulation. The process takes a

magnifying glass to the brand and its multiple expressions over time. To develop a vision for an organization's brand in the future, you must have a sense of its history.

Inevitably, something of worth has been tossed out over time—a tagline, a symbol, a phrase, a point of view—for what seemed to be a good reason at the time. There might be something from the past that should be resuscitated or repurposed. Perhaps a color or a tagline has been in place since the founding of the company. Consider whether this equity should be moved forward.

Examine customer experience first and move to the intersection of strategy, content, and design.

Carla Hall, Creative Director
Carla Hall Design Group

Understand the big picture	> Request materials	> Create a system	> Solicit information	> Examine materials
Markets served	Existing + archival	Organization	Contextual/historical background	Business papers
Sales + distribution	Identity standards	Retrieval	Marketing management	Electronic communications
Marketing management	Business papers	Documentation	Communications functions	Sales + marketing
Communications functions	Sales + marketing	Review	Attitudes toward brand	Internal communications
Internal technology	Electronic communications		Attitudes toward identity	Environments
Challenges	Internal communications			Packaging
	Signage			
	Packaging			

Request materials

The following is the broad range of materials to request. It is important to create an effective organization and retrieval system since in all probability you will be amassing a large collection. It is important to have a person provide background about what has worked and what has not worked.

Organizing audits

Create a war room, and put everything on the walls.

Buy file boxes and create hanging files for categories.

Devise a standard system to capture findings.

Take a "before" picture.

Brand identity
All versions of all identities ever used

All signatures, marks, logotypes

Company names

Division names

Product names

All taglines

All trademarks owned

Standards and guidelines

Business papers
Letterhead, envelopes, labels, business cards

Fax forms

Invoices, statements

Proposal covers

Folders

Forms

Electronic communications
Website

Intranet

Extranet

Video

Banners

Blogs

Sales and marketing
Sales and product literature

Newsletters

Advertising campaigns

Investor relations materials

Annual reports

Seminar literature

PowerPoint presentations

Internal communications
Employee communications

Ephemera (T-shirts, baseball caps, pens)

Holiday greetings

Environmental applications
External signage

Internal signage

Store interiors

Banners

Trade show booths

Retail
Packaging

Promotions

Shopping bags

Menus

Merchandise

Displays

> **Examine identity**

Marks

Logotypes

Color

Imagery

Typography

Look and feel

> **Examine how things happen**

Process

Decision making

Communications responsibility

In-house + webmaster

Production

Advertising agency

> **Document learnings**

Equity

Brand architecture

Positioning

Key messages

Visual language

A competitive audit is a dynamic, data-gathering process. Simply put, this audit examines the competition's brands, key messages, and identity in the marketplace, from its brandmarks and taglines, to their ads and websites. More than ever, it is easy to gather information on the Internet; however, a company should not stop there. Finding ways to experience the competition as a customer often provides valuable insights.

The greater the insight into the competition, the greater the competitive edge. Positioning the company in relationship to the competition is both a marketing and a design imperative. "Why should the customer choose our products or services over those of others?" is the marketing challenge. "We need to look and feel different" is the design imperative.

The breadth and depth of this audit can vary widely depending on the nature of the company and the scope of the project. Frequently, a company has its own competitive intelligence. Qualitative or quantitative research that can be a source of critical data need to be reviewed.

An audit is an opportunity to build a complete understanding of the business and establish a context for the branding solution.

David Kendall, Principal
Kendall Ross

Process : competitive audit

Identify competitors	Gather information/research	Determine positioning	Identify key messages	Examine visual identity
Who are leading competitors?	List information needed.	Examine competitive positioning.	Mission	Symbols
Who most closely resembles the client, and in what ways?	Examine existing research and materials.	Identify features/benefits.	Tagline	Meaning
Which companies compete indirectly?	Determine if additional research is required.	Identity strengths/weaknesses.	Descriptors	Shape
	Consider interviews, focus groups, online surveys.	Examine brand personality.	Themes from advertising and collaterals	Color
				Typography

Understanding the competition

Who are they?

What do their brands stand for?

What markets/audiences do they serve?

What advantages (strengths) do they have?

What disadvantages (weaknesses) do they have?

What are their modes of selling and cultivating customers/clients?

How do they position themselves?

How do they characterize their customers/clients?

What are their key messages?

What is their financial condition?

How much market share do they hold?

How do they use brand identity to leverage success?

What do they look and feel like?

Using the competitive audit

Present audit at the end of the research phase.

Use learning to develop new brand and positioning strategy.

Use audit to inform the design process.

Consider meaning, shape, color, form, and content that the competition does not use.

Use audit when presenting new brand identity strategies to demonstrate differentiation.

A competitive audit for a marketing research firm.

> **Document identity**	> **Examine naming strategy**	> **Examine brand hierarchy**	> **Experience the competition**	> **Synthesize learnings**
Identity signatures	Core brand name	What type of brand architecture?	Navigate websites.	Make conclusions.
Marketing collateral materials + website	Naming system for products and services	How integrated or independent is the core brand in relation to subsidiaries or subbrands?	Visit shops and offices.	Start seeing opportunities.
Sales and promotional tools	Descriptors and domains		Purchase and use products.	Organize presentation.
Brand architecture		How are the products and services organized?	Use services.	
Signage			Listen to a sales pitch.	
			Call customer service.	

A company's reputation and goodwill extend beyond its target customers. Identifying key stakeholders and gaining insight into their characteristics, behavior, needs, and perceptions is a critical success factor. Organizational development experts call this type of exercise "360 analysis" since it yields insight into the perspective of the whole community.

"How do you want to be perceived by your various stakeholders?" is a pivotal question for leadership. For example, a nonprofit needs to identify its clients, funding sources, donors, staff, volunteers, strategic alliances, and the media. A financial services company needs to assess its entire distribution channel, including its sales force, and its multilevel selling process of wholesalers and retailers.

"How do the stakeholders perceive the brand?" "How do stakeholders find out about the company?" Answers to these questions illuminate the gap between the present and the future ensuring that the brand is positioned for success.

A lot of companies sabotage themselves by failing to consider the far-reaching impact of their stakeholders.

Lissa Reidel
Folio One

Each organization needs to identify and prioritize the constituencies that affect its success.

As the brand identity process unfolds, research about stakeholders will inform a broad range of solutions from the brand architecture, to the tilt of brand messages, to the launch strategy and plan.

A language audit has many names. Voice audit, message audit, and content audit are among the most popular. Regardless of the moniker, it is the Mount Everest of audits. Every organization aspires to conduct one, but very few accomplish it or go beyond base camp one. Although language is an intrinsic part of the marketing audit, many companies do not tackle "voice" until after they have designed a new brand identity program.

The courageous look at content and design at the same time, revealing the entire spectrum of how language is used. Analyzing the intersection of customer experience, design, and content is an intensive and rigorous endeavor that demands the left brain and right brain to work in tandem.

Vigorous writing is concise.

William Strunk Jr. and E.B. White
The Elements of Style

Process : examining language

Company name—formal
Company name—informal
Descriptors
Taglines
Product names
Process names
Service names
Division names

Identification

Mission
Vision and values
Key messages
Guiding principles
Customer pledges
History
Elevator speak
Boilerplate

Aspiration

Meaning
Voice
Tone
Emphasis
Accuracy
Clarity
Consistency
Positioning
Framework
Hierarchy
Punctuation
Capitalization
Style

Foundation

Criteria for evaluating communications

Developed by Siegel & Gale

Adherence to brand values
Is the tone and look of the information consistent with your brand attributes?

Customization
Is content based on what you already know about the customer?

Structure and navigational ease
Is the purpose of the document readily apparent, and is the document easy to use?

Educational value
Did you take the opportunity to anticipate unfamiliar concepts or terminology?

Loyalty support
Does the communication thank customers for their business or in some way reward them for extending their relationship with you?

Visual appeal
Does the document look inviting and in keeping with a company's positioning?

Marketing potential
Does the communication seize the opportunity to cross-sell products in a meaningful, informed way?

Utility
Is the document well suited to its function?

Call to action Phone numbers URLs Email signatures Voice mail messages Titles Addresses Diagrams Forms Directions

Navigation

News releases FAQs Press kits Annual reports Brochures Shareholder communications Call center scripts Customer service scripts Sales scripts Presentations Announcements Web content Blog content Blast emails Advertising campaigns Direct mail

Information

An audit readout signals the end of the research and analysis phase. It is a formal presentation made to the key decision makers that synthesizes key learnings from the interviews, research, and audits. The biggest challenge is organizing a vast amount of information into a succinct and strategic presentation. The audit readout is a valuable assessment tool for senior management, and a critical tool for the creative team to do responsible, differentiated work. It is a tool used as a reference throughout the entire process.

It is rare that an audit readout does not engender epiphanies. Although marketing and communications may not be top of mind for some management teams, seeing a lack of consistency across media, or seeing how much more discipline the competition uses in its marketing systems, is a real eye-opener. The objective of the audit is to open up the possibilities that a more strategic, focused brand identity system can bring.

We see the opportunity. Others see how far the brand voice has strayed.

Joe Duffy, Chairman
Duffy & Partners

We presented ACLU's visual history at the national and affiliate level: identity, imagery, printed donor materials, and the identities of other advocacy groups. We summarized our interview findings, other research and our analysis. We ended the presentation with the new design directives.

Sylvia Harris
Information design strategist

Process: synthesize learnings

Interviews	>	Brand	>	Marketing research	>	Marketing audit	>	Language audit
Stakeholder categories		Strategy		Brand recognition		Logos + signatures		Voice + tone
Key learnings		Positioning		Survey results		Brand architecture		Clarity
Customer insights		Essence		Focus group findings		Across marketing channels, media, product lines		Naming
Excerpts				Perceptual mapping		Look and feel		Taglines
				SWOTs		Imagery		Key messages
				Gap analysis		Color		Navigation
				Benchmarking		Typography		Hierarchy
								Descriptors

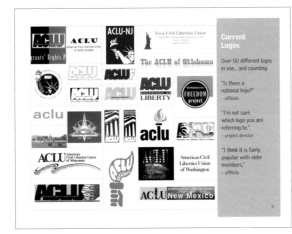

ACLU audit readout presentation

Essential characteristics

Focuses leaders on the possibilities

Jumpstarts robust conversations

Identifies gaps between positioning and expression

Builds commitment to doing things right in the future

Uncovers inconsistencies

Reveals need for more differentiation

Adds value and sense of urgency to the process

Informs the creative team

Unearths brilliant and forgotten ideas, images, and words

Analysis requires an ability to listen, read between the lines, observe what others don't see, make connections, see patterns and identify opportunities.
Blake Deutsch

I can't believe we are using the same stock images as our biggest competitors.
Anonymous

Holy smokes! What do you mean we haven't trademarked our product name?
Anonymous

> **Competitive audit**	> **Intellectual property audit**	> **Process audit**
Positioning	Trademarks	Existing guidelines
Logos	Compliance issues	Technology
Brand architecture		Collaboration
Taglines		
Key messages		
Look and feel		
Imagery		
Color		
Typography		

Clarifying brand strategy involves both methodical examination and strategic imagination. Phase 2 is like looking into a microscope with one eye and a telescope with the other. It is about analysis, discovery, synthesis, simplicity, and clarity. This combination of rational thinking and creative intelligence characterizes the best strategies, which go where others have not.

In Phase 2, all of the learnings from the research and audits are distilled into a unifying idea and a positioning strategy. Agreement is solidified about target markets, competitive advantage, brand core values, brand attributes, and project goals. More often than not, the definitions of the problem and its challenges have evolved. Although many companies have their values and attributes in place, they may not have taken the time to articu-

late and refine them, or to share them beyond an offsite management retreat. The role of the consultant here is to identify, articulate, illuminate, weave, and play back the possibilities.

Phase 2 can lead to a number of possible outcomes. In a merger, a new brand strategy for the combined enterprise is necessary. Other scenarios require a unifying idea that will be effective across business lines in a new brand identity program. A brand brief is created, and a discussion about findings and epiphanies follows. When there is openness and candor between the client and the consultant, true collaboration can produce the exceptional. Key success factors during this phase are trust and mutual respect.

The client is the author. We are the interpreter.

Bart Crosby, Principal
Crosby Associates

Phase 2 scenarios

Different scenarios determine the scope of services during the second phase.

A clearly defined brand strategy

When Turner Duckworth worked with Amazon.com and Jeff Bezos, brand strategy was already clearly defined and articulated. What Amazon needed was a world class brand identity. When Sandstrom Design was brought in by Steve Sandoz, a creative director at Weiden Kennedy, to work on Tazo tea, a vision that was articulated as "Marco Polo meets Merlin" was already in place. What the Tazo team needed was a firm that knew how to design the product offering and render it "otherworldly." When Bernhardt Fudyma worked with Nabisco to evaluate its familiar red triangle trademark design, the firm conducted an in-depth evaluation process, which did not require strategy development.

A need to redefine brand strategy

When Harley-Davidson set out to turn around its business and reinvent itself, senior leadership decided to build a brand strategy based on existing rider passion. Over the years they worked collaboratively with David Aaker, a preeminent brand strategist, as well as their agencies, VSA Partners and Carmichael Lynch, to evolve and express their strategy. When the Tate in the United Kingdom wanted to enhance its appeal and attract more visitors to its four museums, Sir Nicholas Serota, the Tate's director, and his communications staff worked closely with Wolff Olins to develop a central brand idea that would unify the different museums. "Look again, think again" was an invitation to visitors to reconsider their experience of art.

A need to create brand strategy

Aside from new business creation, mergers are by far the most challenging scenarios that require new brand strategy. Determining a unified strategy and a new name for two companies that may have been competitors, and working with a transition team in a compressed timeframe, takes extraordinary skill and diplomacy. VSA Partners created a brand strategy and a new name, Cingular, for the joint venture of Bell South Mobility and SBC Wireless in six weeks. The new name would represent eleven former brands and more than 21 million customers. The brand strategy positioned Cingular as the embodiment of human expression since VSA viewed the wireless space evolving from a features-and-functions buying decision to a lifestyle choice.

Revisit the vision

Interviews with senior management, employees, customers, and industry experts provide an intimate glance into the uniqueness of a company. If you are lucky, the CEO is a visionary who has a clear picture of an ideal future and all its possibilities. Often, such visionaries are hard to find. It is important to look for the gold— sometimes a business is so busy servicing its customers that it has forgotten the core ideas around why it is so successful. Sometimes it takes a customer's loyalty and clarity to bring it back. Sometimes listening to a sales presenta- tion by the company's most successful rep provides valuable insight.

Look at the really big picture

It is never enough to examine a company's business strategy, core values, target markets, competitors, distribution channels, technology, and competitive advantage. It is important to stand back and look at trends that are affecting the future, whether they are economic, sociopo- litical, global, or lifestyle. It is also important to observe other brands outside the industry sector, and how they express their brand strategy. Finally, it is important, in the case of a mature company, to look back historically and to take note of which drivers have made this company successful.

A brand becomes stronger when you narrow the focus.

Al Ries and Laura Ries
The 22 Immutable Laws of Branding

If you want to build a brand, you must focus your branding efforts on owning a word in the prospect's mind. A word that no one else owns. What prestige is to Mercedes, safety is to Volvo.

Al Ries and Laura Ries
The 22 Immutable Laws of Branding

As the mass and volume of information increases, people search for a clear signal—one that gives pattern, shape, direction to the voice.

Bruce Mau
Designer

Engage in meaningful dialogue

It is so easy to be caught up in daily tasks that companies frequently do not take the time to revisit who they are and what they are about. The beauty of this process is that it gives senior managers an explicit reason to go off-site and spin a dream. It is a worthwhile exercise, even if offsite turns out to be just the conference room with no calls and no distractions. Superb consultants know how to facilitate a dialogue between core leaders in which various brand scenarios are explored and brand attributes surface.

Uncover brand essence (or simple truth)

What does a company do that is best in world? Why do its customers choose it over its competition? What business are they in? How are they really different than their most successful competitor? What are three adjectives that summarize how this company wants to be perceived? What are its strengths and weaknesses? The clarity of these answers is an important driver in this phase.

Develop a positioning platform

Subsequent to information gathering and analysis are the development and refinement of a positioning strategy. Perceptual mapping is frequently a technique used to brainstorm a positioning strategy. On which dimension can a company compete? What can it own? Where can it go that is different from where the competition goes?

Create the big idea

The big idea can always be expressed in one sentence, although the rationale could usually fill a book. Sometimes the big idea becomes the tagline or the battle cry (like *Think different*), and sometimes it is purely aspirational. The big idea must be simple and transportable. It must carry enough ambiguity to allow for future developments that cannot be predicted. It must create an emotional connection, and it must be easy to talk about, whether you are the CEO or an employee.

Play it back

Sometimes old ideas that are framed in a new way do not resonate immediately. The consultant needs to hold up a mirror and say, "This is what you have told me and I heard it again from your customers and your sales force. And this is why it is powerful."

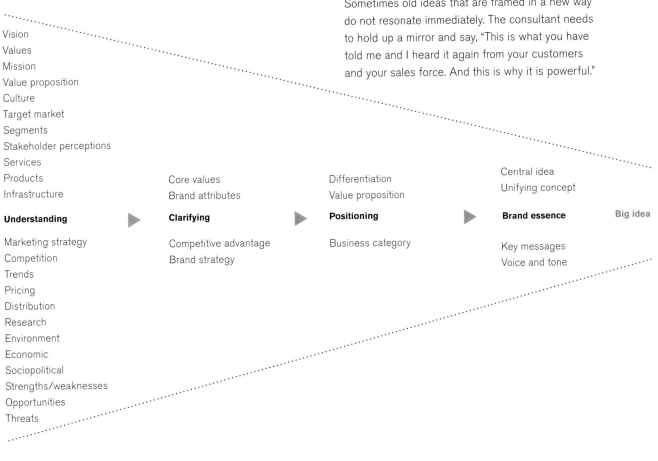

Vision
Values
Mission
Value proposition
Culture
Target market
Segments
Stakeholder perceptions
Services
Products
Infrastructure

Understanding

Marketing strategy
Competition
Trends
Pricing
Distribution
Research
Environment
Economic
Sociopolitical
Strengths/weaknesses
Opportunities
Threats

Core values
Brand attributes

Clarifying

Competitive advantage
Brand strategy

Differentiation
Value proposition

Positioning

Business category

Central idea
Unifying concept

Brand essence   Big idea

Key messages
Voice and tone

Articulating a company's core values, its mission, or its brand attributes appears to be a fairly simple exercise for the leadership of an organization. It is actually a difficult and strategic process characterized by extensive dialogue. A skilled facilitator, experienced in building consensus and getting closure, is needed to ask the right questions. The result of this work is a critical component in the realization of a compelling brand strategy and a differentiated brand identity.

The best big idea statements are simply worded and function as an organizational totem pole around which behavior, actions, and communications are aligned. These statements may be used internally as an affirmation of a distinctive culture and externally as a competitive advantage. They are a springboard for responsible creative work (thinking, designing, naming) or a litmus test against which success is measured. Following are examples of how some organizations express their brand attributes, brand values, principles, or big ideas. The simplicity of the language is deceptive because the process of getting there is inevitably complex.

For GE, imagination at work is more than a slogan or a tagline. It is a reason for being.

Jeffrey R. Immelt, CEO
GE

A successful brand is all about detail. Every facet of a brand must be apparent in an organization's communications, behavior, products and environment.

Brian Boylan
Chairman
Wolff Olins

It's not what you stand in. It's what you stand for.

Kenneth Cole
Founder
Kenneth Cole Productions

The New School

Siegel & Gale identified six groups of ideas, which were then expressed as personality traits or brand attributes.

Activist

The New School has a unique history of social activism, progressive thinking, and internationalism. The New School has always strived for positive and meaningful change.

Eclectic

The New School is unconventional and different, with a constant appetite for the new and experimental.

Open

The New School is multifaceted, diverse, and international, and it appreciates the ranges of ages, origins, and cultures.

Street-Smart

The New School is not an insulated institution. It is a part of New York City and of the larger world. It is urban, vibrant, and dynamic.

Articulate

The New School fosters personal expression and choice, challenging students to be in active dialogue with the world around them.

Creative

The New School is made of writers, thinkers, and artists creating their own worlds and systems of ideas.

Courageous

The New School, since its founding, has been a place where people are not afraid to take a stand on what they think is right.

Martha Stewart

My founding big idea was that the subject of living is indeed a limitless subject, one that can be expanded and expounded upon, and enlarged and extolled.

Martha Stewart
Founder
Martha Stewart Living Omnimedia

Target

At the heart of the strategy is our commitment to delight our guests by consistently delivering the right combination of innovation, design and value in our merchandising, in our marketing, and in our stores. This is the essence of our 'Expect more. Pay less.' brand promise.

Bob Ulrich
Chairman and CEO
Target

The Wild Center

The Wild Center is among a select group of museums built in the middle of their subject matter. Being in the largest temperate forest of its kind in the world changes a museum experience in a fundamental way.

Donald K. Clifford, Jr.
President
The Natural History Museum of the Adirondacks

Brand identity projects involve enormous amounts of data gathering—the team is unearthing the past in the audits and research and listening to aspirations for the future. An important deadline is looming ahead, and everyone wants to know when are they going to see something or find out the new name of the company.

The biggest objective of Phase 2 is to achieve a unified vision of what the brand stands for, which is achieved in the sign-off on the brand brief. The second objective is to write the creative brief, which will provide a road map for the creative team.

The best briefs are succinct and strategic, and approved by the most senior levels in an organization early in the process. If these briefs are approved, the balance of the project is more likely to be on track and successful.

The briefs are a result of a collaborative process—that is, a result of the best thinking and an ability to agree on brand attributes and positioning first, and the desired endpoint and criteria of the process second.

Diagramming our vision, core beliefs, and methods helped our trustees focus on brand decisions.

Pamela Thompson, Vice President Communications
John Templeton Foundation

Documentation
Writing a brief is an iterative process and it is important to have version control. This means that each version should be saved and have a version number on it.

Brand brief

Some organizations have brand briefs in place that have been recently approved by senior decision makers. Other organizations use Phase 2 to initiate a process to document, for example, their vision, mission, attributes, and brand essence. Many entrepreneurial companies have visionaries who walk around with this information in their heads; getting it on paper helps anyone who has the responsibility to execute the vision. This is a hard task but well worth the time invested because a sustainable tool is created.

Writing the brief invariably includes meetings, numerous emails, and versions. The actual document is most effective when it can be captured on one page (11 x 17 inch) as a diagram. When the final version is a Word document, the temptation is to keep changing it.

Content

Vision

Mission

Brand essence or big idea

Brand attributes

Value proposition

Guiding principles/key beliefs

Target audience

Key markets

Key competitors

Competitive advantage

Stakeholders

Creative brief

While the brand brief is an agreement about the brand essence and attributes, the creative brief synthesizes what the creative team needs to know in order to do responsible work aligned with the overall objectives of the project. This brief needs to be signed off by key decision makers before any conceptual or creative work is done. The best briefs are a result of collaboration between the client and the consulting firm. Creative work includes the range of brand identity from naming, logo redesign, key message development, brand architecture, and packaging design, to integrated system design.

The creative brief cannot be written until the audit readout is complete and the brand brief is approved. Each member of the creative team must have a copy of both briefs, as well as a copy of the audit readout.

Content

Team goals

Communications goals of all brand identity elements

Critical application list

Functional and performance criteria

Mind map or SWOTs

Positioning

Protocols

Confidentiality statement

Documentation system

Benchmarks and presentation dates

Other briefs

Large companies will create positioning briefs for marketing segments or business lines. Large research studies are also synthesized in briefs that highlight key learnings.

Naming is not for the weak of heart. It is a complex, creative, and iterative process requiring experience in linguistics, marketing, research, and trademark law. Even for the experts, finding a name for today's company, product, or service that can be legally protected presents a formidable challenge.

Various brainstorming techniques are used to generate hundreds, if not thousands, of options. Culling the large list takes skill and patience.

Names need to be judged against positioning goals, performance criteria, and availability within a sector. It is natural to want to fall in love with a name, but the bottom line is that meaning and associations are built over time. Agreement is not easy to achieve, especially when choices seem limited. Contextual testing is smart, and helps decision making.

The ability to foster consensus among decision makers is as critical as creativity in the naming process.

Lori Kapner, President
Kapner Consulting

Process : naming

Revisit positioning	Get organized	Create naming criteria	Brainstorm solutions	Conduct initial screening
Examine brand goals and target market needs.	Develop timeline.	Performance criteria	Create numerous names.	Positioning
Evaluate existing names.	Determine team.	Positioning criteria	Organize in categories and themes.	Linguistic
Examine competitor names.	Identify brainstorming techniques.	Legal criteria	Look at hybrids and mimetics.	Legal
	Determine search mechanisms.	Regulatory criteria, if any	Be prolific.	Common-law databases
	Develop decision-making process.		Explore variations/iterations on a theme.	Online search engines
	Organize reference resources.			Online phone directories
				Domain registration
				Creating a short list

Naming basics

Brand names are valuable assets.

When you are brainstorming, there are no stupid ideas.

Always examine a name in context.

Consider sound, cadence, and ease of pronunciation.

Be methodical in tracking name selections.

Determine smartest searching techniques.

Review all the criteria before you reject a name.

Naming trivia
Although only 934,000 names are registered, more than 20 million .com domains were registered as of 2002

Remember
Names may be registered in different classes of goods and services.

Inspiration

Language

Meaning

Personality

Dictionaries

Googling

Thesauruses

Latin

Greek

Foreign languages

Mass culture

Poetry

Television

Music

History

Art

Commerce

Colors

Symbols

Metaphors

Analogies

Sounds

Science

Technology

Astronomy

Myths

Stories

Values

Dreams

> **Conduct contextual testing**   > **Testing**

Say the name.

Leave a voice mail.

E-mail the name.

Put it on a business card.

Put it in an ad headline.

Put it into the voice of the stakeholders.

Determine methods to trust.

Check for red flags.

Unearth trademark conflicts.

Check language connotations.

Check cultural connotations.

Do linguistic analysis.

> **Final legal screen**

Domestic

International

Domain

Regulatory

Registration

Investigation and analysis are complete; the brand brief has been agreed upon, and the creative design process begins in Phase 3. Design is an iterative process that seeks to integrate meaning with form. The best designers work at the intersection of strategic imagination, intuition, design excellence, and experience. Reducing a complex idea to its visual essence requires skill, focus, patience, and unending discipline. A designer may examine hundreds of ideas before focusing on a final choice. Even after a final idea emerges, testing its viability begins yet another round of exploration. It is an enormous responsibility to design something that in all probability will be reproduced hundreds of thousands, if not millions, of times and has a lifetime of twenty years or more.

Creativity takes many roads. In some offices numerous designers work on the same idea, whereas in other offices each designer might develop a different idea or positioning strategy. Routinely hundreds of sketches are put up on the wall for a group discussion. Each preliminary

approach can be a catalyst to a new approach. It is difficult to create a simple form that is bold, memorable, and appropriate because we live in an oversaturated visual environment, making it critical to ensure that the solution is unique and differentiated. In addition an identity will need to be a workhorse across various media and applications.

In projects that involve redesign the designer must also carefully examine the equity of the existing form and understand what it has meant to a company's culture. Paul Rand's logos for UPS, Westinghouse, and Cummins were all redesigns. In each case Rand's genius was finding a way to maintain elements from the original identity and to transform them into bigger ideas and stronger, more sustainable visual forms. His strategy was always to present one idea. His brilliant design sensibility was matched by his strategic presentations, in which he traced the evolution of his recommendation.

Examine

Meaning

Attributes

Acronyms

Inspiration

History

Form

Counterform

Abstract

Pictorial

Letterform

Wordmark

Combination

Time

Space

Light

Still

Motion

Transition

Perspective

Reality

Fantasy

Straight

Curve

Angle

Intersection

Patterns

In 1946, the Herman Miller logo was designed by the George Nelson office. Irving Harper, the designer, had stylized the "M" in Miller to create this mark. Over the years it has evolved. The Nelson Office reworked it in 1960 and John Massey reworked it in 1968. In 1998, the Herman Miller creative team designed the one currently in use.

Steve Frykholm
Vice President, Creative Director
Herman Miller

A designer's perspective

Paul Rand
as excerpted from *Paul Rand* by Steven Heller

Rand designed logos for endurance. 'I think permanence is something you find out,' he once said. 'It isn't something you design for. You design for durability, for function, for usefulness, for rightness, for beauty. But permanence is up to God and time.'

Per Mollerup
as excerpted from *Marks of Excellence*

The study of trademarks has its roots in fields as diverse as anthropology, history, heraldry, psychology, marketing, semiotics, communication theory, and of course, graphic design.

Identification, description, and the creation of value are just some of the possible functions of a trademark.

Steff Geissbuhler

We have run out of abstract, geometric marks and symbols, where an artificially adopted notion of growth, global business and aggressive, forward-moving technology becomes meaningless and overused, because it's everybody's strategy, mission, and positioning.

We have found that our audiences react much more directly and emotionally to recognizable symbols and cultural icons with clear connotations, characteristics, and qualities.

The trademark, although a most important key element, can never tell the whole story. At best it conveys one or two notions or aspects of the business. The identity has to be supported by a visual language and a vocabulary.

Paula Scher
My best idea is always my first idea.

Hans-U. Allemann

We usually begin with very predictable and obvious ideas, but the beauty of the identity design process is that it is totally unpredictable. We never know what the process will reveal. I have been designing marks for 40 years, and the process still astonishes me.

The best identity designers have a strong understanding of how to communicate effectively through the use of signs and symbols, have a keen sense of form and letterforms, and an understanding of the history of design.

Malcolm Grear

Form and counterform. Light and tension. Expanded meaning that is not exhausted at first glance. These are the things that fascinate me.

You need to know the enterprise inside and out.

Beyond mere legibility, we aspire to convey our client's essential nature through imagery that is strong, profound and elegant.

Meejoo Kwon
The design process is a triangle created from public perception, client insight and designer's intuition.

A logotype is a word (or words) in a determined font, which may be standard, modified, or entirely redrawn. Frequently, a logotype is juxtaposed with a symbol in a formal relationship called the signature. Logotypes not only need to be distinctive, but also need to be durable and sustainable. Legibility at various scales and in a range of media is imperative, whether a logotype is silk-screened on the side of a ballpoint pen or illuminated in an external sign twenty stories off the ground.

The best logotypes are a result of careful typographic exploration. Designers consider the attributes of each letterform, as well as the relationships between letterforms. In the best logotypes, letterforms may be redrawn, modified, and manipulated in order to express the appropriate personality and positioning of the company.

The designer begins his or her process by examining hundreds of typographic variations. Beginning with the basics—for example, whether the name should be set in all caps or caps and lowercase—the designer proceeds to look at classic and modern typefaces, roman and italic variations, and various weights, scales, and combinations. The designer then proceeds to manipulate and customize the logotype. Each decision is driven by visual and performance considerations, as well as by what the typography itself communicates.

A signature is the specific and nonnegotiable designed combination of the brandmark and the logotype. The best signatures have specific isolation zones to protect their presence. A company may have numerous signatures, for various business lines or with and without a tagline.

Signature

Mark/avatar

Logotype

Chambers Group: Stellarvisions

Signature with tagline

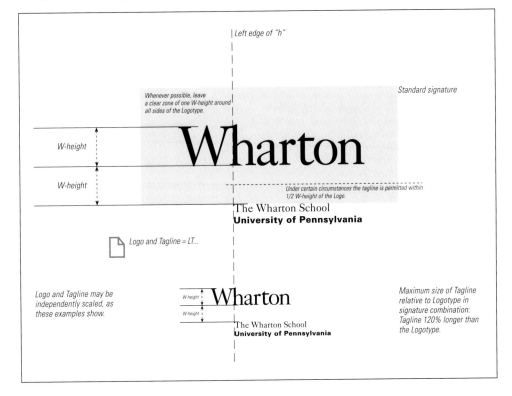

The Wharton identity program, designed by Joel Katz Design Associates, features the word "Wharton" set in a distinctive type treatment. The letterforms, including the "Wh" ligature, were redrawn and reproportioned. The wordmark exists in two versions: "large" for use at sizes larger than 1/2" high, and "small" for use at 1/2" and smaller. A number of signatures were created, including wordmark and tagline signatures, division and program signatures, and joint venture signatures. The above is excerpted from Wharton's identity manual and style guide, created in 2001.

A school bus by any another color is no longer a school bus. Its essence is expressed by the color yellow. As consumers we depend on the familiarity of Coca-Cola cans that are red and UPS trucks that are brown. A person does not need to read the type on a Tiffany gift box in order to know where the gift was purchased. Tiffany's signature blue sets off a series of immediate impressions that are aligned with the company's overall positioning and brand identity strategy.

In the sequence of visual perception, the brain reads color after it registers a shape and before it reads content. Choosing a color for a new identity requires a core understanding of color theory, a clear vision of how the brand needs to be perceived and differentiated, and an ability to master consistency and meaning over a broad range of media.

Color is used to evoke emotion, express personality, and stimulate brand association. While some colors are used to unify an identity, other colors may be used functionally to clarify brand architecture, through differentiating products or business lines. Designers formulate special and unique brand identity color strategies. Traditionally the primary brand color is assigned to the symbol, and the secondary color is assigned to the logotype, business descriptor, or tagline. In addition to the core brand colors, system color palettes are developed to support a broad range of communications needs. Ensuring optimum reproduction of the brand color is an integral element of basic standards and part of the challenge as new media tools proliferate.

Color creates emotion, triggers memory, and gives sensation.

Gael Towey, Creative Director
Martha Stewart Living Omnimedia

BP: Landor Associates

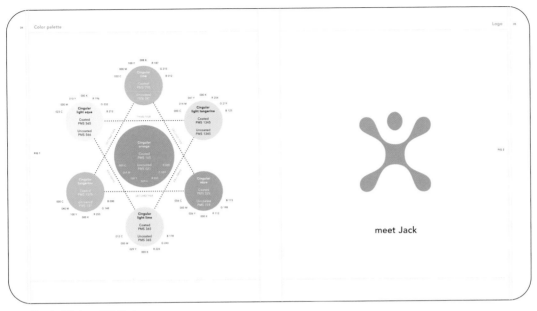

Cingular Wireless: VSA Partners

Color brand identity basics

The ultimate goal is to own a color—a color that facilitates recognition and builds brand equity.

Different viewers experience color differently in various environments. The designer is the ultimate arbiter for setting consistency across platforms.

Ensuring consistency across multiple media is an enormous challenge, and there is no off-the-shelf solution.

Color is dramatically affected by various file formats and reproduction media. Test. Test. Test.

Remember, most of the world uses a PC and PowerPoint.

A commitment to quality reproduction and execution needs to be a top-down initiative in order to ensure that the brand identity asset is protected.

Sixty percent of the decision to buy a product is based on color.

You can never know enough about color. Depend on your basic color theory knowledge: warm, cool; values, hues; tints, shades; complementary colors, contrasting colors.

Develop the best tools to ensure the proper use of brand color.

Colors have different connotations in different cultures. Do your due diligence and research the appropriate markets and cultures.

Use color to build meaning and expand connotation.

You don't have to like a color. You just have to determine if it is doing what you need it to do.
Laura Silverman
Communications consultant

More color

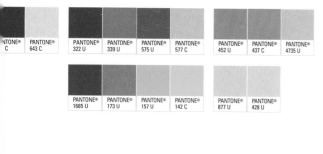

PANTONE® C | PANTONE® 643 C

PANTONE® 322 U | PANTONE® 339 U | PANTONE® 575 U | PANTONE® 577 C

PANTONE® 452 U | PANTONE® 437 C | PANTONE® 4735 U

PANTONE® 1685 U | PANTONE® 173 U | PANTONE® 157 U | PANTONE® 142 C

PANTONE® 877 U | PANTONE® 428 U

PANTONE® 5 C | PANTONE® 359 C | PANTONE® 128 U | PANTONE® 291 U | PANTONE® 1485 C | PANTONE® 325 U

PANTONE® 032 C

More color

Testing the effectiveness of a color strategy

Is the color distinctive?

Is the color differentiated from that of competitors?

Is the color appropriate to the type of business?

Is the color aligned with brand strategy?

What do you want the color to communicate?

Will the color have sustainability?

What meaning have you assigned to the color?

Does the color have positive connotations in the target markets?

Does the color have positive or negative connotations in foreign markets?

Is the color reminiscent of any other product or service?

Will the color facilitate recognition and recall?

Did you consider a specially formulated color?

Can the color be legally protected?

Does the color work on white?

Can you reverse the mark out of black and still maintain the original intention?

What background colors are possible?

What background values are necessary?

How does scale affect the color?

When you have a one-color application, such as a fax or the newspaper, how will you adjust the color so that it reads?

Are there technical challenges to getting the color right?

Can you achieve consistency across media?

Have you tested the color on a range of monitors, PC and Mac?

Have you looked at ink draws on coated and uncoated stock?

Have you considered that the PMS color may look dramatically different for coated and uncoated?

Will this color work in signage?

What are the color equivalents on the web?

Is there a vinyl binder color that is compatible?

Have you tested the color in the environment in which it will be used?

Have you created the appropriate color electronic files?

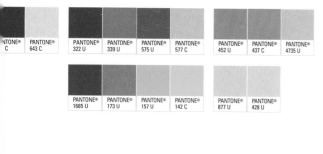

PANTONE® C | PANTONE® 643 C

PANTONE® 322 U | PANTONE® 339 U | PANTONE® 575 U | PANTONE® 577 C

PANTONE® 452 U | PANTONE® 437 C | PANTONE® 4735 U

PANTONE® 1685 U | PANTONE® 173 U | PANTONE® 157 U | PANTONE® 142 C

PANTONE® 877 U | PANTONE® 428 U

PANTONE® 5 C | PANTONE® 359 C | PANTONE® 128 U | PANTONE® 291 U | PANTONE® 1485 C | PANTONE® 325 U

PANTONE® 032 C

Color systems

Will the color system be flexible enough to allow for a range of dynamic applications?

Does the color system support a consistent experience of the brand?

Does the color system support the brand architecture?

Is the color system differentiated from that of the competition?

Have you examined the benefits and disadvantages of:

> using color to differentiate products?

> using color to identify business lines?

> using color to help users navigate decisions?

> using color to categorize information?

Do you need both a bold palette and a pastel palette?

Can you reproduce these colors?

Have you developed both a web palette and a print palette?

Have you named your colors?

Have you created identity standards that make it easy to use the color system?

Mergers, acquisitions, redesign

Have you examined the historical use of color?

Is there equity that should be preserved?

Is the color aligned with the new brand strategy?

Is there a symbolic color that communicates the positive outcome of the merged entities?

Will developing a new color for the company send a new and immediate signal about the future?

Will retiring an existing color confuse existing customers?

Color trivia
Kodak was the first company to trademark a signature color.

Bianchi created a special color green for its bicycles.

When British Petroleum and Amoco merged to form BP, British Petroleum's distinctive green and yellow colors were kept.

Our primary brand color is CIGNA teal. It is a specially formulated color that is unique to our industry. We want CIGNA to be strongly associated with CIGNA teal. Therefore, all businesses are encouraged to use this color broadly across their communications.
CIGNA Brand Identity Guidelines

Typography is a core building block of an effective identity program. Companies like Apple, Mercedes-Benz, and Citi are immediately recognizable in great part due to the distinctive and consistent typographical style that is used with intelligence and purpose throughout thousands of applications over time. A unified and coherent company image is not possible without typography that has a unique personality and an inherent legibility. Typography must support the positioning strategy and information hierarchy. Identity program typography needs to be sustainable and not on the curve of a fad.

Thousands of fonts have been created by renowned typographers, designers, and type foundries over the centuries, and new typefaces are being created each day. Some identity firms routinely design a proprietary font for a client. Choosing the right font requires a basic knowledge of the breadth of options and a core understanding of how effective typography functions. Issues of functionality differ dramatically on a form, a pharmaceutical package, a magazine ad, and a website. The typeface needs to be flexible and easy to use, and it must provide a wide range of expression. Clarity and legibility are the drivers.

Type is magical. It not only communicates a word's information, but it conveys a subliminal message.

Erik Spiekermann
Stop Stealing Sheep

JETS BOLD
ABCDEFGHI
JKLMNOP
QRSTUVWXYZ
1234567890

THE TYPEFACE: Pictured above is the character set for Jets Bold, the primary typeface of the New York Jets brand identity. It is a custom drawn font inspired by the original four letters, J-E-T-S, in the classic logotype. This typeface is available for both PC and Macintosh operating systems and is approved for use across all applications and mediums. As with everything, the way this typeface is used is critical. Sample stylistic treatments are displayed on the following spread to give an idea of it's intended usage.

The New York Jets retained Pentagram to design a brand book to unify and strengthen existing identity elements used in multimedia and merchandising. Hoefler & Frere-Jones, a firm that specializes in designing original typography, created a proprietary Jets alphabet and numbers based on the four letters in the team's original logo.

Typeface family basics

Typefaces are chosen for their legibility, their unique character, and their range of weights and widths.

Intelligent typography supports information hierarchy.

Typeface families must be chosen to complement the signature, not necessarily to replicate the signature.

The best standards identify a range of fonts but give the users flexibility to choose the appropriate font, weight, and size for the message conveyed.

Limiting the number of fonts that a company uses is cost-effective since licensing fonts is legally required.

The number of typeface families in a system is a matter of choice. Many companies choose serif and sans serif faces; some companies choose one font for everything.

Basic standards sometimes allow special display faces for unique situations.

A company website may require its own set of typefaces and typography standards.

The best typographers examine a level of detail that includes numerals and bullets.

Many companies identify separate typefaces for internally produced word-processed documents and electronic presentations.

Certain industries have compliance requirements regarding type size for certain consumer products and communications.

The character of a typeface changes dramatically with different letter spacing, word spacing, and leading.
Matthew Barthlomew
Designer/typographer/teacher

Examine typefaces which

Convey feeling and reflect positioning

Cover the range of application needs

Work in a range of sizes

Work in black and white and color

Differ from the competition's

Are compatible with the signature

Are legible

Have personality

Are sustainable

Reflect culture

Examine
Serif
Sans serif
Size
Weight
Curves
Rhythm
Descenders
Ascenders
Capitalization
Headlines
Subheads
Text
Titles
Callouts
Captions
Bulleted lists
Leading
Line length
Letter spacing
Numerals
Symbols
Quotation marks

Type trivia
Frutiger was designed for an airport.

Matthew Carter designed Bell Gothic to increase legibility in the phone book.

Meta was designed by Meta Design for the German post office but never used.

Wolff Olins designed Tate for Tate Modern in London.

115

● ● ● ● ●

As bandwidth increases, sound is quickly becoming the next frontier for brand identity. Many of our appliances and devices talk to us, voice-activated prompts let us order FedEx without human interface, and the elegant voice of James Earl Jones is the gateway to Verizon Nationwide 411.

The ring tone revolution is upon us. Individuals program their cell phones so that distinctive rings signal a certain someone, and a huge industry has been born in 30 second slices of sound. Quicktime videos populate websites and emails. The sound of silence is a has-been.

Whether you are at the Buddha Bar in Paris or the shoe department at Nordstrom, sound puts you in the mood. Sound also sends a signal: "Hail to the Chief" announces the President's arrival, and a Looney Tunes cartoon always ends with a "Tha-a-a-t's all folks." A foreign accent adds cachet to almost any brand. Being put on hold might mean a little Bach cantata, a humorous sound sales pitch, or a radio station (don't you hate that?).

Designing and integrating the right sound enhances the experience of a brand.

Kenny Kahn, Vice President of Marketing
Musak

What is audio architecture?

Audio architecture is the integration of music, voice and sound to create experiences between companies and customers.
Muzak

No one who saw *2001: A Space Odyssey* will ever forget the voice that said, "Open the pod bay doors, Hal."

Fundamentals of sonic branding

Excerpted from "Sonic Branding Finds Its Voice"
Kim Barnet, on Interbrand's Brand Channel

Sound needs to be complementary to the existing brand

Sound can intensify the experience of a brand

Music can trigger an emotional response

Sound, especially music, heightens the brain's speed of recall

Music can transcend cultures and language

Aural and visual branding are becoming increasingly complementary

Many businesses compose original music

Many audio effects are subliminal

Motors
Harley-Davidson motorcycles tried to trademark its distinctive purr. When Miata designed the first hot sports car in the moderate price category, the sound of the motor was reminiscent of a classic upscale sportscar.

Retail environments
From cafés, to supermarkets, to fashion boutiques, music is used to appeal to a particular customer and put him or her in the mood to shop or revel in the experience.

Talking products
Technology is making the way for pill dispensers that gently remind you to take a pill, and cars that remind you to fill the tank, get service, or turn left. A Mercedes will definitely sound different than a Volkswagen.

Spokespersons
Famous people have been used throughout advertising history to endorse a product. Also, a receptionist with a great voice and a friendly personality can become the spokesperson of a small firm.

Recorded messages
Great museums are paying attention to the voices they choose for audio tours. Companies specialize in targeted messages while you're on hold.

Signals
The Intel chip has its own musical bleeps, and AOL's "You've got mail" ditty became so much a part of the culture that it became the name of a movie love story with Meg Ryan and Tom Hanks.

Multimedia presentations
Interactivity and new media require the integration of sound. Testimonials are given by real customers. Video clips of company visionaries are shown to employees.

Websites and games
Sound is being used increasingly to aid navigation, as well as to delight the user. Sound effects on computer games heighten the adventure, and avatars can be customized by the user.

Jingles
Catchy messages set to music that stick in the mind of the consumer.

Characters
While the Aflac duck has a memorable quack, many characters, like Elmer of Elmer's Glue, are still silent.

Bringing brands to life is facilitated by a world in which bandwidth no longer constricts creativity and communication. Although the tools and skills to animate trademarks are available, very few creative professionals have taken full advantage of the medium to communicate a competitive difference.Ideally, the animated version of an identity is part of the initial conceptualization, rather than an afterthought. Motion must support the essence and meaning of an identity, not trivialize it.

Avatar: a brand icon designed to move, morph, or otherwise operate freely across various media.

Dictionary of Brand

Rand did not foresee the animated potential of the Westinghouse logo when he first designed it, but the possibilities for bringing it to life soon became perfectly clear.

Steven Heller
Paul Rand

The motion designer's control of time and timing supports surprise and enhances storytelling.

Chris Pullman, Vice President of Design
WGBH

When graphics set sail, they allow us to convey ideas over time, Whether with type or with image, the added elements of progression and drama create a memorable expression.

Sagi Haviv
Chermayeff & Geismar Studio

Logo motion principles

Developed by Sagi Haviv, Principal, Chermayeff & Geismar Studio

Essential

There must be a reason behind every decision made in the process of creating motion graphics, just like any other facet of design. Any nonessential element must be removed to ensure excellence.

Strategic

Animation should support brand essence, strive to communicate the brand's personality, and elaborate on its agenda expressed in the static mark. By ensuring the expression is appropriate to the brand positioning, the animation will protect brand equity.

Harmonious

Animation should evolve from the visual language of the brand identity. Often when looking at the static mark, an expert can identify what the mark "wants to do," namely what motion is innate in its graphic characteristics.

Communicates

Animation should tell a story—progression and drama, build-up, climax and payoff are essential to captivate the audience and deliver the message.

Resonates

In this medium, movement is the expression and special care should be given to rhythm, speed and transitions which define the mood and the emotional appeal of the piece.

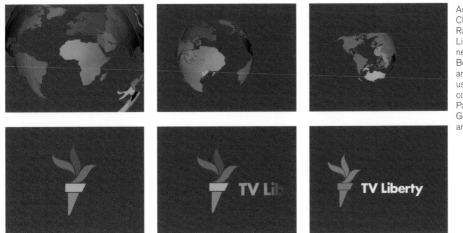

An animation created by Chermayeff & Geismar for Radio Free Europe/Radio Liberty introduced the new identity to the global Board of Governors. The animation was expanded for use in broadcast in various countries. Steff Geissbuhler, Partner, Chermayeff & Geismar, designed the mark and led the process.

The design of the core brand identity elements—e.g., the mark and the logotype—is only the beginning of the identity design process. Marks should not be shown to the client until rigorous testing and exploration of the concept's viability are complete. From a design perspective, what may work in isolation may not meet the rigors of an entire system design. Seeing a signature out of context on a blank sheet of paper does not help sell: Clients need to envision the possibilities.

Key applications that represent real future scenarios need to be identified. Frequently, these are outlined in a contractual agreement. A typical list for a small engagement might include a business card, a home page, an advertisement, a brochure cover, a letterhead, and something fun,

like a baseball cap. On larger projects, the designer needs to demonstrate the effectiveness of brand extensions and the ability of the identity to work across business lines and markets served. In retail projects, the designer needs to explore how this identity would work within a retail environment and affect the customer experience.

Design exploration helps build a case for a particular design concept by demonstrating that it will support the marketing and communications needs of the company into the future. Flexibility, consistency, and sustainability are essential. The magic of an idea becomes real and easier to approve.

Dwell in possibilities.

Emily Dickinson

Studio 360:
Opto Design

Testing the concept

Choose the most visible applications.

Choose the most challenging applications.

Examine the flexibility of the identity.

Examine how to express coherence and consistency.

Does the signature work?

Is it differentiated enough from the competition's?

Is it scalable?

Does it maintain impact?

Does it stay legible at a small scale?

Will it work in different media?

Will it work on the Internet?

Can it move?

Will it work both in color and in black and white?

Will it be conducive to brand extensions?

It works with the parent; will it work with the divisions?

Can it accommodate a tagline in the signature?

Will it work in other cultures?

Identity design testing basics

Use real scenarios and real text for application testing.

Continue asking the big questions in regard to appropriate meaning, sustainability, and flexibility.

Start thinking about the implications for the entire system of color and typeface families.

Always examine best-case and worst-case scenarios.

Remember, this is an iterative process.

If something does not work, deal with it immediately. Go back to the beginning if necessary to examine the core concept. The signature might need to be reworked.

Date and assign a version number to the entire sketch process; be obsessive about organization of this phase.

Think ahead to production: How will this look on a screen? Test it on a PC.

Solicit feedback from trusted colleagues—designers and nondesigners—to reveal any connotations that may not be apparent.

Anticipate what you will need to present the design strategy; start envisioning the presentation.

Continue to actively think about the future: five or ten years out is sooner than you think.

When we presented our vision for Studio 360's identity, it was important to explore a range of applications and engage the decision makers to imagine the possibilities for the radio show.

John Klotnia
Opto Design

The first major design presentation is the decisive moment. A design team has worked hard to get to this point, and it is the culmination of months of work. The expectations and stakes are high. Clients are usually impatient during the planning and analysis phase since they are so focused on the end goal, which is their new brand identity. There is usually a sense of urgency around scheduling this meeting. Everyone is ready to hit the ground running, even though the implementation phase of the work is not imminent.

Careful planning is essential to ensure the success of the outcome of the meeting. The smartest, most appropriate, and most creative solutions can get annihilated in a mismanaged presentation. The larger the group of decision makers, the more difficult the meeting and the decision are to manage. Even presenting to one decision maker alone demands planning in advance.

Delivering a good presentation is something that a professional learns through experience and observation. The best presentations stay focused on the agenda, keep the meeting moving within the scheduled time, set out clear and reasonable expectations, and are based on a decision-making process that has been predetermined. The best presenters are well prepared and have practiced in advance. They are prepared to deal with any objections and can discuss the design solutions strategically, aligning them with the overall brand goals of the company. Larger projects routinely involve more than one presentation and numerous levels of building consensus.

Don't expect the work to speak for itself. Even the most ingenious solutions must be sold.

Suzanne Young
Communications strategist

Dosirak:
Welcomm Publicis Worldwide
Kbrand Associates

Presentation basics

Agree in advance about the agenda and the decision-making process.

Clarify who will attend the meeting and the role they will play. Individuals who have not participated in the early part of the process may derail the process.

Circulate the agenda in advance. Be sure to include the overall goals of the meeting.

Create an in-depth outline of your presentation and practice in advance. Create a handout if appropriate.

Look at the room's physical layout in advance to decide where you want to present from and where you want others to sit.

Arrive well in advance to set up the room and to be there to greet all the attendees.

If the company is going to provide any equipment for the meeting, test it in advance. Familiarize yourself with the lighting and temperature controls in the room.

Presentation strategies

Begin the meeting with a review of the decisions made to date, including overall brand identity goals, definition of target audience, and positioning statement.

Present each approach as a strategy with a unique positioning concept. Talk about meaning, not aesthetics. Each strategy should be presented within several actual contexts (ad, home page, business card, etc.), as well as juxtaposed with the competition.

Always have a point of view. When presenting numerous solutions (never more than three), be ready to explain which one you would choose and why.

Be prepared to deal with objections: steer the conversation away from aesthetic criticism and toward functional and marketing criteria.

Never present anything that you do not believe in.

Never allow voting.

Be prepared to present next steps, including design development, trademarking, and application design.

Follow up the presentation with a memo outlining all decisions that were made.

The brand identity design concept has been approved, and a sense of urgency generates a fusillade of questions: "When we will get business cards?", followed by "How soon can we get our standards online?" Now that the major decisions have been made, most companies want to hit the ground running. The challenge to the identity firm is to keep the momentum going while ensuring that critical details are finalized.

Phase 4 is about design refinement and design development. In Phase 3, hypothetical applications were designed in order to test the ideas, and to help sell the core concepts. The highest priority now is to refine and finalize the elements of the identity and to create signatures. This work requires an obsessive attention to detail; the files created are permanent. Final testing of the signature(s) in a variety of sizes and media is critical. Decisions about typeface families, color palettes, and secondary visual elements are finalized during this phase.

While the design team is fine-tuning, the company is organizing its final list of applications that need to be designed and produced. Core applications are prioritized, and content is either provided or developed. The intellectual property firm begins the trademark process, confirming what needs to be registered and in which industry classes. The lawyers confirm that there are no conflicting marks.

A brand identity program encompasses a unique visual language that will express itself across all applications. Regardless of the medium, the applications need to work in harmony. The challenge is to design the right balance between flexibility of expression and consistency in communications.

Design is intelligence made visible.

Lou Danziger
Designer and educator

In a diameter of one half inch, we see the name of the orchard, a trademark, a code, a URL, Product of USA, and a union bug.

This label is a glimpse into the future—when immediate recognition of a brand is needed on a miniature scale while we surf the web on our wristwatches.

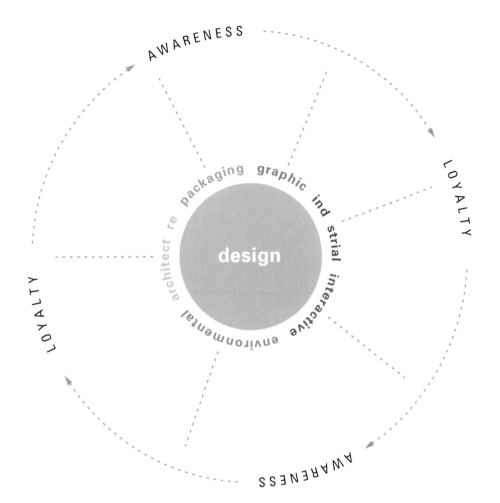

The diagram shows a central circle labeled "design" surrounded by the words: architect re packaging graphic ind strial interactive environmental. The outer ring is labeled AWARENESS and LOYALTY (repeated), connected with dashed arrows forming a circular flow.

Application design essentials

Convey the brand personality.

Align with positioning strategy.

Create a point of view and a look and feel.

Make the design system work across all media.

Demonstrate understanding of the target customer.

Differentiate. Differentiate. Differentiate.

Design development basics

Design is an iterative process between the big picture and minutiae.

Designing real applications and the identity system are simultaneous.

Ensure that all assumptions are achievable.

Be open to additional discovery as it gets more real.

Application design imperatives

Seize every opportunity to manage perception.

Create a unified visual language.

Start thinking about launch strategy.

Create balance between consistency and flexibility.

Produce real applications before finalizing standards.

Work on the highest-visibility applications first.

Know when to identify outside experts for collaboration.

Use spreadsheets to keep track of numerous applications.

Never show any application without showing alignment with brand strategy.

Be obsessive about quality.

Gather notes during this phase for standards and guidelines.

A brand identity that is distinctive and differentiated from its competitors will always help a client legally protect this valuable and critical asset. Almost anything that serves to distinguish products or services from those of a competitor can serve as a trademark. Names, symbols, logotypes, taglines, slogans, packaging and product design, color, and sound are all brand identity assets that can be registered with the federal government and protected from future litigation.

Federal registration is in place to ensure that the consumer is not confused or misled by trademarks that are too similar. The government agency responsible is called the U.S. Patent and Trademark Office (USPTO). Trademarks are always registered within industry classes, of which there are forty-five, and may be registered in more than one class. Intellectual property is the name of the legal discipline that specializes in providing the broadest scope of protection for brand identity assets. Intellectual property assets also include copyrights and patents.

There are different points in the brand identity process when research is conducted to determine whether there are any conflicting marks, names, or taglines. The various types of searches include common-law, federal, and state. Experienced legal counsel is needed to assess the risk of trademark infringement.

A distinctive identity is worth nothing unless you can protect it.

Roberta Jacobs-Meadway
Ballard Spahr Andrews & Ingersoll

Process : trademark search and registration

Establish legal needs	> Establish legal resources	> Decide on type of search	> Conduct preliminary research	> Conduct comprehensive research
Determine what needs to be protected: name, symbol, logotype, product design.	Identify client legal counsel.	Common-law (anyone can conduct)	Determine quickly other ownership.	Identify comprehensive database resources for naming, symbols, taglines, trade dress (package design), product design, color, sound.
Determine type of registration: federal, state, country.	Identify intellectual property lawyer.	Short screening (level 1)	Search domain registration sites, newspapers, search engines, telephone directories.	
Identify key dates.	Review other proprietary assets.	Comprehensive		Conduct and review searches.
Identify any regulatory constraints.	Research search services.	Visual (for symbols, package, products)	Create short list for comprehensive search.	Determine availability.
Determine industry class(es).				Choose what to eliminate or contest.
Assign search responsibilities.				
Set up documentation system.				

Brand identity legal basics

The more differentiated an identity is from those of its competitors, the easier it is to protect from a legal perspective.

Registering a mark gives clients extra rights and the broadest scope of protection. Although trademark rights may be established by actual use, federal registration ultimately secures more benefits in trademark infringement.

Registration is done at the federal and state levels. State registrations are usually less expensive than federal registrations but are more subject to challenge.

Protection for marks in other countries must be sought country by country since legal protection differs from country to country.

An individual, a corporation, a joint venture, or a partnership can own a trademark. A trademark cannot have two independent owners.

In the case of litigation, defendants failure to do a competent search may be evidence of bad faith.

Intellectual property is a specialty, and identifying a lawyer who has experience in this is critical. Anyone can search the USPTO or other databases on the web for federal registrations, but lawyers are trained to assess the risk of a brand identity strategy.

Certain industries, such as the financial industry, require state registrations with designated commissioners for product names that are sold nationally. What works in one state will not necessarily work in another.

Mergers usually have their own set of requirements that affect information sharing. Parties may request to restrict access to certain documents.

By the end of 2001, the USPTO had 1,063,164 active registrations for trademarks.

® may be used only when marks have been federally registered.

™ is used to alert the public and does not require filing federal applications. It means trademark, which is a claim of ownership for goods and packaging.

SM means service mark and refers to a unique service. This appears on any form of advertising and promotional literature. It does not require filing federal registration.

> **Conduct registration**

Finalize list of registrations.

Create documents as required.

Federal

State

Country

> **Monitor and educate**

Develop plan to monitor intellectual property assets.

Conduct annual intellectual property audits.

Educate employees and vendors.

Publish standards that clarify proper usage.

Make it easy to adhere to legal usage.

The art of correspondence and the letterhead have lasted from the quill pen, to the typewriter and the computer. Although voice mails and e-mails have become the most widely used form of communication, the letterhead is not yet obsolete in the beginning of the twenty-first century. The letter still comes to us in the same way that it has been coming to us since Ben Franklin became the first U.S. postmaster—unless, of course, it comes via FedEx, or as an attachment.

The letterhead, offset-printed on fine paper, remains a core application in the brand identity system even with electronic letterheads. The letterhead with an original signature is still an important conduit for doing business. It is regarded as a credible proof of being in business, and it frequently carries an important message or contractual agreement. It is still regarded as the most formal type of business communication and has an implicit dignity. For many years banks required businesses to write a letter on their letterhead in order to open an account.

In America the standard letterhead size is 8.5" by 11". This size is referred to as the U.S. standard size and is also used in Canada and Mexico. The rest of the world, however, uses letterhead and envelopes based on the metric system.

Characters:
Summerford Design

Process: letterhead design

Clarify use		Determine need		Get content		Develop design		Identify paper
Letters, short and long	>	Corporate only	>	Best-case scenario	>	Use real letter.	>	Appropriate surface
Contracts		Division letterhead		Worst-case scenario		Show actual size.		Availability
Memos		Personal letterhead		Unify abbreviations		Examine iterations.		Laser compatibility
Invoices		Size		Tagline		Design envelopes.		Color
				Regulatory information				
				Parent				
				Professional affiliation				

Letterhead design basics

Never design a letterhead without an actual letter on the page.

Never present a letterhead design without a real letter on it.

Take into consideration the location of the folds.

Get an ink draw on the paper that you have chosen.

Do a fax test.

Design a second sheet.

Research the right size for a foreign country.

Feel the paper, and identify the proper weight.

Find out biases regarding formats.

Provide templates for letter positioning, type style, and size.

Always test the paper and envelopes on a laser printer.

The world of abbreviations
There are no universal abbreviations. Consistency is the rule.

Telephone
Phone
Tel
P
T
Voice
V

Facsimile
Fax
F

Mobile
Cellular
M
C

E-mail
e-mail
e
(just address)

Website
Web
(just URL)

Home
Home

Characters' extensive paper application system builds on its core identity. Characters provides computer-generated production services.

> **Determine production method**

Printing

Engraving

Foil stamping

Embossing

Watermark

> **Manage production**

Review proofs.

Watch first run on press.

Develop electronic templates.

Each day millions of people all over the world are asking others, "May I have your card?" This commonplace business ritual looks different around the globe. In Korea you show respect for a colleague by presenting a business card in two hands. In the Far East most corporate business cards are two-sided, with one side, for example, in Korean, and the other side in English. The Western-size business card is slowly becoming the standard around the world, although many countries are still using variations of a larger card.

In the nineteenth century, Victorian calling cards were elaborately decorated and oversized by present American standards. They were designed to showcase a name only. Today the designer is faced with so much information to include—from e-mail to voice mail to mobile phone and 800 numbers, double addresses and domains—that the small business card is a challenge even for the most experienced designers. Information, by necessity, is flowing to the back side.

The business card is a small and portable marketing tool. The quality and intelligence of the information are a reflection on the card holder and her company. Digital business cards are gaining in popularity. These mini CDs have the capacity to hold a multimedia presentation on the size of a credit card. In the future a high-tech business card may double as an identification card and include a user's fingerprint or other biometric data.

Like the best packages, the best calling cards convey trustworthiness and WOW at once.

Tom Peters
Brand You

Process : business card design

Clarify positioning	Determine need	Finalize content	Develop design	Identify paper
Revisit positioning goals.	Who uses a card?	Best-case scenario	Use real text.	Appropriate surface
Revisit competitive audit.	How frequent is the need?	Worst-case scenario	Show actual size.	Weight
Revisit internal audit.	What is the quantity required?	Unify abbreviations	Examine iterations.	Availability
Understand brand hierarchy.	What is the critical information?	Tagline	Consider the back.	Color
		Regulatory info	Develop color strategy.	Quality
		Parent		
		Professional affiliation		

Business card design basics

Think of a business card as a marketing tool.

Make it easy for the receiver of a card to retrieve information.

Make it easy for new cards to be produced.

Minimize the amount of information, within reason.

Consider using the back as a place for more information or a marketing message.

Carefully choose the weight of the paper to convey quality.

Feel the paper and the surface.

Make sure that all abbreviations are consistent.

Make sure that the titles are consistent.

Make sure that the typographic use of upper- and lowercase is consistent.

Develop system formats.

Do not consider an unusual size unless the company is a restaurant or a fashion house.

> **Determine production method**

Printing

Engraving

Foil stamping

Embossing

> **Manage production**

Review proofs.

Watch first run on press.

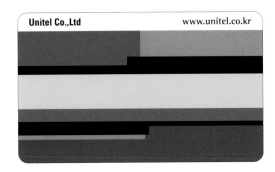

Unitel Co.,Ltd   www.unitel.co.kr

유니텔 주식회사
서울특별시 서초구 서초동 1449-6번지 한원빌딩, 137-070
4th Fl, Hanwon Bldg., 1449-6, Seocho-dong, Seocho-gu, Seoul, Korea
Tel : 02-3415-6948   Fax : 02-3415-6101
e-mail : chulsoo@unitel.co.kr

김 철 수 Chulsoo Kim
책임/전략기획 Planning Manager
마케팅팀 Marketing Team

UNITEL

Infinite, a strategic identity and image management firm in Seoul, Korea, designed these bilingual, two-sided business cards for Daehan Investment Trust Securities and Unitel, an internet provider.

150-705 서울특별시 영등포구 여의도동 27-3번지
Tel : 02-3771-7091 Fax : 02-782-8606 H.P : 011-3283-0154
E-mail : chulsoo@daetoo.com www.daetoo.com

김 철 수 홍보실/차장

대한투자 신탁 증권

27-3 Yoido-Dong, Youngdungpo-Ku, Seoul 150-705, Korea
Tel : 82-2-3771-7091 Fax : 82-2-782-8606 H.P : 011-3283-0154
E-mail : chulsoo@daetoo.com www.daetoo.com

Chulsoo Kim Planning Manager/Marketing Team

You are waiting for your café latte and see brochures in a stylish rack. You rip open your monthly mutual fund statement, and there it is—an insert. You unpack your new iPod, and there is a tiny booklet. You go to the doctor, and each aspect of your health care has its own publication. You contact a consultant, and he encourages you to download his company's brochure. Brochures are omnipresent.

Brochures continue to be popular marketing and information tools. The best brochures invite readership since they are easy to understand and user-friendly. Designing a unified system ensures that the identity of the company is consistently presented and communicates familiarity to the existing customer. Designing a grid and typographic system that allows flexibility is not only smart from a branding perspective, but also efficient from a cost and resources perspective.

Empire Blue Cross & Blue Shield: Bernhardt Fudyma Design Group

Process : brochure system design

Revisit the big picture	Design a cover system	Determine typographic system	Determine artwork	Design color family
Examine positioning goals.	Examine signature scenarios:	One typeface family or many	Photography	Two-color
Examine competitive audit.	Signature in primary and constant place	Title typeface	Illustration	Four-color
Examine internal audit.	Split signature	Cover descriptor typeface	Collage	Flat colors
Identify functional needs, i.e., how brochures are used and distributed.	Signature not used on cover	Header typeface	Typographic	Web colors
Understand how brochures are produced within the company.	Signature used on back only	Subhead typeface	Abstract	
Identify challenges.	Signature used in secondary position with product name in primary position	Text typeface	Identity derivative	
		Caption typeface		

Brochure system basics

Unified brochure systems increase brand recognition.

Effective brochure systems are differentiated from the competition's.

Brochures are an extension of a company's identity and brand architecture.

Effective brochures make it easy for customers to understand information and to buy products and services.

By making information accessible, a company demonstrates its understanding of its customers' needs and preferences.

Effective brochures make it easier for the sales force to sell.

Effective systems anticipate future change.

System standards should be easy for managers, design professionals, and advertising agencies to understand.

Systems should include flexible elements but not waver on clear, absolute standards regarding signatures.

Great design is effective only if it can be reproduced at the highest quality.

The best brochures are well written and present appropriate amounts of information.

Systems should include a consistent call for action that gives customers choices and access.

Bernhardt Fudyma Design Group created a flexible graphic system for Empire Blue Cross & Blue Shield that unified all marketing and communication materials and positioned its client as New York State's leading provider of health insurance.

> **Choose standard formats**	> **Choose paper**	> **Develop prototypes**	> **Develop guidelines**
4 x 9	Examine functionality.	Use real copy.	Articulate goals.
6 x 9	Examine price points.	Look at best- and worst-case scenarios.	Create grids.
8.5 x 11	Decide on family of papers.	Edit language as needed.	Explain system.
Other	Have dummies made.	Demonstrate flexibility of system.	Develop templates.
PDF	Feel the paper.	Decide on signature configurations.	Monitor execution.
	Consider weight if needed.		

The best packages become one with our brand experience. Packages are brands that you trust enough to take into your home. For baby boomers, they reside forever in their childhood memories—from the Whitman's Sampler box and the Beatles' "White Album" cover, to the glass Coca-Cola bottle and the Tiffany box. For Generation X, packages themselves have evolved into status symbols. The lexicon of cool includes the Absolut vodka bottle, the wavy and futuristic Gatorade bottle, the iPod packaging, and the Tiffany box.

We are continually comforted and cajoled by packaging shapes, graphics, colors, messages, and containers. The shelf is probably the most

competitive marketing environment that exists. From new brands to extending or revitalizing existing product lines, considerations of brand equity, cost, time, and competition are often complex.

Packaging design is a specialty, and it routinely involves collaboration with industrial designers, packaging engineers, and manufacturers. In the food and pharmaceutical industry, it is regulated by the government. Package design is only one part of the puzzle involved in a product launch. Timetables include packaging approval and production, sales force meetings, manufacturing and distribution, and advertising.

In the average half-hour trip to the supermarket, 30,000 products vie for the shopper's attention.

Thomas Hine
The Total Package

First I bought it because it looked cool. Later I bought it because it tasted good.
Michael Grillo
Age 14

Process : packaging design

Clarify goals + positioning	Conduct audits + identify expert team	Conduct research as needed	Research legal requirements	Research functional criteria
Establishing goals and defining problem	Competitive (category)	Understand brand equity.	Brand + corporate standards	Product stability
Brand equity	Retail (point of sale)	Determine brand standards.	Product-specific	Tamper or theft resistance
Competition	Brand (internal, existing product line)	Examine brand architecture.	Net weight	Shelf footprint
Existing brands in product line	Packaging designer	Clarify target consumer.	Drug facts	Durability
Price point	Packaging engineer	Confirm need for product—does product benefit resonate?	Nutrition facts	Usage
Target consumer	Packaging manufacturers	Confirm language—how should benefit be expressed?	Ingredients	Packability
Product benefit	Industrial designers		Warnings	Fillability
	Regulatory legal department		Claims	

Zours : The Bailey Group

Packaging basics

The shelf is the most competitive marketing environment that exists.

Good design sells. It is a competitive advantage.

Positioning relative to the competition and to the other members of the product line is critical for developing a packaging strategy.

A disciplined, coherent approach leads to a unified, powerful brand presence.

Structure and graphics can be developed concurrently. It is a chicken-and-egg debate.

Brand extensions are always a strategic tug-of-war between differentiation and coherence within a product line.

Consider the entire life cycle of the package and its relationship to the product: source, print, assemble, pack, preserve, ship, display, purchase, use, recycle/dispose.

Devise timetables involving packaging approval and production, sales force meetings, product sell in to stores, manufacturing, and distribution.

Developing a new structure takes a long time and is very expensive, but it offers a unique competitive advantage.

It's no longer enough to just research the competition. One needs to think beyond the category when designing a new structure. We live at a time when one buys tuna in a bag, bath salts in a paint can, and wine in a carton.

Steve Perry
The Bailey Group

Clean & Clear:
The Bailey Group

> **Determine printing specs**	> **Determine structural design**	> **Finalize copy**	> **Design and prototype**	> **Evaluate solution + manage production**
Method: flexo, litho, roto	Design new structure or use stock?	Product name	Start with face panels (2D renderings).	In a retail/competitive environment
Application: direct, label, shrink-wrap label	Choose forms (e.g., carton, bottle, can, tube, jar, tin, blister packs).	Benefit copy	Get prototypes made.	As a member of the product line
Other: number of colors, divinyl, UPC code, minimums for knockouts	Choose possible materials, substrates, or finishes.	Ingredients	Narrow option(s).	Consumer testing
	Source stock and get samples.	Nutrition facts/drug facts	Design rest of package.	Finalizing files
		Net contents	Simulate reality: use actual structure/substrate with contents.	Overseeing production
		Claims		
		Warnings		
		Distributed by		
		Manufactured in		
		UPC code		

⬤ ⬤ ⬤ ⬤ ⬤

Engaging content, sound, movement, and color create a walking, talking interactive company experience, bringing the brand personality to life. A website is the next best thing to reality, and in some cases it is more efficient, more user-friendly, and faster. The customer is in charge. The internet provides the customer with a no-pressure sales environment, and at the click of a mouse, a competitor is waiting.

The best websites understand their customers and respect their needs and preferences. A company's website should quickly answer these questions: "Who is this company? Why does anyone need to know? What's in it for me?" Expressing an authentic brand identity on the web is still a new frontier that communication architects, information architects, designers, and engineers are just beginning to conquer. Websites are increasingly used as portals for media tools. From logos to message points, downloading from a site enables employees to jumpstart marketing and communications from anywhere in the world.

The number one Internet myth is "Build it and they will come."

Richard Kauffman
Panoptic Communications

Interactive experiences require nonlinear thinking, inviting interfaces, and creative intelligence.

Stella Gassaway, Visionary and Creative Principal
Stellarvisions

Characteristics of the best websites
Easy to use
Meets visitor expectations
Communicates visually

Process: website design

Compiled by Stellarvisions

Initiate plan	> Build groundwork	> Define structure	> Prepare content	> Create visual design
Set goals.	Conduct competitive audit.	Outline content.	Set editorial calendar.	Color palette, tone, metaphor
Establish project team.	Gather data about audience.	Map content.	Decide how often content changes.	Grid and element placement
Identify audiences.	Consider content sources.	Define logical relationships.	Identify existing content.	Graphic elements + text styles
Define key messages.	Explore technological issues.	Create user personas + scenarios.	Rewrite text for web.	Navigational cues
Revisit positioning.	Assess resources for ongoing site updates.	Postulate visitor's mental model.	Commission new content, visual, or media assets.	Layouts of key screens
Set priorities.	Evaluate existing site.	Build wire-frame prototypes.	Approve content, including legal signoff.	Planning display on small screen devices
Rough out project plan.	Revisit goals + set strategies.	Test prototypes.	Review content in screen context.	Interfacing for functions
Define success.			Edit and proofread text.	Integration of media
				Prototyping and testing with users

Website basics

Keep site goals, audience needs, key messages, and brand personality central to each and every decision about the site.

Anticipate future growth. Measure, evaluate, change.

Site structure should not simply reflect organizational structure.

Begin site structure with content, not a screen design.

Do not force content into counterintuitive groupings.

Write content specifically for the web.

Conduct usability testing.

Observe etiquette. Alert visitors where special technology is needed, where a screen may load slowly, or where a link leaves your site.

Comply with ADA: Arrange for visually impaired visitors to use software to read the site aloud or greatly magnify text.

At each stage ask: Is the message clear? Is the content accessible? Is the experience positive?

Confront internal political agendas that may sabotage site goals.

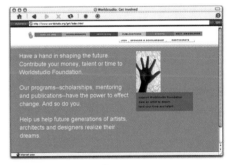

Worldstudio Foundation: Stellarvisions

> **Develop technical design**

Strategy for data integration

Static vs. dynamic screens

Content management option

Transaction flow design

Quality assurance testing plan

Security + scalability

Technical specifications

Prototyping and testing

Locking feature set

> **Finalize development**

Production of screen graphics

Development of HTML templates

Content freeze

Inserting content into screens

Approval of beta site

Quality tests of beta site

User tests of beta site

> **Launch and maintain**

Promote site launch.

Complete style guide.

Optimize site for search engines.

Develop maintenance plan.

Monitor logs and user paths.

Measure success.

Test ongoing usability.

Communication in the environment provides yet another opportunity to build a brand. From city streets and skylines, through museums and airports, signage functions as identification, information, and advertising. There is substantial evidence that effective retail signage increases revenues, and intelligent wayfinding systems support and enhance the experience of a brand, whether it is that of a town, a university, or a business district.

Signage is playing an increasing role in expressing and revitalizing the image and experience of a destination. In Seoul, Korea, large digital billboards grace the sides of skyscrapers to capture our attention. Digital media open the door for interactive storytelling.

In the eighteenth century, laws required innkeepers to have their signs high enough to clear an armored man on horseback. In the twenty-first century, cities and towns around the world routinely revise sign codes in order to create environments that support the image that a community wants to portray, and to regulate standards to protect public safety.

Signage helps people identify, navigate, and understand environments.

Alan Jacobson, Principal
AGS

Process: signage design

Establish goals		Build project team		Conduct research		Establish project criteria		Begin design schematic
Determine project scope.	>	Client facilities manager	>	Site audit: environment	>	Legibility	>	Brand identity system
Understand audience needs + habits.		Information design firm		Site audit: building type		Placement		Color, scale, format
Clarify positioning.		Fabricator		User habits and patterns		Visibility		Typography
Clarify function.		Architect or space designer		Local codes and zoning		Sustainability		Lighting
Develop time frame + budget.		Lighting consultant		Consideration for the disabled		Safety		Materials and finishes
				Weather + traffic conditions		Maintenance		Fabrication techniques
				Materials and finishes		Security		Mounting + hardware
				Fabrication processes		Modularity		Placement

Signage basics

Signage expresses the brand and builds on understanding the needs and habits of users in the environment.

Legibility, visibility, durability, and positioning must drive the design process. Distance, speed, light, color, and contrast affect legibility.

Signage is a mass communications medium that works 24/7 and can attract new customers, influence purchasing decisions, and increase sales.

Exterior signage must consider both vehicular and pedestrian traffic.

Every community, industrial park, and shopping mall develops its own signage code; there are no universal codes.

Signage codes affect material, illumination (electrical), and structural choices; zoning or land use issues affect placement and size of signage.

Zoning constraints need to be understood prior to design development.

Permit and variance applications should include the benefit to the land-use planning scheme.

Signage requires a long-term commitment, and maintenance plans and contracts are critical to protecting the investment.

Developing prototypes minimizes risk by testing design prior to fabrication.

Signage should always complement the overall architecture and land use of a site.

Signage standards manuals include various configurations, materials, supplier selections, and production, installation, and maintenance details.

Vanderbilt University: Malcolm Grear Designers

> **Develop design**	> **Complete documentation**	> **Manage fabrication + maintenance**
Begin variance process.	Complete working drawings	Check shop drawings.
Prepare prototypes or models.	Construction, mounting, and elevation details	Inspect work.
Finalize content.		Manage fabrication.
Create drawings or renderings.	Final specifications	Manage installation.
Choose materials + color samples.	Placement plans	Develop maintenance plan.
	Bid documents	
	Permit applications	

Since Silk Road traders described the benefits of jade and silk in lyrical song, merchants have created a sense of longing and entitlement by communicating about their products. Today we call it advertising and despite TiVo and the decline of print, it is still the way consumers learn about new products, services, and ideas.

Our society has a love-hate relationship with advertising. Pundits issue warnings about its ubiquity and the cynicism of an increasingly skeptical audience. But who can resist the latest catalog or ignore sumptuous magazine ads? Advertising is influence, information, persuasion, communication, and dramatization. It is also an art and a science, determining new ways to create a relationship between the consumer and the product.

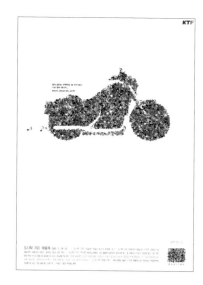

Unless your campaign contains a big idea, it will pass like ships in the night.

David Ogilvy
Ogilvy on Advertising

Process : advertising

Developed by Ritter Strategic Marketing

> Conduct research	> Develop strategy	> Develop creative	> Test creative	> Develop media plan
Define objectives + target audience.	Define strategic objective + customer benefit(s).	Define creative strategy.	Determine testing approach.	Develop alternative strategies.
Review or develop brand vision + positioning.	Explore creative strategies.	Develop integrated theme.	Conduct consumer communication verification checks.	Determine reach, frequency, benefits, budgets.
Review past creative + results.	Develop media strategy.	Develop copy concepts.	Modify concepts as necessary.	Review + finalize plan + budget.
Analyze marketplace.	Weigh evolutionary vs. revolutionary approaches.	Develop visual approaches.	Develop production schedule.	Place media buy.
Review competition + trends.	Define brand personality.	Distill the best ideas.		Provide content to media.
Develop target demographics.	Revitalize positioning.	Explore integration across media.		Review media verification + invoices.
Identify opportunities + unmet needs.	Validate priorities + assumptions.			
Review analysis and findings.	Establish budget.			

Anything that is screen-based will be able to be used as an ad-serving mechanism.

Andy Jung
Director of Advertising and Media
Kellogg's

I do not regard advertising as entertainment or an art form, but as a medium of information. When I write an advertisement, I don't want you to tell me that you find it "creative". I want you to find it so interesting that you buy the product. When Aeschines spoke, they said, "How well he speaks." But when Demosthenes spoke, they said, "Let us march against Philip."

David Ogilvy
Ogilvy on Advertising

Welcomm Publicis Worldwide's advertising campaign for Dosirak features everyday objects filled with the Dosirak musical texture from its logo, like great sound filling the air. The campaign's conceptual simplicity ensures unending possibilities in creative expression. The identity was designed by Kbrand Associates.

> **Manage production**

Assemble production specifications + requirements.

Develop production schedule.

Review with client or test with consumer.

Clear with legal.

Review, modify, + edit as necessary.

> **Implement campaign**

Communicate plan to client team.

Conduct road show for client field outposts.

Launch integrated campaign.

Conduct consumer communication checks.

Capture key learnings.

Document improvement opportunities.

Manage ongoing program.

> **Monitor impact**

Track impact across all media.

Compare sales activity to that of prior campaigns.

Review costs relative to budget.

Assemble findings for discussion.

Modify campaign for future.

From a luxury car showroom, to the inside of an airplane or a supermarket, smart businesses seize every opportunity to manage the experience and expectations of customers by branding the environment. Fabergé, the goldsmith known for the splendid jeweled eggs for the czar, was one of the first global entrepreneurs to understand that a well-conceived showroom appeals to customers and increases sales. We live at a time when it is not unusual for the design and ambience of a restaurant to be a greater attraction than the culinary art, or for a financial services company, such as ING Direct, to open a hip café to serve up good coffee and financial advice.

The exterior architecture represents yet another opportunity to stimulate immediate recognition and attract customers. In the 1950s, an orange tile roof in the distance sent an immediate and welcoming signal that there was a Howard Johnson's restaurant ahead. At the opposite end of the cultural spectrum, the architecture of the Guggenheim Museum at Bilbao is the brand and a powerful magnet that draws millions of visitors.

Architects, space designers, graphic designers, industrial designers, lighting experts, structural and mechanical engineers, general contractors, subcontractors, and a host of manufacturer's reps collaborate with client development teams to create unique environments and experiences that make their clients more successful. Memorable and unique color, texture, scale, light, sound, movement, comfort, smell, and accessible information manage perception in the environment.

Apple store

Aveda salon, Tokyo

Branded environment imperatives

Understand the needs, preferences, habits, and aspirations of the target audience.

Create a unique experience that is aligned with brand positioning.

Experience and study the competition, and learn from their successes and failures.

Create an experience and environment that make it easy for customers to buy, and that inspire them to come back again and again.

Align the quality and speed of service with the experience of the environment.

Create an environment that helps the sales force sell and makes it easy to complete a transaction.

Consider the dimensions of space: visual, auditory, olfactory, tactile, and thermal.

Understand the psychological effect of light and lighting sources, and consider energy efficiency whenever possible.

Consider all operational needs so that the client can deliver on the brand promise.

Understand traffic flow, the volume of business, and economic considerations.

Align merchandising strategies with displays, advertising, and sales strategies.

Design a space that is sustainable, durable, and easy to maintain and clean.

Consider the needs of handicapped customers.

Bank of New York: Lippincott Mercer

We're starved for Wow! For experiences that coddle, comfort, cajole, and generally show us a darn good time. That's what we want for the money. I want decent vittles, mind you, but food we can get anywhere.

Hilary Jay
Director
The Design Center
Philadelphia University

Gucci has redesigned their retail experience. It's not a radical jump—it has to do with who they are, and it builds on their history with a new eye to the future—and a streamlined presence.

Trish Thompson
Fashion Consultant

Wherever I may wander
Wherever I may roam
When I walk into a
Starbucks
I'm suddenly back at home.

Cathy Jooste
Global Citizen

Building brand awareness on the road is easier than ever. Vehicles are a new, large, moving canvas on which almost any type of communication is possible. Whether on an urban thruway at rush hour or a remote country road at sunset, the goal remains the same: make the brand identity immediately recognizable, and do it within a few seconds.

From trains, to planes, to large vans and small delivery trucks, vehicles are omnipresent. Vehicle graphics are experienced from ground level; from other vehicles, such as cars and buses and from the windows of buildings. Designers need to consider scale, legibility, distance, surface color, and the effects of movement, speed, and light. Designers also need to consider the life of the vehicle, the durability of the signage medium, and safety requirements and regulations that may vary state by state.

The Goodyear blimp and the hot-air balloons are brand identities taking flight. Many vehicles carry other messages, from taglines and phone numbers, to graphic elements and vehicle identification numbers. Simplicity should rule the road.

Process : vehicle signage

Plan	Design	Determine	Examine	Implement
Audit vehicle types.	Choose base color for vehicle.	Fabrication methods: Decal and wrap	Impact on insurance rates	Create files done to spec.
Revisit positioning.	Design placement of signature.	Vinyl	Life of vehicle	Prepare documentation for installer.
Research fabrication methods.	Determine other messages: Phone number or domain.	Magnetic Hand-painted	Life of sign type	Examine output.
Research installers.	Vehicle ID number.		Cost and time	Test colors.
Receive technical specifications.	Tagline.		Safety or other regulations	Manage installation.
Get vehicle drawings.	Explore other graphic elements.			

Fresh produce from local farmers and wholesalers are delivered door to door by Westside Organics, inspiring their customers to "Save time, save gas, save the environment."

Westside Organics: Grapefruit

Clothing communicates. From the friendly orange apron at Home Depot, to a UPS deliveryperson in brown, a visible and distinctive uniform simplifies customer transactions. A uniform can also signal authority and identification. From the airline captain, to the security guard, uniforms make customers more at ease. Finding a waiter in a restaurant may be as simple as finding the person with the black T-shirt and the white pants. On the playing field, professional teams require uniforms that will not only distinguish them from their competitors, but also look good on television. A lab coat is required in a laboratory, as are scrubs

in an operating room, and both are subject to regulations and compliance standards.

The best uniforms engender pride and are appropriate to the workplace and environment. Their designers are respectful of the individuals who need to wear them and carefully consider performance criteria, such as durability and mobility. The way an employee is dressed affects the way that the individual and her organization are perceived. The reproduction method, placement, and scale of the identity are critical decisions that build awareness.

We branded the country, and people will actually end up wearing the brand.

Joe Duffy, Founder
Duffy & Partners

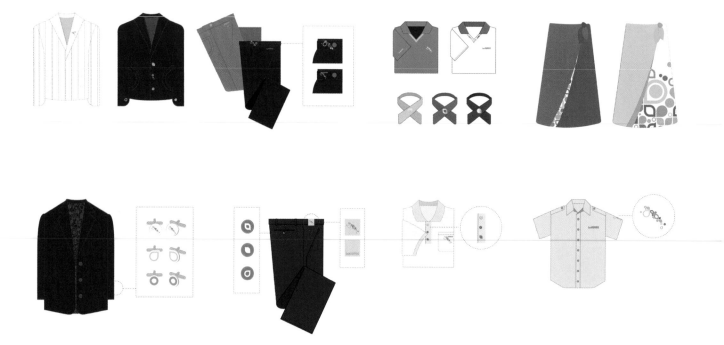

Uniform performance criteria

Functional: Does the uniform take into consideration the nature of the job?

Durability: Is the uniform well made?

Ease: Is the uniform machine washable or easy to clean?

Mobility: Can employees do their tasks easily?

Comfort: Is the uniform comfortable?

Visibility: Is the uniform immediately recognizable?

Wearability: Is the uniform easy to put on?

Weight: Has the weight been considered?

Temperature: Does the uniform consider weather factors?

Pride: Does the uniform engender pride?

Respect: Does the uniform respect different body sizes?

Safety: Does the uniform adhere to regulations?

Brand: Is the uniform a reflection of the desired image?

Who needs uniforms?
Public safety officers
Security guards
Transportation personnel
Couriers
Bank tellers
Volunteers
Health care workers
Hospitality workers
Retail personnel
Restaurant personnel
Sports teams
Sports facilities personnel
Laboratory workers
Special events personnel

Methods
Off the shelf
Custom design
Custom fabrication
Embroidery
Screen printing
Patches
Striping

Uniform possibilities
Aprons
Belts
Pants
Shorts
Skirts
Turtlenecks
Golf shirts
T-shirts
Vests
Neckwear
Outerwear
Rainwear
Blazers
Blouses
Bows
Gloves
Boots
Helmets
Shoes
Socks
Tights
ID badges
Accessories
Scarves
Fleece
Windwear
Visors
Baseball caps
Scrub apparel
Patient gowns
Lab coats

The Bahamas' Ministry of Tourism uniform program in conceptual development.

Duffy & Partners

Welcome to the twenty-first century. Technological innovation offers a voice to individuals and builds new, unusual, global communities. Mobile technology and broadband have made the world a smaller place. User groups give consumers unprecedented clout. Blogs enable individuals who have no resources beyond their convictions to brand themselves, celebrate their individuality, and broadcast their views.

As software engineers churn out new technologies, marketers and designers seize on them to differentiate brands and outpace the competition.

Unlike earlier times, when people learned a skill and applied it the same way for life, members of our society are continually acquiring new skills and bending new media to wring out every possible innovation and permutation, before moving on to the next new thing. The new media of today becomes the mainstream media of tomorrow and the discarded, dated debris of next year.

You can spend a lot of money on technology, but unless you spend money on interface design, you are just throwing it away.

George Graves, former Chief Technologist
QVC

Favicons
A short icon, associated with a particular website or webpage, that appears in the web browser's URL bar, next to the site's name.

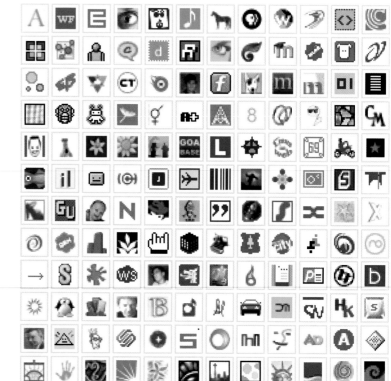

The Possibilities

Avatars

Blogs

Podcasting

Social communication tools

Wikis

Electronic banners

V-logs

IM-ing

Favicons

Blast emails

Search engines

Blog search engines

Online communities

Pop-ups

Motorola RAZR

My cell phone is my life.
Tessa Wheeler
Age 18

Favicon art: Michael Pierce

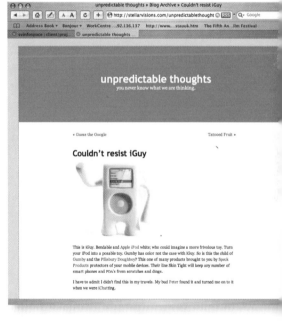

My blog is a brain dump. It's the totally nonlinear, unpredictable thoughts that inform my intuitive decisions.
Stella Gassaway, visionary

A trade show is not a trade show without giveaways. The best booths give you canvas bags to store all your goodies, from squeezy stress balls, to commuter cups, to baseball caps, to mouse pads. You wonder how you ever lived without this memorabilia.

Ephemera is defined as objects with a short life, or more simply put, stuff. Companies frequently use marketing and promotion items. Done right, these tchotchkes build brand awareness and are good public relations and thank-yous. Many large companies have company stores on their websites so that employees can be completely outfitted in any weather condition. The best clothing that carries an identity is tastefully designed and produced with quality. For example, a nice polo shirt can engender pride, and it can also be a nice client gift.

Reproduction is rarely simple. Special techniques, such as embroidering a golf shirt or leather stamping onto a portfolio, usually require a custom signature that understands the needs of the production technique. The best way to control quality is to examine a proof.

Illustrating a core belief that all design is interactive, Stellarvisions created these promotional buttons (shown actual size).

Categories	Production methods
Thank-you	Silk screening
Appreciation	Imprinting
Recognition	Debossing
Special event	Foil stamping
Trade show	Color filled
Grand opening	Engraving
Affiliation	Etching
Pride	Embroidering
Motivation	Leather stamping

The possibilities

Alarm clocks	Cases	Flying saucers	Lip balm	Pillows	Stopwatches
Albums	Certificates	Flyswatters	Lipsticks	Piñatas	Stress relievers
Aprons	Chairs	Foam novelties	Liquid motion products	Pins	Stuffed animals
Auto/travel stuff	Christmas decorations	Folders	Locks	Pitchers	Sun catchers
Awards	Cigars	Food/beverages	Luggage/tags	Place mats	Sun visors
Awnings	Clipboards	Frames	Lunch boxes/kits	Planners	Sunglasses
Badge holders	Clocks	Games	Magnets	Plants	Sweaters
Badges/buttons	Clothing	Gauges	Magnifiers	Plaques	T-shirts
Bag clips	Coasters	Gavels	Maps/atlases	Plates	Tablecloths
Bags	Coffee pots	Gift baskets	Markers	Playing cards	Tags
Balloons	Coin holders	Gift cards/wrap	Masks	Pointers	Tape measures
Balls	Coins/medallions	Glass specialties	Matches	Poker chips	Tattoos
Bandanas	Coloring books	Globes	Mats	Portfolios	Teapots
Banks	Combs	Gloves	Measuring devices	Postcards	Telescopes
Banners/pennants	Compact discs	Glow products	Medals	Puppets	Thermometers
Bar stuff	Compasses	Goggles	Medical information products	Purses	Tiaras/crowns
Barbecue stuff	Computer stuff	Golf stuff	Megaphones	Puzzles/tricks	Ties
Barometers/hygrometers	Condoms	Greeting cards	Membership cards	Radios	Tiles
Baskets	Containers	Handkerchiefs	Memo cubes	Rainwear	Timers
Bathrobes	Cookware	Hangers	Memo pads	Recorders	Tins
Batteries	Corkscrews	Hardware tools	Menus/menu covers	Recycled products	Tissues
Beauty aids	Cosmetics	Headbands	Metal specialties	Reflectors	Toolkits
Belt buckles	Coupon keepers	Headphones	Microphones	Religious goods	Toothbrushes
Beverage holders	Covers	Headrests	Miniatures	Ribbons	Tops/spinners
Bibs	Crayons	Highlighters	Mirrors	Rubber stamps	Toys/novelties
Binoculars	Crystal products	Holders	Money clips	Rulers	Travel stuff
Blankets	Cups	Holograms	Money converters	Safety products	Trays
Bookends	Cushions	Horseshoes	Mouse pads	Sandals	Trophies/loving cups
Bookmarks	Decals	Hotel amenities	Mugs	Scarves	Umbrellas
Books	Decanters	Ice buckets	Musical specialties	Scissors	Uniforms
Bottle holders	Decorations	Ice packs	Nameplates	Scoops/scrapers	USB/flash drives
Bottle stoppers	Desk stuff	Ice scrapers	Napkin rings	Scratch-off cards	Utensils
Bottles	Dials/slide charts	ID holders	Napkins	Seals	Utility clips
Bowls	Diaries/journals	Inflatables	Noisemakers	Seats (folding)	Valuable paper holders
Boxer shorts	Dice	Invitations	Office supplies	Seeds	Vests
Boxes	Dishes	Jackets	Openers	Sewing stuff	Vinyl plastic specialties
Breath mints	Dispensers	Jars	Organizers	Shirts	Voice recorders
Briefcases	Doctor/druggist aids	Jewelry	Ornaments	Shoes/shoehorns	Wallets
Buckets	Dog tags	Jewelry boxes	Packaging	Shovels	Wands/scepters
Bulletin boards	Drink stirrers/sticks	Kaleidoscopes	Pads	Signs/displays	Watch fobs
Bumper stickers	Drinkware	Kazoos	Pajamas	Slippers	Watches
Business card holders	Easels	Key cases/tags	Pamphlets	Snow domes	Water
Business cards	Electronic devices	Key holders	Paper specialties	Soap	Weather instruments
Calculators	Emblems	Kitchen	Paperweights	Socks	Whistles
Calendar pads	Embroidery	Kites	Party favors	Special packaging	Wind socks
Calendars	Emergency first aids kits	Labels	Pedometers	Sponges	Wine stuff
Cameras	Envelopes	Lamps/lanterns	Pen/pencil sets	Spoons	Wood specialties
Camping equipment	Erasers	Lanyards	Pepper mills	Sports equipment	Wrist rest
Candle holders	Exercise/fitness	Lapel pins	Pet stuff	Sports memorabilia	Wristbands
Candles	Eyeglasses	Lawn/garden stuff	Phone calling cards	Sports schedules	Yo-yos
Candy	Eyeglasses–3D	Leather specialties	Photo cards	Squeegees	Zipper/pulls
Canisters	Fans	Leis	Photo cubes	Stamp pads	
Cans	Figurines	Letter openers	Phone stuff	Stamps	List provided by:
Caps/hats	Flags	License plates/frames	Phones	Staple removers	Advertising Specialty Institute
Carabiners	Flashlights	Lighters	Physical/therapeutic aids	Staplers	
Carafes	Flasks	Lights	Picnic coolers	Stationery/business forms	
Cards	Flowers	Lint removers	Pictures/paintings	Stones	

Managing brand identity assets requires enlightened leadership and a long-term commitment to doing everything possible to build the brand. The mandate to build the brand must come from the top. If management's commitment is tepid and the resources committed are minimal, the original investment will most likely deliver a dismal rate of return.

To the surprise of many clients, the brand identity process does not end after corporate letterhead and business cards are printed. This is when the work really begins. Because it takes quite a while to get to this point of visible accomplishment, many managers assume that the time, money, and energy spent thus far represent the majority of the investment. Wrong. This is just the beginning. Creating the brand identity was the easy part. Managing these assets well is harder.

Key initiatives

Conduct an internal launch.

Communicate with employees about the new brand identity.

Create standards and guidelines to ensure that all future applications adhere to the intention of the program.

Launch the new brand identity externally to key stakeholders.

Create accountability.

Identify those people who champion the brand.

Develop a checks-and-balances method to audit progress.

The brand is a living animate object. It needs to be continually monitored, ensuring differentiation and relevance.

Clay Timon, former CEO
Landor Associates

JoongAng Ilbo is one of the leading daily newspapers from Korea. Its brand identity, designed by Infinite, features the letter "J" in the shape of an ear in the middle of a circle. The tagline, "We will be the eyes and ears of the public" is reinforced by the circle, which stands for the earth. The identity places JoongAng Ilbo at the center of the world. Their standards are extensive and anticipate every category of applications.

JoongAng Ilbo:
Infinite

Rare is the person in an organization who embraces change. Introducing a new name and identity to an existing organization or to merged entities is exponentially more difficult than creating a brand for a new company. Changing brand identity means that whatever was on a manager's plate now doubles. The to-do list is extremely long, even in a small company. New brand identity implementation requires a vigilant strategic focus, advance planning, and obsession with detail.

Routinely the director of marketing and public relations will oversee the change. In larger organizations an individual may be retained to focus exclusively on implementation. The skills required are knowledge of branding, public relations, communications, identity design, production, and organizational management. Military mobilization skills come in handy, and boundless optimism helps.

Managing brand identity change has the potential to enhance brand perception–by increasing awareness among constituencies, increasing preference, and building loyalty.

Patricia M. Baldridge, Vice President, Marketing and Public Relations
Philadelphia University

Biggest challenges

Developed by Patricia M. Baldridge

Time and money: planning enough advance time and an adequate budget

Deciding whether to go for a mega-launch or a phased-in launch

Internal buy-in and support

Keeping a strategic focus on all communications

Helping people to make the connection from old to new

Honoring one's heritage while celebrating the new

Identifying the broadest list of stakeholders affected by the change

Helping people who have trouble with the change through a transition

Effectively communicating the essence of the brand within time and money constraints

Creating and maintaining message consistency

Reaching all audiences

Building excitement and understanding

Key beliefs

A strategic focus centers on the brand.

Brand identity can help to center a company on its mission.

A mega-launch means less chance for confusion and complications.

Clarity about key messages surrounding the launch is critical.

Go internal before you go external.

Once is never enough to communicate a new idea.

You need to sell a new name and build meaning.

Different audiences may require different messages.

Do whatever you can to keep the momentum going.

Recognize that an identity program is more than a new name or new logo.

Name change essentials

A sound reason for changing the name is the first and most critical step.

The change must have the potential to enhance, among others, the company's public perception, recognition, recruitment, customer relations, partnerships.

Accept the fact that there will be resistance.

Keep the momentum going by creating an air of excitement.

Targeted messages are better but cost more.

New brand identity affect

Stationery, business cards, forms

Faxes, e-mail signatures

Signage

Advertising

Website

Marketing materials

Uniforms, name tags

Customers, vendors, contractors

Directory listings

Voice mail, how you answer the phone

Get ready. Get set. Launch. A launch represents a huge marketing opportunity to communicate. Smart organizations seize this opportunity to build brand awareness and synergy.

Different circumstances demand different launch strategies—from multimedia campaigns, company-wide meetings, and road tours, to a T-shirt for each employee. Some organizations execute massive visible change, including external signage and vehicles, virtually overnight, while others choose a phased approach.

Small organizations may not have the budget for a multimedia campaign. Smart organizations create a sales call opportunity to present a new card, or send a PDF announcement to each customer, colleague, and vendor. Others use existing marketing channels, such as inserting brochures with monthly statements.

In nearly every launch, the most important audience is a company's employees. Regardless of the scope and budget, a launch requires a comprehensive communications plan. Rarely is the best launch strategy no strategy, which is the business-as-usual or un-launch. Occasionally an organization may not want to draw attention from the financial community or its shareholders, so it may choose to do nothing.

Who needs to know?
What do they need to know?
Why do they need to know?
Does the change affect them?
How are they going to find out?
When are they going to find out?

Key pre-launch questions

Strategic launch goals

Increase brand awareness and understanding among all stakeholders, including the general public.

Increase preference for the company, products, and services.

Build loyalty for the company.

Promote the new identity as a brand.

Create an emotional connection with stakeholders.

Positively influence your constituents' choices and/or behavior.

Comprehensive plan elements

Goals and objectives of the new brand identity

Communications activities supporting brand implementation

Timeline for implementation and budget

The way identity is aligned with company goals

The way identity is aligned with research

Target audiences

Key messages

Communications strategies, including internal communications, public relations, advertising, and direct marketing

Internal training strategy for employees

Standards and guidelines strategy

Methods

Organization-wide meetings

Press releases

Special events

Q & A hotline on website

Script of consistent messages

Print, radio, TV ads

Trade publications

Direct mail

Launch website

External launch basics

Timing is everything. Find the window.

Create consistent messages.

Target messages.

Create the right media mix.

Leverage public relations, marketing, and customer service.

Make sure your sales force knows the launch strategy.

Be customer-focused.

Schedule a lot of advance time.

Seize every opportunity to garner marketing synergy.

Tell them, tell them again, and then tell them again.

Internal launch basics

Make a moment. Create a buzz.

Communicate why this is important.

Reiterate what the brand stands for.

Tell employees why you did it.

Communicate what it means.

Talk about future goals and mission.

Review identity basics: meaning, sustainability.

Convey that this is a top-down initiative.

Make employees brand champions and ambassadors.

Show concrete examples of how employees can live the brand.

Give employees a sense of ownership.

Give something tangible, such as a card or a T-shirt.

Brand identity systems are a long-term investment of time, human resources, and capital. Each positive experience with a brand helps build its brand equity and increases the likelihood of repeat purchasing and lifelong customer relationships. A return on investment is achieved, in part, through making it easier and more appealing for the customer to buy, making it easier for the sales force to sell, and being vigilant about the customer experience. Clarity about the brand, a clear process, and smart tools for employees, fuels success.

Decision makers frequently ask, "Why should we make this investment? Can you prove to me that it has a return?" It's difficult to isolate the impact of a new logo, a better brand architecture, or an integrated marketing communications system. It is critical that companies develop their own measures of success. Those who don't expect instant results, and think in the cumulative long term, understand the value of incremental change and focus.

It takes a whole company to build a brand.

Blake Deutsch

Human capital

Once they understood our vision, our employees accepted responsibility enthusiastically, which sparked numerous simultaneous and energetic developments in the company.

Jan Carlzon
Former CEO
Scandinavian Airlines Group
Moments of Truth

Brand is about real value — value in human terms, which doesn't mean only numbers. It's what people do, usually together, to fulfill an implied promise.

Ken Roberts
Chairman and CEO
Lippincott Mercer

Engagement happens when employees hear the message, believe the message, and then live or act upon it.

Enterprise IG

Communication tools must be culture-driven, designed to support and express your core values. This results in increased job satisfaction, productivity and loyalty.

Stella Gassaway
Stellarvisions

Pride

Wow factor

I get it

Confidence

Your boss is happy

The CEO gets it

Metrics for brand management Source: Prophet

Perception metrics

Awareness
Are customers *aware* of your brand?

Familiarity + consideration
What do customers *think* and *feel* about the brand?

Saliency
Brand recognition

Differentiation
Relevance
Credibility
Likability
Perceived quality
Purchase intent

Performance metrics

Purchase decision
How do customers *act*?

Loyalty
How do customers *behave over time*?

Customer leads
Customer acquisition
Trial
Repeat
Preference
Price premium

Customer satisfaction
Retention
Revenue per customer
Share of wallet
Customer lifetime value (LTV)
Referrals
ROI
Cost savings

Financial metrics

Value creation
How does customer behavior *create tangible economic value*?

Market share
Revenue
Operating cash flow
Market cap
Analyst ratings
Brand valuation

Metrics for isolated touchpoints

Advertising
Awareness
Conversion
Revenues

Electronic banners
Clickstreams

Public relations
Buzz
Awareness

Intellectual property
Protecting assets
Preventing litigation
Adhering to compliance

Websites
Number of visitors
Returning visitors
Length of time spent on site
Clickstreams (where prospect has been)
Cost per visitor (CPV)
Sales per visitor
Leads or inquiries per visitor
Site traffic
Usage patterns
Page views (impressions)
Fewer calls to customer service
Usability studies

Direct mail
Response rate

Trade shows
Number of leads generated
Number of sales
Number of inquiries

Licensing
Revenues
Protecting assets

Product placement
Reach
Impressions
Awareness

Signage

Packaging
Market share vis-à-vis competition
Sales change after new packaging
Compare sales change to overall project cost
Money saved because of engineering and materials
Eye-tracking studies, to track what they see first (shelf impact)
More shelf space
Home usage/observation consumer/field test
Entrée to a new retailer
Press coverage; buzz
Number of line extensions
Product placement
Sales cycle time
Consumer feedback
Influence on purchasing decision

Online branding tools
Visits to site
Amount of time on site
Reduction in production time
Increased adherence to guidelines
Less decision making time
More efficient ordering
Number of transactions
More compliance

Standards + guidelines
More consistent marketing and communications
Customer receives "one company"
More efficient use of time
Less decision making
Fewer corrections
Reduction in legal costs

Metrics rethought

Design

The Design Council study of share prices of UK quoted companies over the last decade found that a group of companies, recognized as effective users of design, outperformed key FTSE indices by 200%.

Steady investment in, and commitment to, design is rewarded by lasting competitiveness rather than isolated successes.

The Design Council

Evidence-based design

Research has demonstrated that more thoughtfully designed health care environments have a positive effect on an individual's health and wellness.

Mergers

In the UK, over 70% of what was paid in the acquisition of companies was for the goodwill from intangibles including corporate brand value.

Turnbridge Consulting

Six Sigma

Six Sigma is a methodology used to improve business processes. Originally developed by Motorola, it is currently being used by Honeywell, Vanguard, and DuPont to reduce variation in brand communications.

Sustainability

Eco-friendly packaging
Reducing e-waste and trash
Reducing hazardous materials in product design
Saving energy

Everyone wants to know in the beginning of an engagement that there is a clear measurement program, even though at the end of the project they never do it.

Anonymous

Engaging employees in the meaning of the brand and the thinking behind it is one of the best investments that a company can make. Organizational development consultants have long known that long-term success is directly influenced by the way employees share in their company's culture—its values, stories, symbols, and heroes. Traditionally the CEO and the marketing department were the most visible brand champions—individuals who understood and could articulate a company's core values, vision, and brand essence. Enlisting employees as brand champions builds on the underlying concept of aligning culture, behavior, and performance.

"It's not just values, it's the extensive sharing of them that makes a difference," say Terrence Deal and Allan Kennedy in *Corporate Cultures: The Rites and Rituals of Corporate Life.* Companies all around the world are beginning to develop compelling ways of sharing the brand essence— from road shows, to online branding tools and guides, to special events. What was once a standards and guidelines toolkit for creative firms has evolved into a brand-building tool for all employees.

1 + 1 = 11

Marty Neumeier, President
Neutron SF
Author, *The Brand Gap*

Online resource can help build brands

Developed by Monigle Associates

Communicates strategies and objectives for the brand in an organization

Provides help and best practices as opposed to rules (tools, not rules)

Saves users time

Provides resources people need to participate in the brand-building process

Pulls together often disparate subjects into one online resource center

Tracks user activity to help support future investments

Can reengineer many costly processes, reducing cost from strategy to implementation

Builds consistent implementation

Demystifies brand and identity systems

ARAMARK and the road show

Public companies routinely use road shows to bring their messages directly to key investors and analysts. Road shows are also an effective tactic for launching brand initiatives. ARAMARK chairman and CEO Joe Neubauer traveled to seven cities to speak to 5,000 frontline managers to launch his company's new brand and to align employees with the vision of the company. "If employees are excited and mobilized, then more than half the branding battle has been won," said Bruce Berkowitz, former director of advertising for ARAMARK. "Employees carry the company's culture and character into the marketplace."

ARAMARK worked with a meeting planning company to produce a one-hour road show. The show included a skit performed by Broadway actors and a multimedia presentation of the political, cultural, and economic milestones that gave a context for the company's metamorphosis. Neubauer reinforced key messages about the company's heritage and its leadership in the industry. His overarching message, "Employees are the heart of our success and convey our company's top-tier delivery of services," was supported by a new brandmark. Designed by the Schechter Group (now part of Interbrand), the mark embodies the star quality of the employees and supports the new brand promise of "managed services, managed better."

Managers were fully prepped on the new brand vision and strategy. They received an "Ambassadors Kit" that contained a company history, copies of the new advertising campaign, a merchandise catalog, and a graphic standards manual. In addition, the materials included a manager's checklist and a media launch schedule with explicit instructions on how to handle the launch, how to explain it to staff members, and how to implement the brand identity change. The CEO's presence and passion combined with accessible brand building tools were a powerful combination that fueled ARAMARK's growth.

WGBH mission statement and video

The mission statement of WGBH, the Boston affiliate of the Public Broadcasting System (PBS), can easily be found on its website and is frequently seen in the signature block of employee e-mail. It reads as follows: "WGBH enriches people's lives through programs and services that educate, inspire, and entertain, fostering citizenship and culture, the joy of learning, and the power of diverse perspectives."

A prominent and easily accessible mission statement is a simple tool that creates a sense of purpose and keeps employees focused on the vision. On the website, the mission statement is followed by a list of commitments that present the unified values of WGBH. In the "About Us" section a QuickTime video describes the station as a window on the world and a storyteller to the nation, and cites its commitment to lifelong learning. When internal messages are aligned with external expression, the brand synergy created is evident and the result is profound.

Jenner & Block

Smart companies communicate about the brand to each employee. Crosby Associates designed a high-quality brochure for Jenner & Block that communicates the firm's mission and values, and displays how the brand is expressed through a variety of marketing communication channels.

The Little Red Book

In 1981, SAS (Scandinavian Airlines Group) distributed a small book to 20,000 employees. The purpose of the book was to simply and succinctly communicate the vision and strategy of the company at a time of organizational change. The book, well written and designed, not only informed the employees, but also inspired them to work toward the same goals.

ARAMARK: Interbrand

Companies that value design and the contributions of designers get more effective, strategic, and intelligent marketing and communications solutions. Many companies believe that greater control, efficiency, and cost savings may be garnered through bringing creative work—design, writing, and production—in-house. Brand identity programs are more often than not developed by outside firms that have the experience, staffing, and qualifications to develop new branding strategies. In-house designers often implement the bulk of an identity program once it has been launched and standards are in place.

Understanding the role that the internal design department will play in implementing and managing a new brand identity is critical to the success of the program. The new brand identity is an asset that needs to be managed and nurtured. First and foremost, the identity system itself must be easy to understand and to implement. The balance between consistency and flexibility must be clear at the outset.

Coordinating the identity program standards between the external identity firm and the internal design department is necessary. The new program and its rationale must be introduced to the internal team, who should have access to the external firm for questions, clarifications, and unforeseen circumstances. The linchpin for implementation is the project manager, the person who coordinates the identity program between the external design firm and the internal design resources. The project manager should have tremendous management and organizational skills, as well as a proven ability to work with creative teams. Another good investment is to bring in the external firm for periodic implementation reviews.

WGBH recognized that design needed to be a function that reported directly to the CEO.

Chris Pullman, Vice President of Design
WGBH

Internal creative teams need to seize the "insider advantage" by using deep knowledge of the brand—execution and insights—to leverage their strategic value to the corporation.

Moira Cullen
Design Director
Coca-Cola Company

Act like an agency. Commit to excellence and innovation. Be entrepreneurial and market yourselves.

Lynn Whittemore
Design Director
HealthInk

Essential characteristics

Valued by senior management

Staffed by experienced designers (creative and technical expertise)

Well managed (managed by a creative or design director)

Multifunctional (experience across all media)

Multilevel experience (senior level and junior level)

Open channels of communication with senior management

Clearly defined roles and responsibilities for staff members

Clearly defined and proven processes and procedures for producing work

Commitment to brand identity standards and vision

Ability to design with creativity and innovation within system

Ability to explain the rationale behind design solutions

Teamwork; open and clear communication within the group and beyond it

Biggest challenges

Overcoming political hurdles

Getting access to senior management

Getting senior management respect for in-house design

Overcoming design-by-committee thinking and actions

Focusing on high quality rather than the bottom line

Debunking the myth that high quality means high cost

Giving hands-on designers access to external design firms when developing standards (e.g., design firm develops something that cannot be produced in-house because the two parties did not talk)

Too much work for too small a staff

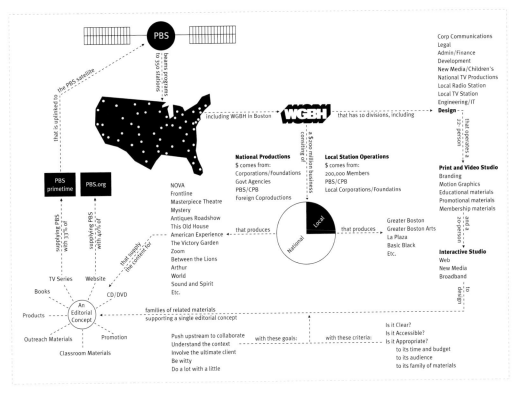

Chris Pullman, WGBH vice president of design, developed this chart to communicate the role of design at WGBH Boston.

Brand books, spirit books, and thought books inspire, educate and build brand awareness. Brand strategy can't influence anyone if it stays in a conference room, in someone's head, or on page 3 of a marketing plan. The vision of a company and the meaning of a brand need a communications vehicle that is accessible, portable and personal. Increasingly, companies are also producing brand essence multimedia. Intranets and online brand sites are beginning to juxtapose the fundamentals, i.e., "Who are we" and "What our brand stands for," in addition to standards, templates and guidelines.

Timing is everything. Companies in the midst of organizational change need to convey "where the ship is going." Frequently, the brand identity process sparks a new clarity about brand essence. Communicating about how each employee can help build the brand provides a context for success.

A spirit book is a compelling way to express the essence of a brand.

Ken Carbone, Principal
Carbone Smolan Agency

Peninsula Papagayo

A COLLABORATION WITH NATURE

Peninsula Papagayo

Carbone Smolan Agency designed a limited-edition, handbound spirit book for Peninsula Papagayo that captured the brand essence and the look and feel of a luxurious 2,300-acre sanctuary and resort in Costa Rica. The purpose of the spirit book was to inspire high-end developers and architects and to be a nontraditional, effective marketing tool. Frequently, before a company has the time to create real standards, it decides to make the investment in capturing the personality, the attributes, or the aspirations of a new brand.

WGBH

WGBH gave each employee a passport-sized brochure titled "WGBH Branding Guidelines" to "take advantage of the wide recognition and powerful positive associations people have with the WGBH brandmark in all of our activities and links with the outside world." This user-friendly guide helps employees more effectively manage WGBH brand assets and defines branding and other brand terms. This cost-effective tool underscores the fact that everyone plays a role in building the brand.

Citigroup

When Pentagram met with Citigroup's global advertising agency and global signage design firm, it presented a thought book that communicated the central unifying principles of the program. Pentagram believes that this encouraged the highest degree of flexibility and creativity in the future. The thought book was an 11 x 17 wire-bound booklet designed to inspire.

Mutual of Omaha

Mutual of Omaha disseminated a poster to each employee that announced the new revitalized brand identity and engaged everyone to take part in building the brand. Crosby Associates' design dramatically announced the new corporate color: "We're new. We're blue." Employee engagement and understanding are the first steps toward adhering to brand identity standards.

Peninsula Papagayo: Carbone Smolan Agency

Designing, specifying, ordering, and printing or fabricating elements of a new brand identity system are all dependent on a set of intelligent standards and guidelines. Good solid standards save time, money, and frustration. The size and nature of an organization affect the depth and breadth of the content and how marketing materials are conceived and produced in the future.

Following is an in-depth composite that can be used as a reference for building an outline. Usually printing and fabrication specifications accompany design specifications. Legal and nomenclature guideline considerations are critical to include. Some guidelines include order forms for business cards and other applications.

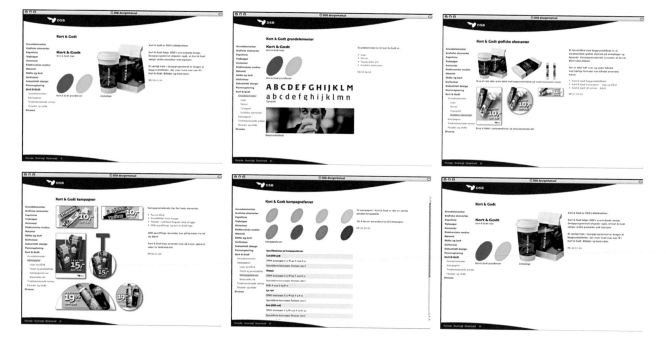

Kort & Godt online identity guide: Kontrapunkt

Contents

Managing consistency and the integrity of a brand identity system is facilitated by intelligent standards and guidelines that are easily accessible to all internal and external partners who have the responsibility to communicate about the brand. Brand identity guidelines have become more accessible, dynamic, and easier to produce. The range of formats includes online standards, CDs, posters, fact sheets, PDFs, brochures, and binders. Now even the smallest nonprofit can provide streamlined standards, reproduction files, and electronic templates.

Building a brand is progressively viewed as the shared responsibility of each and every employee. Adhering to the guidelines requires discipline and vigilance. More importantly, it saves money, time, frustration, and helps build the brand. The best branding tools communicate, "What does the brand stand for," in addition to providing brand identity information.

Adhering to the guidelines must unequivocally be a top-down priority.

Blake Deutsch

Who needs to understand what the brand stands for?

Everyone

Who needs to access guidelines?

Internal employees

Marketing

Communication

Design

Legal

Web gurus

PR

Product designers

Anyone creating a PowerPoint presentation

External creative partners

Branding firms

Design firms

Advertising agencies

Information architects

Technologists

Packaging design firms

Architects

Writers

Co-branding partners

Online branding sites

The web has made it easy to consolidate brand management in one place, giving employees and vendors user-friendly tools to brand resources. While most large corporations have these sites, smaller companies and nonprofits cannot afford this software investment yet. People look forward to the day when they will be able to download files, templates, and images in a proprietary shopping. The day is soon.

Media relations portals

Many corporations have downloadable logo files in the media relations section of their websites. These files are often accompanied by extensive legalese that outline usage that is allowed or, in some cases, a licensing agreement.

Marketing and sales toolkits

Companies that have independent distributors and dealerships need effective ways to control the look and feel at the point of sale. VSA Partners has created standards and marketing resources for Harley-Davidson that help independent dealerships achieve a distinctive and memorable retail presence through their exterior signage, retail displays, and advertising.

Identity standards manuals

Traditionally smaller companies used offset printing. Today such companies are beginning to produce limited-edition manuals using laser printers. Although correct color is usually not attainable, the spirit of the program can be communicated effectively. The binder format allows changes to be made by replacing or adding pages. A CD that carries reproduction files and templates is placed in the back.

CDs

The CD, with its large storage capacity and portable format, is a great solution for those companies that cannot yet justify putting their standards online. Many companies are putting standards into a PDF format on a CD. It is easy to produce and cost-effective. Brinker Capital, an investment firm, needed a smart standards program to disseminate to its agencies and creative firms. Rev Group produced a limited-edition CD that is updated annually as the company grows and its needs evolve. The CD includes everything from business papers and marketing tools to trade show booths.

Newsletters

Some organizations take advantage of their existing marketing and communication channels to launch and communicate information about a new identity. Princeton announced and displayed its new athletics program identity system designed by Pentagram in the centerfold of a newsletter that went out to all alumni. By showing the entire system of components, and explaining the rationale, Princeton positions this system as sustainable and valuable.

Characteristics of the best standards and guidelines

Are clear, easy to understand

Have content that is current, easy to apply

Provide accurate information

Include "what the brand stands for"

Talk about meaning of the identity

Balance consistency with flexibility

Are accessible to internal and external users

Build brand awareness

Consolidate all necessary files, templates, + guidelines

Promise positive return on investment contribution

Provide point person for questions

Capture the spirit of the program

Feature prototypes (best-in-class examples)

The web has transformed brand management, consolidating brand assets and establishing 24/7 access to user-friendly guidelines, tools and templates. Scalable, modular sites are always current, evolving as a company grows. Many sites feature brand vision and attributes, helping to build a shared vocabulary. Robust sites support strategic marketing, consistent communications, and quality execution. Initially envisioned to house logos and image libraries, sites now encompass brand strategy, content development guidelines, and web resources.

Creative firms and external vendors are assigned passwords to access key messages, logos, image libraries, glossaries, intellectual property compliance, and a panoply of smart resources and content. Sites may also be used for online ordering and transactions. Access to certain sections may be limited to user groups. The success of online branding tools is easily monitored through usage statistics.

Our Brand Space site is engaging, educational and a valuable asset to our global staff and agencies.

Mark Allatt, Global Brand Director
Deloitte London

A typical site for a large company could include 1,000 screen files, 300 images in an image library, 50 downloadable templates, and 700 signature files.

Process : online branding site

Developed by Monigle Associates

Initiate plan	Build groundwork	Launch project	Prepare content	Design and program
Determine goals.	Review status of assets + standards.	Conduct launch meeting	Determine author and status of content.	Identify interface + navigation style.
Identify brand management problems and issues.	Determine content approval process.	Develop:	Set editorial style guidelines.	Develop and approve site interface.
Identify user groups + profiles.	Prioritize content and functionality.	Site architecture map + functionality.	Develop content update plan if needed.	Initiate programming based on site map.
Identify stakeholders.	Research development options: internal + external.	Project online workroom	Determine content file formatting + exchange requirements.	Develop system functionality.
Create project team + appoint leader.	Develop preliminary budget + timeline.	Timeline + preliminary launch plan.		
Develop team roles, rules, and protocol.	Select site development resource.	User groups + user lists. Access and security plans.		
		Determine IT requirements + hosting plan.		
		Identify brand assets and cataloging scheme.		

Characteristics of the best online sites

Educational, user-friendly. and efficient

Accessible to internal and external users

Builds brand engagement

Consolidates brand management in one place

Scalable and modular

Offers positive return on investment contribution

Database-driven, not PDF-driven

Provides resources: signatures, templates, image library

Always current: new content and functions can be added to improve implementation of the brand

Builds transactional elements into the site, i.e., online ordering improves implementation and lowers cost simultaneously

Flexible in hosting and ongoing maintenance

Provides more rather than less information and resources

Content guidelines

Write concisely. Less is more.

Outline carefully to create a logical order of information.

Know the culture, and write accordingly

Use commonly understood terminology; do not use unnecessary "brand speak."

Provide examples and illustrations.

Support site navigation.

Deloitte's online branding site was developed by Monigle Associates. Enterprise IG designed Deloitte's brand identity.

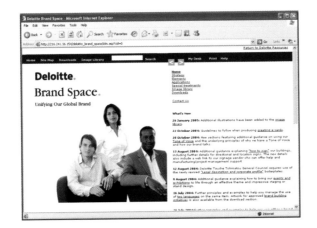

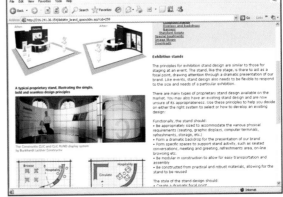

> **Develop database**

Populate database with content and assets.

Program links and required functions.

Edit content and design by core team.

> **Prototype and test**

Core team reviews beta site.

Users test beta site.

Make modifications as necessary.

Approve site launch.

> **Launch**

Finalize launch plan.

Create communications + buzz.

Promote site launch.

Appoint brand champions.

Conduct special training sessions.

> **Monitor success**

Develop maintenance plan.

Assign administrator.

Assess usage trends-user reports.

Identify content updates and process.

Integrate technology and functional advances.

Assign budget for management and upgrades.

Define and measure impact.

Communicate successes.

Maintaining the quality of reproduction in a world where tools are continually changing is an ongoing challenge. Users have urgent needs, different levels of proficiency, various software platforms, and a disparate understanding of digital files, color, and quality. An asset management system needs to be diligent about naming, organization, storage, retrieval, and overall usability of file formats.

The designer's responsibilities are to test all files in numerous formats and to develop a retrievable system that is logical and sustainable. The manager's responsibility is to determine who has access to files and how best to field all requests. It is no longer unusual to download logo files and images from a website's media portal. Clear legal guidelines, forms, and contact information help protect the assets.

You can't always get what you want, but if you try sometimes you might find, you get what you need.

The Rolling Stones

Finding your way around reproduction files

What type of image is it?

Is it a photographic image with continuous tones or is it a graphic image with solid color, crisp edges, and line art?

How is it going to be reproduced?

Professional printing, office printing, and screen display have different file requirements. Some documents may be viewed on screen or printed out.

What color space is needed?

Color information is included in a file and interpreted by the output device.

Professional printing techniques use spot color inks (such as Pantone®) or four-color process inks, which builds color out of cyan, magenta, yellow, and black (CMYK). Color inkjet or laser printers use CMYK toner.

Screens display color with red, blue, and green points of light (RGB). Hex numbers designate RGB colors for HTML code.

What program is being used?

It is important to know the program being used to ensure compatibility and to facilitate use of vector artwork whenever possible.

I can't open it!

Unless you are going to modify the artwork in a design program, image files should be inserted or placed, not opened.

I can't find it!

Files should be named as concisely and informatively as possible so they can be understood at a glance. Consistency is imperative for grouping common attributes and distinguishing unique ones.

File format basics

Vector graphics

Vector graphics are hard-edged images created in a drawing program. Because they are based on mathematically defined lines and curves, they can be manipulated and scaled without losing reproduction quality.

EPS (Encapsulated PostScript)

Vector graphics created in a drawing program are saved or exported as EPS files so that they can be placed into other applications.

The highest-quality output for graphic images with hard edges.

Printers must have Adobe® PostScript®.

When vector graphics are saved as TIFF, JPEG, or other bitmap file format, the hard-edged lines and curves are converted to pixels.

EPS files created in Adobe Photoshop® are bitmap images and will have a loss of clarity when scaled or printed.

Raster or bitmap images

Raster or bitmap images are continuous-tone images that are constructed as a continuous mapping of pixels. These images cannot be scaled, rotated, or skewed outside of an image-editing application without the loss of reproduction quality.

TIFF (Tag Image File Format)

Highest-quality output for photographic images

Best bitmap version of hard-edged graphics—alternative to EPS when an Adobe® PostScript® printer is unavailable

Convenient for exchanging image files between computer platforms

JPEG (Joint Photographic Experts Group)

Compressed file format for on-screen viewing of continuous-tone photographs

Compression adds "artifacts" and smears text, lines, and edges

Not suitable for printing

GIF (Graphics Interchange Format)

Compressed file format for on-screen viewing of graphics and images in HTML

Not suitable for printing

These are just a sample of the most widely used formats.

File format matrix		Photographic images with continuous tones	Graphic images with hard edges
Printing	**Design software** Adobe Illustrator®, Macromedia Freehand®, CorelDRAW®, QuarkXpress®, Adobe InDesign®	TIFF (PNG)	EPS
	Office software Microsoft Word®, Microsoft Excel®	TIFF	TIFF (PNG) Converts vector graphics to bitmap image
Screen	**Design software** Adobe ImageReady®, among others	JPEG	GIF (PNG, TIFF, LZW)
	Office software PowerPoint®	JPEG	TIFF (PNG)

Resolution

The resolution of digital imagery is measured in pixels per inch (ppi), the digital equivalent of dots per inch (dpi). The end use of the image is critical for determining the optimum resolution.

For printing, the higher the resolution the more detail and clarity there is to the image, and the larger the file is in terms of memory. Offset printing typically requires 300 ppi resolution.

For screen display, the pixels in the image map directly to the pixels on the screen. Images for screen display should be 72 ppi (Mac) or 96 ppi (PC), but the physical dimensions will be affected by the resolution of the display itself.

File naming conventions

Filenames should not have more than fifteen characters plus a three-letter file extension (.eps, .jpg, .gif, .doc) indicating what type of file it is.

Do not use uppercase, spaces, or special characters, such as " \ / : * < > ? ¦. Use a period only before the file extension suffix.

Create a system for organizing and identifying those variations of the artwork that are required for different applications, such as signature, color, subbrand entity, and file format.

Metric system basics

In the early 1970s, most major countries, with the exception of the United States, adopted the metric system. The metric system is a decimal system of units based on the meter as the international standard unit of length. The meter is approximately equivalent to 39.37 inches. The benefit of the metric system is that it is more convenient and easier to calculate.

Never assume that any U.S. company uses a standard size in their foreign branches until you have conducted a comprehensive audit.

Conversion formulas

to convert	multiply by
inches to centimeters	2.540
centimeters to inches	.394
inches to millimeters	25.400
millimeters to inches	.039
feet to meters	.305
meters to feet	3.281

Points and picas

12 points = 1 pica	
72 points = 1 inch	
6 picas = 1 inch	

U.S. commercial envelopes

	inches	mm
$6^1/4$	$3^1/2 \times 6$	89 x 152
$6^3/4$	$3^5/8 \times 6^1/2$	92 x 165
$8^5/8$	$3^5/8 \times 8^5/8$	92 x 220
7	$3^3/4 \; 3 \; 6^3/4$	95 x 171
Monarch ($7^3/4$)	$3^7/8 \times 7^1/2$	98 x 190
9	$3^7/8 \times 8^7/8$	98 x 225
10	$4^1/8 \times 9^1/2$	105 x 241
11	$4^1/2 \times 10^3/8$	114 x 264
12	$4^3/4 \times 11$	121 x 279
14	$5 \times 11^1/2$	127 x 292

U.S. A-style envelopes

A-2	$4^3/8 \times 5^3/4$	111 x 146
A-6	$4^3/4 \times 6^1/2$	121 x 165
A-7	$5^1/4 \times 7^1/4$	133 x 184
A-8	$5^1/2 \times 8^1/8$	140 x 206
A-long	$3^7/8 \times 8^7/8$	98 x 225
A-10	$6 \times 9^1/2$	152 x 241

Research compiled by Steff Geissbuhler
Partner, C&G Partners

Metric business correspondence

Letterhead   210 x 297 mm   8¼ x 11¾"

DL envelope   110 x 220 mm   4⁵⁄₁₆ x 8⅝"

Business card

Germany Italy Switzerland	85.5 x 54 mm (standard credit card)	
Germany United Kingdom	85 x 55 mm	
Australia Brazil Hong Kong Japan Spain	90 x 55 mm	
Australia Finland France Israel Norway Russia Spain	90 x 50 mm	
Netherlands	74 x 52 mm	
Spain	110 x 72 mm	

A series

	mm	inches
A0	841 x 1189 (area=1m²)	33¹⁄₈ x 46³⁄₄
A1	594 x 841	23³⁄₈ x 33¹⁄₈
A2	420 x 594	16¹⁄₂ x 33¹⁄₈
A3	297 x 420	11³⁄₄ x 16¹⁄₂
A4	210 x 297	8¹⁄₄ x 11³⁄₄
A5	148 x 210	5⁷⁄₈ x 8¹⁄₄
A6	105 x 148	4¹⁄₈ x 5⁷⁄₈
A7	74 x 105	2⁷⁄₈ x 4¹⁄₈
A8	52 x 74	2 x 2⁷⁄₈
A9	37 x 52	1¹⁄₂ x 2
A10	26 x 37	1 x 1¹⁄₂

B series

B0	1000 x 1414	39³⁄₈ x 55⁵⁄₈
B1	707 x 1000	27⁷⁄₈ x 39³⁄₈
B2	500 x 707	19⁵⁄₈ x 27⁷⁄₈
B3	353 x 500	12⁷⁄₈ x 19⁵⁄₈
B4	250 x 353	9⁷⁄₈ x 12⁷⁄₈
B5	176 x 250	7 x 9⁷⁄₈
B6	125 x 176	5 x 7
B7	88 x 125	3¹⁄₂ x 5
B8	62 x 88	2¹⁄₂ x 3¹⁄₂
B9	44 x 62	1³⁄₄ x 2¹⁄₂
B10	31 x 44	1¹⁄₄ x 1³⁄₄

RA and SRA sizes for printing

R sheets allow for extra trim
SR sheets allow for extra trim and bleed

R A0	860 x 120	33⁷⁄₈ x 48¹⁄₈
R A1	610 x 860	24¹⁄₈ x 33⁷⁄₈
R A2	430 x 610	17 x 24¹⁄₈
R A3	305 x 430	12 x 17
R A4	215 x 305	8¹⁄₂ x 12
SR A0	900 x 1280	35¹⁄₂ x 50³⁄₈
SR A1	640 x 900	25¹⁄₄ x 35¹⁄₂
SR A2	450 x 640	17⁷⁄₈ x 25¹⁄₄
SR A3	320 x 450	12⁵⁄₈ x 17³⁄₄
SR A4	225 x 320	8⁷⁄₈ x 12⁵⁄₈

Metric C series envelopes

C0	917 x 1297	36¹⁄₈ x 51¹⁄₁₆
C1	648 x 917	25¹⁄₂ x 36¹⁄₈
C2	458 x 648	18¹⁄₁₆ x 33¹⁄₈
C3	324 x 458	12³⁄₄ x 18¹⁄₁₆
C4	229 x 324	9 x 12³⁄₄
C5	162 x 229	6³⁄₈ x 9
C6	114 x 162	4¹⁄₂ x 6³⁄₈
C7	81 x 114	3³⁄₁₆ x 4¹⁄₂

Metric special size envelopes

DL	110 x 220	4⁵⁄₁₆ x 8⁵⁄₈
C6/5	114 x 229	4¹⁄₂ x 9
C7/6	81 x 162	3³⁄₁₆ x 6³⁄₈

3 Practice

Part 3 showcases best practices. Local and global, public and private, these highly successful projects, created by branding firms, design consultancies and in-house creative teams, inspire and exemplify original, flexible, lasting solutions.

Case studies

Extraordinary work is done for extraordinary clients.

Milton Glaser
Designer

Our vision is to be the world's most customer-centric company, the place where people discover anything they want to buy online.*

Profile : Originally an online bookstore, Amazon.com is positioned as the "web's biggest retail store," selling music, software, toys, tools, electronics, fashion, and housewares. Founded in 1994, the company has 30 million customers and ships to 150 countries.

Project goals

Create a unique and proprietary identity.

Maintain the brand equity of the original identity.

Position Amazon.com as customer-focused and friendly.

Modify the core identity for global domains.

*Jeff Bezos
Founder and CEO
Amazon.com

A creative brief may describe brand values that are more aspirational goals than reality. At Amazon.com, it was clear that the focus and attitude of the company and its employees truly matched and set the standard for its brand values. The focus on customer service—and in particular friendly, accessible service—was clearly reflected in the work ethic and practice of the CEO himself and his marketing team.

Joanne Chan
Head of Client Services
Turner Duckworth

Why did you name your company Amazon?

Earth's biggest river. Earth's biggest selection.

Jeff Bezos
Founder and CEO
Amazon.com

amazon.com.

Process and strategy

In 1999 Amazon.com retained Turner Duckworth to redesign its brand identity. Amazon.com's positioning as a customer-focused, friendly company was the core of the mission and values. The challenge was to create a unique and proprietary identity that maintained what Amazon.com believed were its brand equities: lowercase type in the logo, and an orange swoosh underneath the name. Turner Duckworth immersed itself in the brand, spent a lot of time on the website, and examined competitor sites. The firm also analyzed what makes a logo effective or ineffective on the web. "Our goal was to infuse personality into the logo, and to create a compelling idea that would convey the brand message," said David Turner, head of design.

Creative solution

The design team developed distinct visual strategies at the first stage; each one emphasized a different aspect of the positioning brief. The final logo design was an evolutionary leap from the old logo. The central idea behind the new logo reflected the client's business strategy of selling more than just books. The design team connected the initial a of "amazon" to the z. This approach clearly communicated "Amazon.com sells everything from A to Z." The graphic device that connects the a and the z also speaks to the brand positioning: customer focus and friendly service. This device forms a cheeky smile with a dimple that pushes up the z. The brown shipper box packaging was considered at every stage of the logo design.

Turner Duckworth designed custom lettering for the wordmark and made the "amazon" more prominent than the ".com." The typography was designed to give the logo a friendlier and unique look. The design team also designed a full alphabet so that Amazon.com could update its international domains, currently in the United Kingdom, Germany, France, and Japan. The project was completed in eight weeks.

Results

Jeff Bezos, the CEO, founder, and visionary, was involved at every presentation and was the key decision maker. Amazon.com had determined that it would execute a "soft launch" of the new identity. The new brand identity was not announced to the press or highlighted on its website. Sensitive to the perceptions of customers and Wall Street analysts, the company felt it was important that Amazon.com did not appear to be a "different" company.

In 2005 Amazon was named the fourth fastest growing brand in the world, with a 35% compounded growth rate in brand value between 2001 and 2005, according to Brand Republic.

Access to the key decision maker, and in particular to the visionary of a company, certainly makes our work easier. Not only does it accelerate the feedback, development and approval processes, but it also allows us to ask questions of the visionary and hear unedited answers.

Joanne Chan
Head of Client Services
Turner Duckworth

The American Civil Liberties Union (ACLU) works to defend the Bill of Rights, mounting court challenges to preserve racial justice, human rights, religious freedom, privacy, and free speech.

Profile : Founded in 1920, the ACLU is a nonprofit, nonpartisan organization with 400,000 members and supporters. The national organization and its fifty state affiliates work in the courts, the legislatures, and communities, handling 6,000 court cases a year. The ACLU is supported by dues, contributions, and grants.

Project goals

Create a unified image for the entire organization.

Develop an integrated, sustainable, and meaningful identity system.

Connect the organization to ideas and ideals.

Differentiate from other public advocacy groups.

Communicate stature and stability.

Facilitate consistent communications.

We have to be one.
Anthony Romero
Executive Director
ACLU

We wanted to help the ACLU look like the guardians of freedom.
Sylvia Harris
Information design strategist

Previous identity

Process and strategy

The ACLU set out to reach a broader constituency and build membership, and asked Fo Wilson Group to customize a team to build a unified, meaningful identity. The Fo Wilson Group, a design consultancy, was joined by Sylvia Harris, an information design strategist, and Michael Hirschhorn, an organizational dynamics expert. In the audit, the team found more than fifty logos. Every state affiliate had its own logo, website design, and architecture, with little connection to the national organization. Other advocacy organizations were studied, and Harris found that "ACLU represents a set of principles, while most other advocacy groups represent a constituency." The team interviewed a wide range of stakeholders, including affiliates, communications staff, and members. The most frequently mentioned attribute that defined the ACLU was "principled," followed by "justice" and "guardian." A survey conducted in 2000 by Belden, Russonello & Stewart found that "over 8 out of 10 Americans (85%) had heard of the ACLU." The team realized that the ACLU identity needed to be recognized in a wide variety of arenas, from town halls, to courtrooms and campuses.

Creative solution

The design directive was to capitalize on a highly recognizable acronym, and to connect ACLU principles and the spirit of freedom to the acronym. Fo Wilson Group designed a series of signatures with a contemporary logotype and expressive symbolism. Several options were tested for the modular system that used patriotic imagery. During the audit, the team found that the ACLU's original symbol from the 1930s was the Statue of Liberty, and it had been dropped in the 1980s. The Statue of Liberty tested the best, and although other advocacy groups used the symbol, the ACLU decided to return to its legacy and history. A unique photographic perspective of the statue's face was stylized, and a photographic signature was adopted to work in the digital environment. A range of applications demonstrated how the system worked, from website architecture, to newsletters and membership cards. The flexible system needed to work for the national office, the affiliates, the foundations, and special projects.

Results

ACLU's leadership group championed the identity initiative from the early planning through the analysis, decision making, and roll out. The identity team conducted a series of phone conference presentations to roll out the new program with the affiliates. Educational programs for staff were conducted at the headquarters. The group was instrumental in getting forty-nine of the fifty affiliates to adopt the new identity system. The national organization paid to have new letterhead printed for the affiliates. Opto Design was retained to finalize the design system, produce all the preliminary applications, and develop an ACLU Identity Guidelines website. Membership has increased to its highest rate in its eighty-five year history, the budget has doubled, and the national staff has increased by 75 percent.

Although the ACLU had historically been strong in media relations, communications was a new function that was needed.
Emily Tyne
Communications Director
ACLU

With a complex national organizational model such as ACLU, it is important to strategize thoughtfully how to gather input, test out ideas, and roll out new plans across the 50+ offices nationally.
Michael Hirschhorn
Organizational dynamics expert

National identity

Affiliate identity

Foundation identity

American Girl Place brings American Girl dolls to life, combining education, entertainment, and retailing in a setting designed to appeal to girls.

Profile : American Girl Place offers dolls, books, clothing, and accessories, inspired by the dolls' historical, fictional characters, which are coveted by girls seven to twelve. Pleasant Company, founded in 1986 by Pleasant Rowland, an educator, was acquired by Mattel in 1998.

Project goals

Design and build a 35,000-square-foot retail flagship destination.

Create an uplifting, positive experience for young girls and the people who love them.

Reflect the past, present, and future of American girlhood.

Present product offerings in a memorable, subtle experience.

Create a destination that incorporates education, entertainment, and retail.

American Girl characters
Kaya
Felicity
Josefina
Kirsten
Addy
Samantha
Nellie
Kit
Molly

We conducted focus groups and discovered that girls like black and white, too, not just pink and pastels.
Michael Keith
President
Michael Keith Design Group, LTD

Process and strategy

"Every detail in the store was designed with girls seven and up in mind, from the bookshelves to the restaurant seats," says Nancye Green, principal of Donovan/Green. "We worked closely with Pleasant Rowland, whose vision was the creation of an open-ended journey into a young girl's imagination." Donovan/Green was retained as designer/builder for the flagship shore in Chicago. Along with concept development, programming, and architectural and graphic design, Donovan/Green was responsible for selecting the contractor, managing the construction, and supervising a multidisciplinary team, including merchandising and theater consultants, in a compressed time frame. Rowland envisioned a peaceful and calm space, not a typical toy store filled to the brim with merchandise.

Creative solution

Donovan/Green's design focuses on the experience for young girls and the grown-ups who love them. The merchandise is secondary. The first floor, focusing on the past, features dioramas explaining the historical perspective of each character. The design is classical and is a contrast to the second floor, which has a very modern and whimsical design. The café, designed in elegant black and white for lunch, afternoon tea, and dinner, has special seats that enable girls to have their dolls at the table. The menus feature food from the characters' stories, and the intimate theater shows a lively musical revue that plays out scenes from the books. At the photo studio the girls can get a memento of their visit, with their picture on the cover of *American Girl* magazine. The upper level is dedicated to modern girls. Large portrait shots of pre-teen girls are juxtaposed with museum-like maple cases and provide a segue to the shop, which sells merchandise and accessories.

Results

Customers average more than four hours a visit because the destination provides education, entertainment, food, and shopping. The first year in business, American Girl Place had gross sales over $25 million. The Chicago store opened in 1998, the New York store opened in 2003, and the Los Angeles store is scheduled to open in spring 2006. The Chicago and New York stores have welcomed more than 10 million visitors, have been the recipients of numerous awards, and have frequently been cited as one of the most successful retail destinations in America.

The American Girl Place is no retail store; it's an engaging retail experience.

B. Joseph Pine II and James H. Gilmore
The Experience Ecomomy

American Girl Place is all about emotion; it's about girls connecting with each other, their heritage, their parents, themselves and the world around them.

Jill Bensley
President
J.B. Research Company

The American Girl place is the epitome of the branded experience: it has a strong philosophy, clear values, and a founder/visionary who wanted to create the experience of a lifetime for her customers.

Nancye Green
Principal
Donovan/Green

Photos by Hedrich Blessing

183

The successful initial public offering marked a new beginning for Assurant. The company is focused on being a premier provider of specialized insurance products and related services.

Profile : Assurant provides specialty insurance and insurance-related services through its five key businesses: Assurant Employee Benefits; Assurant Health; Assurant Preneed; Assurant Solutions; and Assurant Specialty Property. After operating as the North American independent arm of Fortis Insurance N.V. for 25 years, the company changed its name in connection with its initial public offering in 2004.

Project goals

Design a new brand identity.

Collaborate with the in-house creative team.

Create an ad campaign to launch a new name and brand identity.

Our name and logo may have changed, but our strategy and values have not.

J. Kerry Clayton
President and CEO
Assurant

ASSURANT

Process and strategy

Assurant formed a brand leadership council that worked closely with the president and the CEOs of the individual companies. This council provided strategic leadership, research, and direction to the Carbone Smolan Agency about brand aspirations and structure. The new brand needed to send a strong signal to the business and investment community and distance itself from its parent, Fortis, a Belgo-Dutch multinational corporation.

The identity was to be the first tangible representation of the company and had to be completed in a very compressed time frame. Carbone Smolan Agency conducted an intensive, "rapid response" creative session to get stakeholders to agree quickly about how best to represent the brand visually.

Creative solution

Assurant's new logo design consists of three brightly colored and tightly woven bands, which symbolize the integration of the three core strengths of the company: risk management expertise, customized technology, and long-term client partnerships. The ad campaign with its theme of "bringing clarity to complexity" was visually rendered by using dynamic photographs of common objects that are simple demonstrations of complex laws of physics, such as a yo-yo for gravity. These objects were colored in the Assurant palette to strengthen their visual connection to the new brand identity.

Results

Assurant launched a national advertising campaign to promote its new name and brand identity in national media, including *The Wall Street Journal.* Carbone Smolan Agency created the fundamental brand identity tools and trained Assurant's internal creative staff to use them. Ken Carbone, Principal, conducted a "creative summit" to evaluate the implementation of the new identity, already in use on thousands of applications. Periodic summits provide feedback about what is working and suggestions for the future evolution of the brand identity. An online branding site streamlines operations and manages consistency.

We wanted a branding firm that would create the basic building blocks for our internal creative group to implement in the future. Our employees bring in-depth knowledge as well as passion to our new brand.

Cathy Feierstein
Vice President
Organizational Learning
Assurant

The Olympic Games are a celebration of human spirit and achievement, created to transcend the politics of a fractured world and focus on a shared humanity.

Profile : The Games of the XXVI Olympiad, held in Atlanta in 1996, marked the 100th anniversary of the modern Olympic Games. Muhammad Ali lit the Olympic flame. More than 10,000 athletes from 179 nations competed in almost 300 events, and were documented by more than 15,000 journalists.

Project goals

Design unified system of pictograms for all Olympic events.

Create scalable pictograms.

Express harmony, radiance, and grace.

Receive approval from gold medalist athletes.

Each Olympic country has thematically designed proprietary pictograms.

Process and strategy

Malcolm Grear Designers (MGD) was one of five firms hired to create the look of the Games. The design team attended an intensive three-day Olympic orientation and worked over a period of six months. The team chose "harmony, radiance, and grace" as the big ideas that the Atlanta Games would convey. MGD was commissioned to design 31 sport event pictograms, as well as the Olympic torch. Each sport was researched. After the initial gestural drawings were created, a gold medalist from that sport reviewed them and provided feedback. Numerous committees and sports experts were also part of the complex approval process.

Creative solution

The silhouetted black figures on ancient Greek pottery, called panathenaic amphora, inspired the spirit of the design. Malcolm Grear wanted the pictograms to function as signs without words, both on television and in person in the stadiums. Not only was the body language appropriate to each athletic event, each body pose was appropriate to the way that both women and men played the sport. After the gestures were approved, MGD unified the drawings into simple forms and counterforms to facilitate scalability and reproduction.

Results

The pictograms were used in hundreds of two- and three-dimensional applications, produced in a range of materials and sizes. Neon sculptures were created, 30-foot banners decorated the venues, and the icons were placed on everything from Swatches, to umbrellas. For the first time in Olympic history, they were used on the athletes' medals. The Olympic Committee sold licensing rights to corporate America, and companies like Xerox and Coca-Cola created specialty items for public relations.

We wanted the pictograms to be understood throughout the world as signs without words.

Malcolm Grear
CEO
Malcolm Grear Designers

We envision a connection between beauty, environment, and well-being. We strive to set an example for environmental leadership and responsibility, not just in the world of beauty.*

Profile : Aveda is a beauty line that uses environmentally sound ingredients in hair care, skin care, makeup, perfume, and lifestyle products, available at 6,000 spas and salons in 27 countries. Aveda was founded in 1978 by Austrian environmentalist Horst Rechelbacher. Acquired by Estee Lauder in 1997, the company has retained its unique brand essence and identity.

Project goals

Open the first Aveda salon in Japan.

Create an authentic experience for the future customer.

Achieve brand recognition in Japan.

Research the unique needs of the Japanese customer.

Connect beauty, environment, and well-being.

*Horst Rechelbacher
Founder
Aveda

Process and strategy

Aveda invested in three years of research before launching its brand in Japan. Its strategy was to open its first Aveda Lifestyle Salon and Spa in Tokyo's fashion district. The salon was conceived to build brand awareness and to encourage other salons in Japan to use Aveda products. Setting up shop in a new country meant learning the Japanese way of life and using research to understand the needs, insights, and preferences of the new customers. Aveda learned that many Japanese women prefer light scents, and that the conditioners were not powerful enough to meet the requirements of Asian hair. Aveda products were then modified and reformulated for the Japanese market. The salon design also needed a unique vision to appeal to highly evolved Japanese aesthetics.

Creative solution

All creative solutions were based on Aveda's understanding of and respect for the communities served. One new line of products was named Light Elements to reflect the Japanese love for lightness. Aveda also developed a special formula product line called Damaged Remedy. Aveda used environmentally sound materials from the local area to build the salon. The furniture is made of Tamo oak, a wood that is used to control soil erosion. The flooring and the stairs are made of wood reclaimed from an ancient Japanese farmhouse that had been torn down. The spa room walls are made of straw, soil, and clay from the Kochi area.

Results

Aveda now has the same level of brand recognition in Japan as it does in America. It has become one of the few international companies to have found success in Japan, and has exceeded its business projections. Light Elements and Damaged Remedy products filled a need for Aveda's new Japanese customers and are now sold throughout the world. Since 2003 new salons have opened, and the products have received good press and have been sold in other spas.

The Aveda customer transcends demographics. Our profile is about individuals who have an affinity with Aveda's ideals.

Chris Hacker
SVP, Global Marketing and Design
Aveda

We believe in beauty with a purpose. Our ingredients must be not only high-quality, but high-integrity. We are dedicated to changing the way the world does business.*

Profile : Aveda is a beauty line that uses environmentally sound ingredients in its hair care, skin care, makeup, perfume, and lifestyle products, available at 6,000 spas and salons in 27 countries. Aveda was founded in 1978 by Austrian artist and environmentalist Horst Rechelbacher and acquired by Estee Lauder in 1997.

Project goals

Develop a new makeup line from an authentic source.

Connect beauty, the environment, and well-being.

Create an aesthetically pleasing packaging solution with 100% recycled materials.

*Dominique Conseil
 President
 Aveda

This Aveda Uruku packaging combines aesthetic excellence and environmentally sensitive engineering.

Process and strategy

Aveda prides itself on using botanicals and plant minerals derived from authentic sources. It also views outsourcing to developing communities as a way of giving back. This philosophy led to a collaboration with an indigenous tribe in South America, the Yawanawa. The western Brazilian tribes use a reddish pigment, derived from the urukum palm tree, to adorn their bodies. Aveda collaborated with the Yawanawa to organically grow the tree, fostering the community's economic and cultural survival. After rigorous research and development, Aveda developed a new line of products using the red uruku pigment derived from the trees. The resulting makeup line, free from any synthetic dyes and fragrances was called Aveda Uruku makeup. Aveda's environmental concerns required a packaging solution created entirely from recycled materials which was also aesthetically pleasing. To accomplish this vision, Aveda's design and marketing team approached Harry Allen and Associates.

Creative solution

Harry Allen's primary goal was to find an eco-friendly material that would make an attractive package and be compatible with Aveda's existing compression molds. Allen approached Material ConneXion for a packaging solution that matched the Aveda philosophy. After checking the available options of environment-friendly materials, Allen selected post-industrial polypropylene made of flax chide, a type of plastic with a woody texture for the cap. A collaboration of Aveda's design team and Harry Allen resulted in a highly styled lipstick case that was refillable and had a pleasing, earthy feel. Recycled aluminum was used for the metal base. The packaging was constructed from molded fiber clamshell made of 100 percent recycled newsprint, applying the process used to make egg cartons.

Results

The packaging design was environmentally sensitive and low cost. Aveda designed a print and web campaign to introduce the Aveda Uruku makeup, to tell the story of the Yawanawa tribes. The product and communications were aligned at every step with Aveda's morals and ideals. Aveda won several accolades for its frontline efforts to create recyclable and renewable cosmetic packaging. In 2002, the Aveda Uruku makeup line won the International Package Design Award "Cosmetic Category Leader."

Customers are increasingly aware that you can look beautiful and make a difference.

Chris Hacker
Senior Vice President, Global Marketing and Design
Aveda

We must be compelling. We must break out of the clutter of destination marketing and advertising. We must celebrate our people, our heritage, culture, music.*

Profile : The Islands of the Bahamas thrive on tourism, which accounts for more than 60% of the GDP and employs half the labor force. The Bahamas' culture is a mixture of European, African, and indigenous Arawak. It is known for the charm and hospitality of its people, its subtropical climate, and the incredible beauty of its above-water and underwater landscapes.

Project goals

Discover, capture, and communicate the unique essence of the Bahamas.

Position the Bahamas as the preferred vacation choice.

Distinguish the Islands of the Bahamas from other sand and sea destinations.

Inspire the tourism office, the souvenir manufacturers, and the media to use the new identity.

*The Honorable
Obie Wilchcombe
Minister of Tourism for the
Bahamas

A brand book unveiled the new identity to Bahamian influentials before the public launch. Equal parts education and inspiration, it presents The Bahamas' unique story.

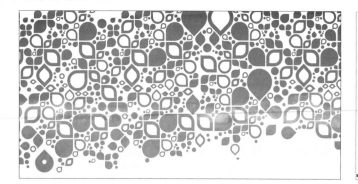

Process and strategy

Duffy began with an exhaustive visual audit of how the existing identity was used. The team then traveled to the islands, returning to their office with hundreds of photos and invaluable first-hand encounters with the sights, sounds, colors, textures, and feeling of the place. The authentic, defining characteristic that emerged from their experience and research was that the Bahamas "is not just one place, but many places." The breadth and diversity of the geography, ecology, cultures, attractions, and activities is what makes a trip to the Bahamas different from trips to other sand and sea destinations. The team realized that there was already a visual manifestation of this truth: the forms of the islands on a map.

Our work reflects the hundreds of islands, thousands of personalities, and millions of experiences people enjoy in the Bahamas.

Tricia Davidson
Managing Partner
Duffy & Partners

Creative solution

The team now had their essence and their framework, but in order to turn the forms of the islands into an identity they had to both simplify the forms and imbue them with the flavor of the islands themselves. The result is a stylized, abstracted translation of the islands with organic forms and tropical colors. However, the identity goes beyond a specific arrangement of forms. Because the forms and colors are so distinctive, they retain their connection to the identity even when they are presented as textures. In addition to representing the Bahamas as the sum of these diverse destinations, variations of the identity are used to highlight and orient viewers to specific islands. The power of this identity is that it is not just a logo but a flexible, visual language with infinite applications. Its authenticity guarantees that the experience will match the perception.

Results

The identity for the Bahamas became the foundation for a $5 million promotional campaign, "Island Hopping." The campaign includes the slogan, "Just off the coast of the familiar," to highlight the proximity to the United States. The Ministry of Tourism is committed to putting intense efforts behind the brand and campaign. A website is the cornerstone of these efforts. The ministry solicited agreements from the private sector to use the new identity on all future promotions and advertisements.

Strong branding elegantly captures what is unique, special, and enduring about the product.

We branded the country, and people will actually end up wearing the brand. Every single element working together will contribute to differentiation and a stronger brand.

Joe Duffy
Founder
Duffy & Partners

To break away.
To reconnect.

THE ISLANDS OF THE
bahamas

We strive to be the acknowledged global leader and preferred partner in helping our clients succeed in the world's rapidly evolving markets.*

Profile : The Bank of New York Company, founded in 1784, provides a comprehensive range of services that enable financial institutions, corporations, endowments, foundations, and government entities to move and manage financial assets in more than 100 markets worldwide. Its core competencies include securities servicing, investment management, treasury management, and individual and regional banking services. In 2005, the bank had $101.8 billion assets under management.

Project goals

Research perceptions, awareness, and familiarity.

Position the bank as a global service leader.

Design a new identity and brand architecture.

Develop a system for brand outreach and governance.

*Vision Statement
 The Bank of New York Company

We strive to act as a full-fledged client partner, helping to navigate the complexities of global markets and unlock the full potential of our clients' assets and their enterprises.

Thomas A. Renyi
Chairman and CEO
The Bank of New York Company

The interwoven lines reflect the movement and vitality of today's financial markets. The interior white square symbolizes the focus on leveraging the bank's expertise and experience.

Alex de Jánosi
Partner
Lippincott Mercer

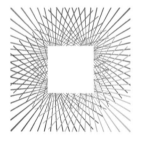

The BANK
of NEW YORK

Process and strategy

The Bank of New York's rapid evolution from a regional icon to a global service provider in the decade following the mid-90s required a new positioning strategy and identity. Lippincott Mercer began by measuring awareness, perceptions, and familiarity. Research revealed that internal audiences were familiar with the global strategy, but not clear about their role in building the brand. Although highly regarded by clients, the bank's breadth of capabilities was not fully recognized. Lippincott Mercer created a brand platform that articulated a unified vision for eighty acquisitions. The platform also defined the bank's unique personality, tone, manner, and style. Key messages were written to enhance clarity and credibility in the global marketplace.

Creative solution

The design team envisioned an identity dramatically differentiated from the bold iconic trademarks that characterized twentieth-century financial services. "We were inspired by the intricate patterns of global currency. The radiating lines and colors are dynamic like the assets that the bank moves and manages, and reflect the comprehensive array of services that the bank offers its clients around the world," said Alex de Jánosi, a partner at Lippincott Mercer and the lead designer for the project. The creative team proceeded to design and build a unified system, extending through print, interactive communications, and the corporate website. Lippincott's information architects designed a new interface and organizing principles for www.bankofny.com. The identity system included stationery, signage, and brochures. The logotype combines traditional and modern typefaces.

Results

Lippincott Mercer's work was part of a successful global initiative supporting the bank's evolution to a broad-based, global financial services firm. The new brand architecture has helped employees promote cross-selling of services by streamlining the bank's divisions, businesses, and product offerings. An online brand center was launched to insure that the brand would continue to be understood by employees, communicators, and design professionals. Web guidelines, organizing principles, and new information architecture have provided cost-effective in-house maintenance. In addition, Lippincott collaborated with The Bank of New York to ensure global web governance. A cross-divisional group of senior managers was formed to develop policies and procedures for the web.

We need to reinvent the energy business, to go beyond petroleum. Not by abandoning oil and gas, but by improving the ways in which it is used and produced so that our business is aligned with the long–term needs of the world.*

Profile : The 1998 merger of British Petroleum and Amoco created one of the world's largest oil and petrochemical groups, providing its customers with energy for heat and light, fuel for transportation, retail services, and petrochemical products.

Project goals

Develop a brand identity that would unite BP Amoco's employees from two merged companies.

Signal to the world that the merged company is a new strong global brand.

Align the company's business with its external expressions and its internal culture.

Create an online resource and other tools to ensure that actions are aligned with BP's core values.

*Lord John Browne
Group Chief Executive
BP

In a global marketplace, branding is crucial in attracting customers and business. It is not just a matter of a few gas stations or the logo on pole signs. It is about the identity of the company and the values that underpin everything that you do and every relationship that you have.

Lord John Browne
Group Chief Executive
BP

Process and strategy

Landor Associates began by reviewing BP Amoco's existing research and conducting new research on the equity of the existing brands. Landor used a rigorous process to affirm what makes the brand unique, compelling, and differentiated. This included one-on-one interviews with senior managers and culminated in an offsite workshop called Brand Driver. During this workshop senior managers and marketing executives worked collaboratively to substantiate the core values and attributes of the new brand. It led to the affirmation of the already emerging values (performance, innovation, green, and progressive) and a commitment to transform the organization and transcend the petroleum sector.

Creative solution

Landor developed a brief that distilled BP's brand essence for its creative team. After assessing the strengths and weaknesses of numerous naming options, Landor made a strong recommendation to retain the BP name, based on its significant equity, high-quality perception, and global heritage. The theme "Beyond Petroleum", developed by Ogilvy & Mather, was recommended as a central concept to unify all actions, behaviors, and communications for the BP brand. It signaled a BP imperative to go beyond conventional ways of thinking and doing.

Landor designed a series of visual strategies. The CEO and senior management chose the helios strategy, which tested strongly against the qualities of progressive, forward-thinking, innovative, and environmental. The helios trademark shifted the paradigm of how the petroleum industry should look and feel.

Results

Ensuring that 100,000 employees in 100 countries understood how to align their actions with BP's core values was key to the new strategy. Landor developed a series of employee workshops to engage employees in the new vision, and to engender discussions about ways to live the brand in their daily lives. The Brand Centre, an online resource for guidelines, demonstrates how the brand is used throughout BP and helps each employee play a part in building the brand. BP's ongoing commitment involves annual surveys to monitor the brand's impact externally on business performance, and relations with consumers and communities, and internally on brand perception, employee morale, and job satisfaction.

Branding is not about checking the box and moving on. Brands are living, and breathing—they need to be embraced, monitored, and adapted.

Andrew Welch
Landor Associates

BP has 28,500 service stations, and over 100,000 employees.

Center City District is committed to maintaining the district's competitive edge as a regional employment center, a quality place to live, and a premier regional destination for dining, shopping, and culture.*

Profile : Keeping the downtown of America's fifth largest city clean, safe, and attractive is the mission of the Center City District (CCD), a private sector business improvement district established in 1990 by a coalition that included more than 2,000 property owners, commercial tenants, employers, and the city of Philadelphia.

Project goals

Design a unique identity that emphasizes the downtown area.

Create a flexible system that can be applied to signage, uniforms, ads, vehicles, and promotions.

Design uniforms that are immediately identifiable on the city streets.

Develop an identity system that could be approved by the Board of Directors.

*Paul Levy
President and CEO
Center City District

Core identity

Patch

Process and strategy

The design team, led by Joel Katz, worked with the executive director, who championed the new symbol through the Board of Directors, member by member. The biggest hurdle was to overcome the chairman's preference for a skyline. Katz knew that the symbol should reflect the uniqueness of the organization and relate not to the skyline, but to street level, where the CCD would operate. The design team compiled ads from the Yellow Pages to demonstrate that Philadelphia's skyline was used by a wide variety of companies (including a local escort service) and was neither unique nor appropriate.

Originally CCD had planned to buy off-the-shelf, white-shirt-blue-trouser uniforms. Katz persuaded CCD to create a distinctive uniform, knowing that it was imperative for the employees to have the credibility, but not to resemble the police or the parking authority. The uniforms needed to be memorable, accessible, and upscale, and to reinforce a positive image of the city.

Creative solution

The new mark is an interpretation of William Penn's original 1682 five-square plan for Philadelphia (the northwest square became a circle in 1919). That puts the focus of the identity at grade, where the action occurs. Additional interest is generated by rotating the mark the city's 11° off true north.

Katz chose uniform colors designed to be highly visible on a crowded streetscape and unlike the uniforms of most authorities: teal and violet enhance white or teal tops and navy trousers that were part of a coordinated system of rain shells, baseball caps, shoulder bags, fanny packs, shirts, pants, and ties. Katz added a circular embroidered patch that includes the logotype for all uniforms, accessories, and vehicles. There is connection and differentiation between the community service representatives and the cleaning personnel.

Results

CCD's vision for a safe, clean, well-managed Philadelphia is realized daily by residents, tourists, and office workers. Fifteen years after the original design, the look and feel of the program continue to be fresh and immediately recognizable. The distinctive uniforms, which have been described as "walking banners," were the most important aspect of the launch.

CCD's identity has been applied to newsletters, ad campaigns, the website, brochures, maintenance vehicles, information kiosks, banners, and bus shelter advertising. In addition Katz designed a pedestrian wayfinding signage system, Walk!PHILADELPHIA, that features circular color-coded maps on more than 2,200 signs throughout the city. These are being supplemented by bus shelter maps and rapid transit concourse signage programs.

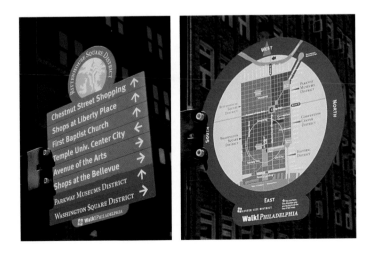

We created Cereality® to celebrate the very personal nature of enjoying a good bowl of cereal, anywhere, anytime. We envisioned Cereality as a fun experience and an opportunity to transform the way people think about cereal.*

Profile : Cereality® Cereal Bar & Cafe is located in college towns, financial districts, airports, and urban hubs. Open from early morning through the evening, Cereality serves 30 brand name cereals and toppings, a variety of milks, and a choice of cereal-inspired snacks, smoothies, and cereal bars.

Project goals

Create a profitable business.

Design a fully integrated brand experience.

Energize the cereal category.

Create buzz.

Maximize the equity of well-known cereal brands.

*David Roth
Rick Bacher
Co-Founders
Cereality

People have relationships with cereals. Not just to a grain, not just to a flake, but to a particular branded product. And this business was inspired by an observation that those relationships are very, very strong, very particular and very personal. And so why not create a retail business that really celebrates those relationships. And our attitude was, don't try and build it, just find it, and celebrate it.

David Roth
CEO and Co-Founder
Cereality

Cereal is served in a "milk-tight bucket"– a container inspired by Chinese take-out containers.

Striped cotton pajamas that declare "Captain of Crunch," baseball caps, and cool mugs are all sold at the cafe.

Process and strategy

The co-founders decided to combine their expertise in brand management, marketing, design, and food to build a unique branded experience. The big idea is simply "all cereal, all day, all ways." An early investor, Quaker Oats, provided Cereality with R&D. ACNielsen marketing research revealed that cereal was the third best-selling item after milk and soft drinks. Ninety-five percent of Americans eat cereal. Cereal is both a snack and a meal other than breakfast. The founders recruited a world-class team from the foodservice and retail industries to turn their vision into a profitable business; this was not a run-of-the mill start-up.

Creative solution

Rick Bacher designed the multicolored logo and the imaginative, light-filled environment, described by the press as "Seinfeldesque." Customers order a custom blend of favorite cereals from pajama-clad Cereologists™. Cereal is served in a "milk-tight bucket," a container inspired by Chinese take-out containers. Behind the counter, cereals are kept in wood and glass kitchen cabinets. A bright red sofa offers a comfy rest, and the farm table seating twelve people is often the choice of a local book club or a birthday party. On Saturday mornings the first family to arrive gets to choose the cartoons shown on the flat screen TV. Cereality merchandise is sold: striped cotton pajamas that declare "Captain of Crunch" or "United Flakes of America," baseball caps, and cool mugs. Everything is branded, and all names are trademarked from Cereality Bars™, to Cereality Bites™ and Slurrealities™, otherwise known as smoothies.

Results

Cereality continues to attract a wide demographic—businesspeople, college students, families with young children—all enjoy a good bowl of cereal in a friendly environment, and a refreshing and healthy fast-food alternative. After the 2003 success of its first kiosk at Arizona State University, Cereality opened another kiosk in University City in Philadelphia in 2004, followed by one in a Chicago financial district location in 2005. Each month the company receives 1,000 emails from customers around the world who want a Cereality in their neighborhoods.

Cereality has energized the cereal category.

Mary Dillon
Former President
Quaker Oats Company

It's always Saturday morning at Cereality®.

Chambers Group's coaching model, 7Chambers, connects the head, heart, and spirit for individuals groups, organizations, and communities across race, gender, sexual orientation, and culture.

Profile : Founded in 2005, Chambers Group is a leadership development firm specializing in executive development, individual and team coaching, and integrating diversity and human capital planning. The founders, Dr. Barbara Riley and Dr. Delyte Frost, have been consultants to Fortune 100 companies for 25 years. Chambers' Leadership Matrix guides leaders in implementing change, achieving power, and realizing measurable results.

Project goals

Express the vision of a new firm.

Create an identity that is fluid and expressive.

Communicate dynamic experience.

Differentiate the offerings.

Achieve balance between business discipline and spiritual values.

We always imagined we could attain a visual identity as rich as our view of the world.

Dr. Delyte Frost
Dr. Barbara Riley
Founders
Chambers Group

Chambers Group

Process and strategy

Chambers Group needed to find a way to balance the social justice and spiritual values of the partners with a strategic business model that would appeal to large companies. Chambers Group's process with Stellarvisions began with a series of conversations that explored the idea of connecting head, heart, mind, and spirit. During these initial meetings, Chambers was evolving and designing its coaching and leadership models. Stellarvisions created a series of personas and scenarios of senior managers and HR professionals who would either choose or refer Chambers Group. These personas activated intensive discussions about the essence and dynamics of the Chambers process, and the needs and perceptions of Chambers clients. The creative team and the partners collaborated to identify unconventional ways to communicate with a broader audience. The number 7 had implicit, explicit, and ancient etymology that was important to the partners.

Creative solution

From the inception of the conversations, Stella Gassaway, firm visionary and creative director, wanted the identity and the web presence to embody the intense, individual, enlightening, and empowering experience of working with the Chambers Group. Stellarvisions immersed itself in thinking through a different cultural space: Jacob's Ladder, the I Ching, yin and yang. The identity needed to express the integration of life and work, and the endless cycle of learning and living. Gassaway instinctively knew that the identity would comprise a wordmark and an avatar. She designed a series of interchangeable elements—called the elements of change—which will be integrated into the coaching process itself as well as into the communications of the company. The new website mimics Chambers' coaching process: a series of questions leads the visitor on a journey and calls on visitors to engage and make choices. Chambers makes people feel safe, heard, and seen. The website uses images and metaphor and is not text heavy.

Results

The meaning and the formation of the elements of change are in constant transformation and engender lively discussions between the partners and the creative principals. The new business was launched in 2005 with an invitation to 7+1 Intensive, a year-long process for intensive change: A multicultural group of women will meet for three days a month for eight months. The new business has launched Chambers into a bright future, with consulting contracts in place for a year out. The website is launched, and the new card and letterheads are in full use. Unlike most consulting groups, the physical becomes spiritual, the yin and yang of Chambers.

**Leadership Matrix
intelligence quotients**

IQ Knowledge Intelligence
EQ Emotional Intelligence
TQ Thinking Intelligence
DQ Diversity Intelligence
PQ Purpose Intelligence
JQ Job Intelligence
SQ Spiritual Intelligence

conscious

context

choice

courage

competence

confidence

create

The University of Chicago Graduate School of Business (Chicago GSB) uses the contextual lenses of sociology, psychology, economics, and statistics to develop disciplined thinkers who can assess any challenge or opportunity.

Profile : Founded in 1898, Chicago GSB is the country's second-oldest business school and the first with permanent campuses in Asia, Europe, and North America. First to offer a Ph.D. in Business and an Executive MBA Program, the school's education and research innovations have produced ideas and leaders to transform business practice.

Project goals

Increase recognition of the school as one of the nation's top-tier graduate business programs.

Create an informal verbal and visual identifier and a single, manageable, and more recognizable brand.

Position Chicago GSB as the most highly respected business school brand.

Differentiate Chicago GSB from other MBA programs.

Encompass dignity, tradition, and the school's core essence.

Process and strategy

Crosby Associates was engaged to develop a comprehensive branding and visual identity program. The audit identified numerous names in use. The school's long name, University of Chicago Graduate School of Business, was frequently transposed; shortened versions ranged from just "Chicago" to "The GSB." The school had a lower profile compared to other top-tier peer institutions. Many had simple one-word communicative names. The university shield was used inconsistently and communications lacked focus and impact. Crosby distilled volumes of research studies and extensive interviews with deans, professors, administrators and students that the school had conducted into a white paper that defined program goals, brand position, and problems that needed resolution.

Crosby presented seven informal name candidates that were already in use. In the presentation, each name was isolated and applied as hypothetical signage on the dominant building on campus. Each candidate was then analyzed for its positive and negative connotations in both the academic environment and the larger world of business leadership.

Creative solution

The final recommended name was Chicago GSB. "It is the most logical choice because it follows the sequence of the institution's formal name," said Bart Crosby, principal of Crosby Associates. Chicago GSB would now become the official wordmark, and act as the primary verbal and visual identifier. Chicago GSB would never stand alone; it would always be accompanied by the complete, official name. The names of programs, centers, institutes, and publications would remain the same in the new system but would be secondary.

The primary visual element in the identity program is the wordmark, which juxtaposes both bold and elegant typography and frames the university shield, which was redrawn and simplified. The new shield lends itself to being a large graphic element; its redrawn features allow it to be printed, hot-stamped, or embossed to add visual texture. Crosby developed a simple, proportional grid system for print and electronic communications.

Results

The new name and integrated program were launched in 1999 and implemented in signage, the website, all marketing communications, and forms. Comprehensive guidelines were published in a perfect-bound brochure format and are available on Chicago GSB's website. The school's Publications Office is always available to field questions about the program.

"A stronger brand name and identity have increased awareness for the business school and has facilitated effective and efficient communications through prominent and consistent use," said Colleen Newquist, Director of Communications, Chicago GSB.

Competition at business schools is always increasing. A stronger brand name increases awareness and facilitates effective communication through prominent and consistent use..

Bart Crosby
Principal
Crosby Associates

When Cingular Wireless launched its brand during the 2001 Super Bowl, its vision was based on human spirit and self-expression rather than technology, features, and benefits.

Profile : Originally formed from the merger of SBC Communications and BellSouth in 2000, Cingular Wireless integrated eleven brands into one network. Cingular is a quintessential twenty-first century brand, born of a merger and continuously evolving. Cingular acquired AT&T in 2004, making it the largest wireless carrier in the United States, connecting more than 50 million customers.

Project goals

Develop a compelling and credible name for the merger.

Create a breakthrough brand presence in the telecommunications industry.

Develop a name that can be owned around the world.

Design a differentiated icon that can be animated.

Our greatest challenge was developing a compelling, credible, and instantly familiar name in a six-week time frame.

Jamie Koval
Principal
VSA Partners

The mark was purposely designed to be both a static and dynamic element—print and electronic. We wanted the overall identity program to feel warm, approachable and simple.

Jamie Koval
Principal
VSA Partners

Process and strategy

VSA Partners worked closely with a small communications team from both companies lead by CEO Stephen Carter. Prior to the merger, Cingular's competitors were positioning themselves around the expected, indistinguishable areas of "access" and "technology." In the short term, Cingular was not offering new technology, products, or services, which meant that the company had to reinforce its position solely through its unique brand essence, name, and identity. Because of the tight time frame, VSA's research was limited to an extensive, global secondary audit of leading competitors. VSA also studied category-defining companies, both inside and outside the telecommunications sector, that were able to build and maintain strong, compelling brands.

"We began to realize that the wireless space was evolving from a features-and-functions buying decision to a lifestyle choice," said Jamie Koval, principal of VSA Partners. VSA's brand strategy was to position Cingular as the embodiment of human expression. Cingular would allow users to "make their mark" by providing intuitive solutions to all wireless wants and needs.

Creative solution

VSA developed the name "Cingular," which was based on a real word with a real meaning—a dramatically differentiated name that communicated the new company's goal of becoming the single source for all wireless needs. Naming was particularly challenging because the domain name needed to be available worldwide, and the name could not start with v,s,a, or n. The Cingular logo was designed to directly reinforce the idea of human expression and help users "make their mark." It is the only anthropomorphic mark in the wireless industry. The brandmark, known internally as "Jack," stands for the pinnacle of individuality. The choice of orange as the corporate color was based on the audit of the competitive set and the desire to put some visual distance between Cingular and its peers.

Results

Neither CEO of the merging companies immediately warmed to the new name. "What they ultimately found convincing was when we presented the full potential of the brand, on packaging, retail environments, and merchandise," Koval said. Once the name and identity were approved, they were presented to Cingular's signage provider and national advertising agency, which ensured that the Cingular brand would be communicated consistently with its original intent. Backed by a $300 million media campaign, the Cingular brand was brought to life, making it an instantly recognizable icon. "It was exhilarating to create the foundation of something so visible and valuable," said Koval, "and to see how it's become imbedded in our culture."

VSA Partners believes that the Cingular program was ultimately successful because it followed the firm's core principles for the project:

The client's desire to achieve a true breakthrough brand

The strategic soundness of a core brand essence and positioning

The appropriateness of an emotional approach to the identity

Consistent access to and support from senior leadership

When Citicorp merged with Travelers Group to form Citigroup in 1998, it was the first financial services company in the U.S. to combine banking, insurance, and investments under one umbrella.

Profile : Sanford Weill, former chairman of Travelers Group, and John Reed, former chairman of Citicorp, envisioned a global financial services giant meeting the needs of individual, corporate, and government customers. In 2005, Citigroup had over $1 trillion in assets, 190 million accounts, and 350,000 employees. The Citibank brand is used on the consumer side of the business. Citigroup, the name of the parent company, is the brand of the corporate investment bank, global wealth management, alternative investments, and the private bank.

Project goals

Develop a unified brand identity for the merged entity.

Maintain the equity in both brands.

Revitalize the consumer brand to be fresh, modern, and relevant.

Create preference for the consumer brand.

Our objective was to exponentially grow the consumer business worldwide, and to connect the business model with something genuinely appealing to the customer.

Susan Avarde
Managing Director, Global Branding
Citigroup Consumer Businesses

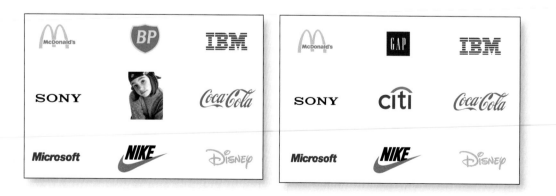

Pentagram showed Melissa and Citi in a field of super brands.

Michael Wolff, a brand strategist, described the vision: "We want to become the bank of the future. We need to imagine talking to our one billionth customer. She is an eleven-year-old girl named Melissa. She thinks of banking services in a whole new way, grows up doing all of her banking online, and expects everything to be simple. She lives in the world of McDonald's, Nike, the Gap, and Coke."

Process and strategy

The process began by examining the equity and marketplace perceptions of Citicorp and Travelers Group within banking, financial services, and the overall consumer world. Anne MacDonald, Chief Marketing Officer, and Susan Avarde, Managing Director, Global Branding, Citigroup Consumer Businesses, were charged with finalizing a name and brand identity of the new entity within ten weeks for the press announcement. They formed a team that included Michael Wolff, an independent brand strategist, and Pentagram partners, Michael Bierut and Paula Scher. The core strategy was to shift the perception that banks were arrogant and intimidating, and that corporate behemoths could be innovative and friendly. Since both merging companies had strong brands and powerful leaders, the challenge was to express the merger's vision and symbolically join the brand equity of each. Avarde and MacDonald created a road show to build awareness about the research, the new positioning strategy, the brand architecture and visual identity. Building new brand champions was a two-year process.

Creative solution

Paula Scher quickly realized the lowercase t in "Citi" could be an umbrella handle. When she put the familiar red arc over the t, which also stood for Travelers, it became the perfect symbol of the merged entity. The logical brand architecture presented "Citi" as the core prefix, which could then accommodate an infinite list of suffix services and products, like CitiFinancial and CitiMortgage. The "blue wave," a core element of Citibank's brand equity, was revitalized and applied across media as a unifying and familiar element. The new identity sent a strong signal of unified financial leadership to all stakeholders.

Results

Merged under one umbrella, the two companies have become one. In 2000, an imaginative advertising campaign was launched by Fallon Worldwide. The "Live Richly" tagliine, used in the advertising signature, positions Citi as an advocate for a healthy approach to money. In 2005, Citi moved from 13th to 12th on *BusinessWeek*/Interbrand's list of the world's most valuable brands. As the top-ranked financial company, it has achieved global consumer brand status alongside Coca-Cola, IBM, GE, Disney, and McDonald's.

Citibank aspired to provide a predictable, recognizable, distinct experience; seamlessly available anytime, anywhere.

Harvard Business School
Case Study: Branding Citigroup's
Consumer Business

We went to meet with regional heads around the world to have conversations, to lay out the possibilities and benefits of revitalizing the consumer brand.

Anne MacDonald
Chief Marketing Officer
Citigroup Consumer Businesses

New retail environment designed by Pentagram.

Columbus Salame is made with the same passion that the partners had when they came from Italy. We can't be the biggest, we can't afford to be the smallest, but whatever we do, we will be the best.*

Profile : Columbus Salame Company is a purveyor of salamis, mortadellas, prosciuttos, roast beefs, and other prepared food products, based in San Francisco. Privately owned by three families, their products are sold nationally in supermarket chains, specialty shops, neighborhood delicatessens, and online.

Project goals

Revitalize the visual identity and introduce new brands.

Design new packaging and point of purchase.

Increase recognition and attract new customers.

Make the products look more distinctive and upscale.

Build on European heritage and existing brand equity.

*Phil Gatto
President
Columbus Salame Company

The more we raised our standards, the more customer appreciation we received. It has made us continue to innovate and create new products.

Phil Gatto
President
Columbus Salame Company

Process and strategy

Phil Gatto, President, Columbus Salame Company, worked closely with Kit Hinrichs, a partner at Pentagram. Columbus wanted to increase its name recognition, market share and profitability. Large nationally advertised brands were dominating the category and simultaneously reducing their prices. Gatto did not want to risk the company's reputation for quality and taste. Hinrichs felt that the 1950s identity no longer appealed to today's sophisticated consumer. "Christopher Columbus had been Betty Crockerized," he said, "rendering it devoid of meaning and character." Pentagram's design team seized the opportunity to illuminate the company's authentic Italian heritage. An old-world European image would differentiate it from the national brands, and reshape it to a more upscale category.

Creative solution

Pentagram's design team transformed Columbus to look more genuine and old-worldly by creating an engraving-like illustration. The red, white, and blue color scheme was maintained and used in an oval frame. The identity utilized two typefaces: the company name was set in a classic face with European connotations, while descriptive text was set in a Bauhaus font that "connoted modernity and commerce." An old, engraved map of Italy was used on hang tags, dry salami case wrapping, point-of-purchase displays, letterhead, and cards. After the first product line was deemed a success, Gatto brought Pentagram back to create a new identity for a premium line of higher margin products. Pentagram named the new line "Renaissance", and designed black product labels with metallic gold lettering and trim placed on fifteenth-century paintings.

Results

The new look of the products increased Columbus' penetration into upscale specialty delicatessens. In addition, mainstream retailers increased their orders because they liked the way Columbus products looked in their cases. Williams Sonoma, the premium kitchen-product retailer, now offers an exclusive Renaissance gift package in their online catalog.

We tried to get inside our designer's head as he got into ours. We have been working with Pentagram for ten years. Kit had never "done" food before, but that was the beauty of it. He took a completely different approach.

Phil Gatto
President
Columbus Salame Company

Through the spirit of challenge and innovation, we will capture customers' hearts with superlative mobile services. We will fulfill our vision of being a Mobile Life Partner, offering customers value, fun, and delight.*

Profile : Dosirak is a musical content website launched in 2005 by KTF, a mobile telecommunications service company with 12 million subscribers. Consumers download MP3 files onto their MP3 cell phones. South Korea is a world leader in mobile media devices, and mobile music delivery is a rapidly expanding market.

Project goals

Build awareness of the new brand.

Attract customers to the website.

Overcome disadvantage as a latecomer to the market.

Convey unlimited possibilities and fun.

*Young-Chu Cho
 President and CEO
 KTF

Process and strategy

KTF named its new service Dosirak, which means lunch box in Korean. The name instantly communicates portability and mobility. *Dosi* also means "city" in Korean and *rak* means "delight" and "music;" those combined mean "delightful music city." The name is also dramatically different from those of their leading competitors.

KTF's brand slogan, "Have a good time," promises consumers fun when they download or listen to Dosirak.

Welcomm Publicis Worldwide determined that the brand identity needed to convey limitless and abundant music, as well as be aligned with KTF's vision for customer life filled with fun and delight.

Creative solutions

Kbrand Associates was retained to design the final brand identity. The final mark is a rectangular formation of densely jumbled, multicolored and vibrant music notes evoking a computer screen about to burst open. The mark becomes an expandable, amorphous texture that inhabits three-dimensional forms and spaces, filling them with fun music. The creative team views the music notes as the brand's core visual code.

Welcomm Publicis Worldwide's advertising campaign features everyday objects, such as shoes, forks, and motorcycles, filled with the Dosirak musical texture, just like great sound filling the air. The campaign's conceptual simplicity ensures unending possibilities in creative expression.

Results

The Dosirak brand was launched in May 2005 with an ad campaign, interactive kiosks and billboards on the streets, and billboards in the subway. In a short time the brand has grown to be a major music contents website in the mobile communications space. Although there are more than fifteen websites for music, Dosirak is the only one that uses music notes as its proprietary visual code.

**KTF Mobile Life
Vision Statement**

It comprises all aspects of customers' lives, including business, personal life, and leisure.

It overcomes time and space barriers.

It is a lifestyle that enables people to lead a freer and more comfortable life.

"Push here if you can't live without music," declares the interactive kiosk in the Seoul subway station where millions of people a day ride the subway.

The Dummies series of books demystifies the unknown and empowers readers with a step-by-step educational and entertaining approach.

Profile : Over 1,000 titles have been published, helping readers navigate the unique challenges of daily life, from finance to feng shui, to personal computers and poker. The Dummies series is available in more than 39 languages and 100 countries. Over 150 million books have been sold worldwide. The brand was acquired by John Wiley & Sons in 2001.

Project goals

Reposition the Dummies brand to include non-technology reference books.

Transform a computer technology publishing brand into a digital lifestyle brand.

Create a sustainable system to differentiate the titles and topics.

Refine the packaging design to reflect and support the Dummies positioning and experience.

Systematize the use of proprietary assets, including color, typography, the Dummies Man and icons.

Dummies Man is not a real character...he is neither liberal nor conservative, neither homeowner or apartment dweller, neither wealthy nor poor, neither old nor young. He does not own any identifiable, branded assets. He is not member of any club, organization or faction.

Excerpted from *Brand Style Guide for Dummies*

The original cover image was a combination blackboard and protest sign, initially conceived as protesting against the arcane jargon of computer technology.

The distinctive yellow and black brand is recognized by 150 million Americans.

The first Dummies book published in 1991.

Process and strategy

In 1994, the business began to expand beyond computing titles with the publication of *Personal Finance for Dummies.* The core brand idea easily transferred to diverse areas of human interest from health and fitness to cooking, games and business. By 1998, Dummies had 50 million books in print. Despite an expanding list of non-technology titles, the marketplace identified the brand with technology. The company realized that certain packaging deficiencies were contributing to that perception. For example, Dr. Ruth Westheimer's *Sex for Dummies* was frequently found in the computing section next to *SQL for Dummies.* The company launched a process that included internal and trade customer interviewing, and consumer focus groups.

Creative solution

In 1999, Landor Associates was retained to analyze the packaging design of the series. They started by restricting the use of the proprietary Dummies typeface to the logotype only. It had been previously used for the entire title. The logotype was also made to work on the spine. The subject area topic (like wine or marketing) was designed in a white sans serif bold type to stand out and to be easily read at a distance. Landor also introduced the systemwide use of photography when appropriate to the topic. When photography was not used, the Dummies Man, previously used only as a navigational icon, became the dominant image on the cover. Variations of the Dummies Man were created by a list of approved artists. Carefully managed, he is viewed as the embodiment of the brand—a reassuring voice and a friend who instills confidence and fun.

Results

In 2005, there were nearly 1,000 active Dummies titles in print and fifty percent of the titles are non-computing. The *Brand Style Guide for Dummies* has been expanded to be a resource for licensee partners, international marketing teams, and custom publishers. The book series is constantly evolving to include new subject areas and new products, from instructional DVDs to kits.

Dummies readers tend to be educated, employed, reasonably well-off. Dummies readers aren't dummies. They are smart, and know what they need to get things up to speed.

Marc Jeffrey Mikulich
Vice President, Brand Management
Wiley

We have done a lot of market research on the consumer, and we know that 64 million people have read a Dummies book. A typical house hold has between 3 and 4 Dummies books.

Marc Jeffrey Mikulich
Vice President, Brand Management
Wiley

Redesigned system, 1999

The founding partners wanted to shift the paradigm of a litigation powerhouse. They envisioned a trim, agile firm with extraordinary client relationships that uses advanced technology and strategic insight to quickly mobilize to big firm capacity.

Profile : Eimer Stahl Klevorn & Solberg LLP (Eimer Stahl) is a national litigation firm in Chicago founded in 2000 to resolve the largest, most complex legal matters for America's corporations. It performs securities and antitrust work, multidistrict environmental and product liability litigation, and high stakes contract disputes. The four founding partners left an established global legal firm to create a different kind of law firm.

Project goals

Build recognition for the new law firm and transcend the category.

Articulate a differentiated brand strategy and positioning.

Create a visual identity system across media.

Establish a fluid, effective, strategic marketplace communication system.

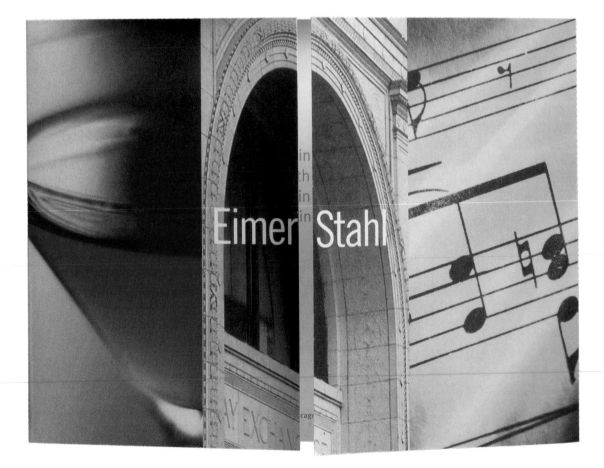

Crosby has designed a system for us that continues to bring our message to the market, in a way that is clever, appropriate, and differentiated.

Nate Eimer
Managing Partner
Eimer Stahl

Process and strategy

Unlike traditional litigation firms, Eimer Stahl wanted to make litigation more cost-effective, more successful, and more enjoyable. Despite their stellar individual reputations, the partners acknowledged that launching a new small law firm was a risk. None of the partners had ever created a new company. They retained Crosby Associates to help them develop a brand value proposition, a mission statement, a positioning platform, and an identity.

Crosby Associates facilitated an offsite meeting with the founding partners to discuss the new firm's goals, philosophy, personality, and unique strengths. Joining Crosby's team was Cheryl Slover-Linett, a strategist and joint facilitator. The team drafted a list of key marketing strategy deliverables, using a hierarchy of brand values and associated client benefits. After the partners' agreement, Crosby began to design.

Creative solution

Crosby designed a very confident, streamlined sans serif logotype and applied a new sensibility across media. Dramatic black-and-white photography is used in the website and in the firm brochure. A marketing system was designed to be sent out regularly to clients and other lawyers. The format, a 4 x 5 gatefold card, is used consistently regardless of the announcement or invitation. But the mailing is always a surprise. The first one was an invitation to a Rolling Stones concert for the band's opening event. Others include newsworthy announcements, such as an open house or a firm anniversary.

Results

Being a small firm with a big firm capability has proven to be a successful strategy. Eimer Stahl was named one of the best boutique firms in the country by *The American Lawyer*, and Crain named it the best law firm in Chicago in 2004. Crosby Associates developed a launch plan to help Eimer Stahl implement its new brand in the legal marketplace. The firm has doubled in size since its founding, from twenty-five to fifty. Marketing is integral to growth.

When we formed Eimer Stahl in 2000, we set out to create a different kind of law firm—one that would deliver outstanding results for clients, but take a more personal, creative approach to getting there. And that's what we've done.

Nate Eimer
Managing Partner
Eimer Stahl

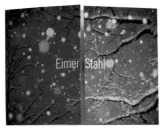

FedEx

FedEx embodies a twenty-first century vision based on a common information interface for all global customers, applying one brand link to a broad spectrum of transportation and logistics services.

Project goals

Conduct worldwide research and analysis.

Position FedEx as a global provider of time-sensitive material.

Collaborate on articulating brand attributes.

Design a new identity and brand architecture.

Facilitate cross-selling.

Develop a brand management resource tool.

Profile : FedEx provides a wide range of business, logistics, and transportation services to customers and businesses in 220 countries and territories through its network of independent operating companies. Six million packages are now delivered each business day—a feat achieved through continuous innovation. FedEx was founded in 1973 by its visionary chairman and CEO, Fred Smith.

Corporation

Express

Ground

Freight

Custom Critical

Trade Networks

The consumers themselves had evolved the brand to FedEx. It had become the Kleenex and the Coke of its category.

Clay Timon
Former CEO
Landor Associates

The success of FedEx branding has been driven by smart instinct, swift decision making and compelling execution, with the role of research often being to validate and provide executional guidance.

Gayle Christensen
Managing Director
Global Brand Management
FedEx

Process and strategy

In a relationship that began in 1993, Landor Associates has co-created two generations of branding transformations for FedEx. The original identity, Federal Express, became a potential impediment to building a global business. By the early 1990s, the company was known as "FedEx" and, unlike the former name, could be said easily by customers who did not speak English. Landor emphasized the organization's global scope, reliability, and speed with a new brand line, "The World on Time," and launched FedEx as the primary verbal and visual identifier. The bold new identity was applied to thousands of uniforms and packages, and fleets of planes and vehicles.

Beginning in 1998, the parent company of FedEx, originally called FDX Corp., acquired a string of shipping and logistics companies to provide transportation, supply chain, and information system services. Each retained its brand name.

Creative solution

Landor began to examine new brand architecture and verbal branding that would make it simpler for customers and prospects to understand the global scope of FedEx and its range of capabilities.

The new brand architecture unified the independent companies under the powerful FedEx brand, accompanied by clear language to differentiate each company service: FedEx Express, FedEx Ground, FedEx Freight, FedEx Custom Critical, and FedEx Trade Networks. Each operating company was also color-coded. This approach was aligned with Fred Smith's vision and requirements to build independent companies that could collectively compete under a strong global brand and symbolize one touchpoint for customers everywhere.

Results

Conversion to the new brand architecture involved a large capital investment during a period of complex organizational and technological change. Landor developed a comprehensive brand resource management website for FedEx, designed to make the core meaning of the brand resonate with employees and creative marketing teams. With more than 3,000 downloads, this website houses the brand assets of all FedEx operating companies. It features a global brand management feedback and approval loop—when a marketing piece is designed and submitted, it is tested against the core brand attributes, and the sponsoring manager receives feedback within 36 hours.

The FedEx Kinko's Office and Print Center brand powerfully redefines the future of the business services marketplace.*

Profile : By acquiring Kinko's in 2003, FedEx has advanced its global business-to-business service brand to include more than 1,200 digitally connected retail centers worldwide. The new network offers digital printing and presentation services, video conferencing, wireless access, computer rentals, office products, and FedEx Express and FedEx Ground shipping services. While FedEx was launching the air express industry, an entrepreneur named Paul Orfala launched Kinko's in a college town and started to build a strong, consumer-friendly culture.

Project goals

Build on the synergy of two recognizable brands.

Name the merged entity.

Position the brand as a one-stop resource for businesses and consumers.

Create a visual identity and retail presence.

Introduce the merger to team members, employees and customers.

*Fred Smith
 Founder, Chairman, and CEO
 FedEx Corp.

The FedEx and Kinko's merger will substantially increase our retail presence worldwide and will enable both companies to take advantage of growth opportunities in the fast-moving digital economy.

The new brand will serve as a beacon to businesses large and small searching for a total business solutions center.

Fred Smith
Founder, Chairman, and CEO
FedEx Corp.

Process and strategy

The challenge presented to Landor Associates by Gayle Christensen, FedEx managing director of brand management, was to convey the strong affinity between the two brands, and to position the new brand as the world's leading provider of document solutions and business services. The firm began its discovery and analysis process by conducting global research on the equity and imagery associated with the brands, and discovered that "the real strength of Kinko's was its name; no other word represented 'a place for overnight copying, computers, video conferencing and WiFi.'"

Key to the new strategy was evolving the FedEx brand to include a retail presence and an engaging customer experience. The new name, FedEx Kinko's Office and Print Center, builds on the strength of both brands.

Creative solution

The name was aligned with FedEx brand architecture. A new signature included a luminous brand icon that sends a bold signal to the marketplace about new offerings. Each color in the icon was designed to convey a service: global shipping express services are orange, ground shipping is green, and the retail centers are blue, inspired by Kinko's primary corporate color. The nexus of the icon is purple, a color that is known by all FedEx companies to symbolize a can-do spirit; purple is also the lead color in all company signatures.

The fresh and friendly look and feel of the new brand was developed and applied to signage, uniforms, stationery systems, vehicles, new office products, and the website. A series of brand engagement launch pieces were developed to introduce the new brand to employees, customers, and shareholders by clearly conveying the new brand's aspirations and character. New standards were developed and added to the comprehensive online FedEx Brand Resource Management tool.

Results

FedEx Kinko's has strengthened the FedEx competitive positioning by broadening its reach and responding to marketplace business trends. The new brand identity was launched in 2004 at an event with team members and employees. The conversion of Kinko's stores to total business solutions centers took place over a year and a half period after the merger announcement to the press.

FedEx Kinko's represents another generation of FedEx branding transformation that anticipates the needs of our customers, whether they are mobile professionals, or large corporations.

Gayle Christiansen
Managing Director
Global Brand Management
FedEx

Our highest objective is to introduce the right people to the right companies. Our company believes in placing people, not resumes, candidates, or employees.*

Profile : Find Great People International is a recruiting firm that finds and places people in professional, technical, and managerial positions on a permanent and contract basis nationally and internationally.

Project goals

Take an established identity from tired to inspired.

Create an emotional connection within the company and its clients.

Fascinate, inspire, reward, and engage kindred spirits.

*John D. Uprichard
 President
 Find Great People International

We believe that a company will be successful if they create an atmosphere that fascinates, inspires, rewards and engages not only everyone who comes into contact with it, but their staff as well.

Robbin Phillips
President
Brains on Fire

Process and strategy

When Phillips International, a recruiting agency, was bought by a younger, energetic management team, the agency was lackluster and looked like it was stuck in the 1960s. The new management hired Brains on Fire, a national identity company based in South Carolina, to suggest a name change and develop a strong brand identity that would cohesively flow with their new vision of a focus-proven agency.

Brains on Fire interviewed clients who had worked with Phillips and other recruiting agencies to find out what companies were looking for in a staffing agency. The identity firm reviewed competitors' websites and materials to get a solid understanding of the recruiting industry. In its research, it learned that most companies were seeking great people to bring on their teams. Brains on Fire immediately recognized the potential and the energy in the phrase "find great people," and recommended that Phillips International adopt the phrase as its new company name.

Initially Phillips hesitated because of the bold guarantee the name promised. Inspired by the vision and energy, Phillips International finally became Find Great People International.

Creative solution

The name change created an internal shift within the company culture. With guidance from Brains on Fire, Find Great People International's staff revised all of the company's written materials, rewriting them in a coherent, simple language that left the tired, traditional placement lingo behind. The staff regularly reads books on business and professional development and uses those books as catalysts for internal discussions about greatness. The previously drab interiors of the Find Great People International offices were changed. Brains on Fire designed a new logo, new business cards, new marketing collateral, and a repurposed website. It trained the staff members to change their vocabulary and incorporate the word "find" in their internal lingo.

Results

The new name acted as a catalyst that inspired and challenged the staff to live up to the brand promise. Find Great People International doubled its staff size in one year and increased its revenues 175% in two years. The branding process ignited the soul of the company, awakening the staff to the true value. In 2005, Find Great People was named one of the fastest growing companies in South Carolina by the accounting firm, Elliott Davis.

Brains on Fire helped us realize that we had to shed our old skin to rediscover the greatness in our company that had been there all along.

John D. Uprichard
President
Find Great People
International

2003

Now

In the spirit of inquiry and discovery embodied by Benjamin Franklin, the mission of The Franklin Institute is to inspire an understanding and passion for science and technology learning.*

Profile : The Franklin Institute Science Museum, founded in 1824, attracts more than one million visitors a year to its interactive presentations and unique historic displays. The museum's hands-on approach to science and technology is popular among both adults and children. The two-story, walk-through heart is one of the top attractions, in addition to the Fels Planetarium, the Tuttleman IMAX Theater, and the science super store.

Project goals

Design an identity that is bold, timeless, and simple.

Design a symbol that appeals to schoolchildren, the global scientific community, and corporate partners.

Appeal to local, national, and international audiences.

Visualize a twenty-first century institution.

Develop alternate signatures for two names.

*Franklin Institute
 Mission Statement

The
Franklin Institute

The Franklin Institute
Science Museum

In the end, the Institute's ability to touch lives— influencing everyday decisions, directing careers and inspiring a lifelong passion for science and technology learning—is the ultimate measure of our success.

Dennis M. Wint
President and CEO
The Franklin Institute Science Museum

Process and strategy

In 1989 The Franklin Institute was expanding dramatically to include a Future Center and an IMAX Theater. Allemann, Almquist + Jones were hired to design a new identity appropriate to the institute's vision and history. AA+J worked closely with a five-member steering committee over a six-month period. The chairman, chief scientist, chief astronomer, and the exhibit director were interviewed about aspirations, uniqueness, and culture. After reviewing the 175-year-old print archive, AA+J experienced the museum's exhibits. It also examined Philadelphia's cultural and entertainment destinations, other institutions that carried the Franklin name, and science museums around the world.

Since The Franklin Institute was brilliant at merging science and technology with a sense of wonder and fun, AA+J believed that a sense of magic was needed. The design team examined the broadest range of possibilities for symbols, from visual translations of the hands-on theme, to various scientific metaphors.

Creative solution

After exploring hundreds of ideas, a number of sketches were analyzed and rethought. AA+J recommended a bold red mark as the primary identifier, with a clean, highly legible treatment for the name. The final mark creates the impression of a sunrise behind a planet and the transient moment of an eclipse. It is a sophisticated mark with layers of meaning and ambiguity, and yet it is inviting, warm, and immediate. When asked about it, a five-year-old said, "Of course, it's the sun, moon, and earth."

Futura Bold, a highly legible font, was redrawn and modified. Hans Allemann created a ligature between the T and the h, altered the relationships of the cap height to the x height, and completely redrew the M. This work was critical because of the name's length and legibility. Three modified versions of the mark were also developed to guarantee reproduction quality at the wide range of sizes required for applications.

Results

The identity, which was created in the late 1980s, continues to be fresh and dynamic. Because of the iconic quality, the mark works at minute scales and as large environmental graphic elements. Its form weaves in and out of layers of visual information without losing its ability to communicate. A recent capital campaign raised more than $60 million for more state-of-the-art exhibits and other renovations. AA+J continues to provide design services for a range of initiatives.

We usually begin with very predictable and obvious ideas, but the beauty of the identity design process is that it is totally unpredictable. We never know what the process will reveal. I have been designing marks for forty years, and the process still astonishes me.

Hans-U. Allemann
Principal, Allemann, Almquist + Jones

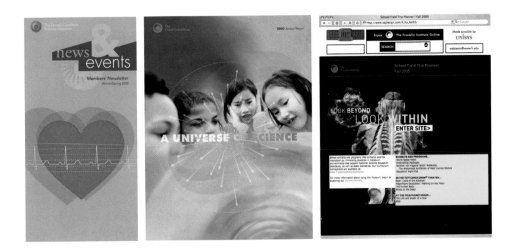

Everything begins with the customer. We focus on all elements of our customer's traveling experience. When we say that we will make it easy for our customers, we mean it.*

Profile : DSB (the Danish state railway system) embarked on a retail initiative for their subbrand, Kort & Godt, creating a new concept in travel kiosks. The kiosks sell not only tickets, but also coffee, pastry, fresh salads, newspapers, and other products to fast-moving travelers. This convenient concept is one expression of DSB values, which are used to drive the business and serve customers.

Project goals

Create a visual identity for the retail concept and subbrand.

Express the value "Making it easy."

Develop a distinct expression in the public space.

Develop a signage, commercials, packaging, and products.

*Keld Sengelov
Chief Executive Officer
DSB

DSB believes that good design is good business. Kort & Godt is an integral part of DSB. Although our retail brand requires a unique graphic personality, it also needs to reflect the DSB program and distinctiveness.

Pia Bech Mathiesen
Director of Design
DSB

Innovation is not about technology alone. It is about understanding real-world people and creating products and services that fulfill human needs in new and better ways.

Kontrapunkt

Process and strategy

When in 2003, DSB decided to create a more customer-friendly environment in railway stations, they repurchased the DSB kiosks. Kontrapunkt worked closely with DSB to create the new concept, combining the purchase of tickets and convenience products in one shop. This strategy was an extension of DSB's consumer promise, "Making it easy." Kort & Godt was a subbrand of DSB and needed to co-exist with the DSB logo and identity system. The project began with a full day briefing from DSB on the project, followed by an internal brainstorming session on the concept of the kiosk. The creative team determined that the success of the concept depended on fast service as well as a range of great products. Transparent walls and upscale positioning were central to the brand's easy and accessible image.

Creative solution

The new logo used a specially designed, expanded version of DSB's Via typeface to underscore the link with DSB. Photography of real people using DSB and Kort & Godt in public places was art directed and photographed. A new color palette was developed from DSB's identity program, and applied to environment and products. Red signals hot food and beverages while green is for cold products. The simple and flexible signage system was designed to be easily adapted to the variety of architectural styles in the stations. It comprises vertical banners and transparent horizontal bands. The transparency of the facades signal openness, and enable the public to look into the shops through dot patterns of colored foils.

Results

DSB views the Kort & Godt shops as an important and tangible expression of their customer commitment for better standards of comfort and convenience. Research has shown that the shops have influenced customer satisfaction and the new subbrand has also resulted in increased revenues.

DSB values drive, service, quality, and new product development:

Makes it easy
We make it easy for customers and for each other

Committed
We identify opportunities

Value-adding

We add value for our customers

Efficient
We will become even better at what we do

Responsible
We acknowledge our responsibilities

Each day, a half million journeys are taken on DSB, which provides rail service within Denmark and across international borders.

Photography: Claus Løgstrop

Kort & Godt means "fast and easy."

227

Inspired by the nineteenth-century farmer who grew crops for flavor rather than high yield, Late July aspires to be the best-tasting organic snack in the world.

Profile : Creating a new business category, Late July was the first company to bring organic crackers to the marketplace. Unlike its conventional counterparts, Late July's products contain no trans fats, hydrogenated oils, preservatives, or artificial flavors or colors. One hundred percent organic, the ingredients are dairy free, vegetarian, and kosher.

Project goals

Design a unique and memorable identity for a new niche market.

Position products as the best-tasting, all-natural snacks in the world.

Design a modular packaging system across product lines.

Communicate the tradition and values of nineteenth-century farming.

Romanticize the cracker.

Express the vision of the founders.

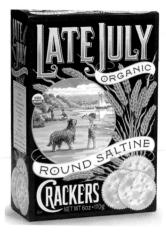

Process and strategy

The name of the company, Late July, came from the founder's childhood memory of lazy long summer days at the beach and nights filled with fireflies and magic. The design process began even before the first cracker was fully developed and produced. In the midst of her pregnancy, co-founder Nicole Dawes retained Louise Fili Ltd.

Fili's extensive knowledge and experience in the food industry, as well as her signature imaginative use of historical reference and superior craft, jumpstarted the brand strategy to reference a bygone era of safe and clean environments. Dawes, the company president, and a passionate entrepreneur, envisioned a small boy on a Cape Cod beach with his dog, a Briard. Fili, whose design office looks more like a nineteenth-century food and flea market, easily immersed her team into the spirit of an earlier century. Although the company launch was based on a cracker line, Fili's team needed to consider all of the brand extensions from the outset to create a sustainable master brand.

Creative solution

Fili knew that everything needed to be vintage. Late July's logotype incorporates a gradation within the lettering and was inspired by turn-of-the-century biscuit tin typography. Chad Roberts, master typographer/designer in Fili's firm, created all of the lettering on the front of the package, including the net weight. A British illustrator, Graham Evernden, was retained to create the boy on a Cape Cod beach because his style approximates chromolithography. Evernden also illustrated the organic, soft winter wheat, grown at family-owned mills. He worked from the first samples of crackers, before they were mass produced. In the cracker world, consumers expect saltine boxes to be blue, and Ritz crackers boxes are always red. This color system was honored in the cracker line. A food copywriter also joined the creative team to ensure that the idea of nostalgic packaging carried through to the language used. Each future package will feature the same organic banner and illustration.

Results

True to the brand, the packaging was printed on recycled stock. Late July was able to get a significant amount of press since it introduced the first organic saltine, classic rich, and cheddar cheese crackers in the marketplace. Eliminating heart-clogging trans fats appeals to a health conscious consumer. Since saltines have been sold for 100 years, and Ritz, the world's most popular cracker, was founded in 1933, the world was ready to have the category transformed. Since the successful launch of the first three crackers, Late July has launched a new line of sandwich crackers for children. These contain organic peanut butter and organic cheddar cheese.

Organic provides a safety net consumers can't find with other products. Buying organic is an easy step that parents can take to protect their families.

Nicole Dawes
President and COO
Late July Organic Snacks

You can design a package that is appropriate to the contents, and it doesn't have to shout.

Louise Fili
Louise Fili Ltd.

Inspiration and information are the heartbeat of the Martha Stewart brand. Quality, beauty, originality, and clarity of information are the guiding principles. We adhere to these principles in every medium.*

Profile : Martha Stewart Living Omnimedia (MSLO), a public company, represents a cluster of unified brands, producing television programming, magazines, and books, as well as home and garden products. *Martha Stewart Living* quickly became a publishing phenomenon, integrating design, cooking, crafts, and gardening into readers' lifestyles. The magazine not only launched a cult-like following, but also served as a springboard for dozens of new initiatives and products.

Project goals

Interpret the brand for the mass market.

Keep content fresh, inventive, and relevant.

Glorify the beauty of everyday objects.

Convey respect for the customer.

*Gael Towey
Executive Vice President and
Creative Director
Martha Stewart Living
Omnimedia

My founding big idea was that the subject of living is indeed a limitless subject, one that can be expanded and expounded upon, and enlarged and extolled.

Martha Stewart
Founder
Martha Stewart Living Omnimedia

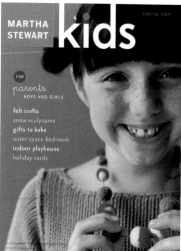

Process and strategy

The company had their own team of experts in various fields such as food, gardening, crafts, decorating, and weddings, but in order to branch out into retailing, they needed to collaborate with individuals who could bring Martha Stewart's vision and sense of style to a new marketing channel. The challenge was to keep these ideals at the heart of the brand experience throughout all mediums, from reading magazines and viewing television broadcasts to strolling down the aisles of Kmart and shopping online.

The how-to information treats the consumer with respect and creates a feeling of mutual trust—whether it is twenty-eight varieties of figs tested, tasted, and photographed for a magazine, or the planting instructions on the back of seed packets. Doyle Partners worked with MSLO to interpret the brand identity for the mass market called Martha Stewart Everyday.

Creative solution

In every category the design is unified by a coherent expression of whiteness and brightness that allows the product itself to dominate. The packaging and environments are now designed exclusively in-house and encompass an intelligent yet whimsical feel. The retail environments have transcended the discount store experience for the customer.

Color was integral not only to the design but also as an element to trigger emotions, memories, and sensations. The use of color in the magazine evolved into a 256-color palette known as Martha Stewart Everyday Colors, a line of interior and exterior paints featuring not-so-everyday names such as Himalayan Eyes, Ursa Minor, and Book Binding Green. Towey brought in a cadre of world-renowned photographers to glorify the beauty of everyday objects, an approach that became intrinsic to the soul of the brand. Under her direction, a common garden hose took on a new elegance when it coiled around a lush garden. The 456 packets in the line of seeds featured photographs of flowers, herbs, or vegetables held in a hand to give the consumer an immediate sense of scale.

Results

Martha Stewart Everyday has been a beacon to democratize good design. A commitment to clarity of information is apparent in each expression of the brand in every medium.

What began as a magazine evolved into books, syndicated and cable TV programs, and hundreds of products. Because the brand vision intuits the potential for beauty and delight in the most ordinary of items, there is no end to the possibilities.

MINI provides an alternative culture of driving—
a closer relationship between driver, car,
and road, and a unique ability to elicit an
emotional reaction.

Profile : Designed to be a four-person, affordable, and safe car by Sir Alex Issogonis in 1959, MINI Cooper had achieved superstar status by the mid-1960s. Minis were owned by the rich and famous from the Beatles to Enzo Ferrari. In 2001 the company decided to relaunch the car in the American market and reintroduce the legend.

Project goals

Launch a small car in the land of SUVs.

Achieve sales targets in North America.

Develop the MINI brand experience.

Create a campaign that generates buzz.

Transform the MINI to American iconic status.

Our work with MINI was to a mindset, not a demographic. Advertising wasn't the answer; innovation was.

Tom Birk
Director of Strategy
Crispin Porter + Bogusky

People need emotional navigation.

Colin Drummond
Crispin Porter + Bogusky

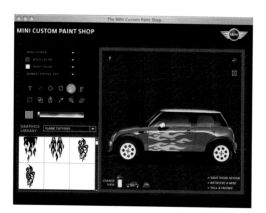

On miniusa.com, you can go to the MINI custom paint shop to personalize your car.

Process and strategy

Crispin Porter + Bogusky (CP+B) was hired as a brand advocacy partner, charged with the mission to launch MINI in the United States, a market where SUVs dominated and small car sales were at a fifteen-year low. The client wanted to prevent the car from being perceived as a fad or as a car that appealed only to women. CP+B looked at fads and icons, from Elvis, to Apple, to understand why icons endure. Tom Birk, Director of Strategy, CP+B, identified ten characteristics of iconic brands and realized that MINI had them all—most important, a defining signature look and a unique ability to elicit a physical or emotional reaction. The car was definitely a smile-generating machine.

CP+B's strategy was to break convention, using nontraditional media and traditional media in unconventional ways. Its goal was to create endless opportunities for people to come in contact with the MINI, and to do it on a budget that was 10% of what a goliath U.S. automobile company would spend.

Creative solution

CP+B developed an integrated grassroots campaign designed to create buzz and a new culture around "motoring." The defining signature look inspired the creative team to think outside the box. "Let's Motor" was the new call to action, and all copy was written to capture the fun and exhilarating driving experience. Audacious media planners rose to the challenge with innovative space purchasing—the first time ever that the borders of editorial pages of national magazines were bought. MINIs rode on top of SUVs in key markets. MINI was a centerfold in *Playboy.* The cover of the *Weekly World News* declared "Mutant steals Mini Cooper car for a joy ride." MINI was launched without a national television campaign, a historical feat.

Results

"One year after the MINI brand was launched in the U.S., its brand awareness has more than quadrupled and sales have exceeded expectations by 50%," said Jack Pitney, Vice President, MINI USA. In 2003 the MINI was named North American Car of the year and generated numerous industry articles. In 2004 the MINI reached 85% awareness. The MINI has surpassed its sales projections every month since the launch.

The characteristics of iconic brands
Developed by Tom Birk,
Crispin Porter + Bogusky

Defining signature look

Ability to elicit a physical or emotional reaction

Tendency to take on characteristics from outside the category

Owning a unique benefit or position within a category or redefining a category altogether

Ability to connect with and reflect the personality, attitudes, and values of a broad user base

Tendency to reinvent themselves to stay salient

Ability to move people beyond mere loyalty to passion and devotion

Often imitated

Always appropriate/never out of style

Hanging out with (borrowing equity from) other icons

MINIs rode piggyback on SUVs in big cities.

We are committed to advancing individualized medicine by discovering, developing, and marketing innovative products to guide and improve treatment of serious viral, immunologic, and oncologic diseases.*

Profile : In 2004 ViroLogic, a biotechnology company, merged with Aclara Biosciences to develop and market innovative products designed to help physicians and pharmaceutical companies optimize treatment regimens for cancer and infectious diseases, leading to better outcomes and reduced costs.

Project goals

Discover and articulate a sustainable positioning strategy for the merged company.

Develop a name and a tagline that underscores its healthcare mission.

Create a differentiated identity and unified image across media.

Design a visual identity system and guidelines for marketing and communications.

*William D. Young
CEO and Chairman
Monogram Biosciences

Process and strategy

Lori Kapner, president of Kapner Consulting, and her team worked closely with the CEO, CFO, and senior management to define the new brand's most compelling attributes. Kapner conducted extensive interviews with customers, physicians, and investors to gain an external perspective on the company's unique characteristics. Ultimately, Kapner recommended that the company visibly "own" the concept of personalized medicine. The new name needed to be dramatically different from others in the competitive arena—Genomic Health, LabCorp, Specialty Labs, Virco, and Vysis. The creative team generated hundreds of name candidates before choosing twenty-nine to present to ViroLogic's management team.

Creative solution

Monogram Biosciences was the new name developed by Kapner to unite the merged entities and convey their common expertise, and competitive difference. Monogram, a word meaning "a person's initials, used as an identifying mark" captures the concept of personalization. The name is easy to understand and remember and use of a real word was intended to set Monogram apart from the fabricated names that populate healthcare. The tagline, "The Mark of Individualized Medicine," was developed to assert the company's leadership in its category.

Kapner worked with design firm DeSantis Breindel to balance the name's approachability with a design that conveys scientific excellence and precision. The logo's uniquely styled "o" represents a cell—the basis of all molecular medicine—and is suggests the important concept of targeted medicine. Each letter in the typeface is hand drawn. Kapner's team created an integrated design system, and guidelines to help the company manage the new system. The website was designed by Ignite Health.

Results

The new identity was launched in September 2005 with a number of coordinated events and communications. All employees received new business cards, T-shirts and clocks with the new logo. Senior management had been briefed in advance, so they could answer all employee questions. The CEO presided over a company-wide celebration and the redesigned website was launched prior to the issuance of a press release, a webcast for the financial community, and a road show to investors and analysts. Industry specialists, physicians, scientists, and pharmaceutical companies received a series of personalized mailings and blast emails, prior to an industry conference. Business partners, collaborators, and vendors also received materials.

> **The visual identity needed to convey a range of attributes given that they are scientists, they are businessmen and they are humanists.**
>
> Brian Fingeret
> Creative Director
> DeSantis Breindel

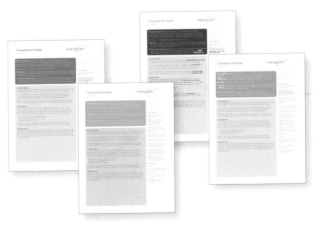

Mutual of Omaha provides life, Medicare supplement, long-term care, and disability insurance for individuals and families. It also offers a full range of employee benefits and retirement plans for businesses.

Profile : Mutual of Omaha launched Wild Kingdom in 1963, one of the most popular televised nature programs of all time. Mutual of Omaha became a well-known American brand for baby boomers and the most recognizable insurance brand. Founded in 1909, the company has assets more than $18.5 billion. Owned by its policyholders, the company distributes its products through agent and brokerage networks.

Project goals

Achieve consistency across marketing and corporate communications.

Bring continuity to the nomenclature.

Unify the visual communications, color, and typography.

Create an imagery archive and approach.

Introduce the branding program to all employees.

We consolidated all brand management functions— Marketing and Corporate Communications, Public Relations, Sponsorships, Multimedia Communications, and Graphic Design—into one department, dedicated to customer communication.

John Hildenbiddle
SVP Global Brand Management and
Public Relations
Mutual of Omaha

Process and strategy

John Hildenbiddle, SVP Global Brand Management and Public Relations, was hired to revitalize the Mutual of Omaha brand and achieve measurable results. The brand management team wrote a positioning statement, building the brand promise into all initiatives. They realized they needed to revitalize and contemporize the brand. The team's goal was twofold: to establish the brand in the minds of a new generation of families, thirty-five and under, and rekindle feelings built on the brand's positive attributes with everyone who grew up watching Mutual of Omaha's "Wild Kingdom." Hildenbiddle retained Crosby Associates to revitalize the brand internally and externally. Hildenbiddle and Crosby collaborated to create a consistent graphic direction that visually communicated the company's new tagline, *Begin Today.*

In 2000 market research revealed that the brand was perceived as positive, caring, and family oriented, a recognition of the company's integrity and values. However, on the flip side, there was the perception on the part of young people that the brand was like your father's Oldsmobile — reliable, but neither snappy nor hip.

Bart Crosby
Principal
Crosby Associates

Creative solution

Crosby Associates designed a simple, coordinated system to visually unify the company and build brand recognition. The symbol and logotype were refined, and the brand architecture for affiliate companies was standardized. Blue was identified as the primary color, supported by a distinctive palette. All communications, from PowerPoint presentations, to promotional literature, were based on a structured framework that used dramatically cropped photography. A visual style for all photography was designed, and a company photo archive was developed.

Results

Hildenbiddle's goal was to enhance the company's reputation and engage each employee in protecting the Mutual of Omaha brand. Before the full-scale consumer launch, eight kick-off meetings were held with all employees to fully explain the new branding initiatives and motivate them to become active Brand Ambassadors.

The new program was launched nationally in 2001 along with the online branding site. A road show was rolled out to thirty key offices. The company installed and promoted an 800 number to field calls: 1-800-One-Look. Every employee, agent, and brokerage in the company received a Begin Today kit, which consisted of a brand promise brochure, an identity standards poster, and a Begin Today T-shirt. The poster's headline was "It's new. It's blue. It's you." Two years after the branding program was launched, metrics reveal a successful outcome. The company moved from twelfth to fifth on "Consideration to buy," moved from fifteenth to sixth on "Unaided Awareness," and achieved an unaided awareness of 99 percent.

The New School stands for critical thinking and civic engagement; creative, disciplined, and collaborative self expression; fearless participation in the debates of the day; and a willingness to embrace change.*

Profile : After World War I, The New School became a strong voice of new political and artistic thought. Based in New York City's Greenwich Village, the university houses eight schools and more than 8,000 undergraduate and graduate students. In 2003 Bob Kerrey, former senator of Nebraska, became its President.

Project goals

Bring The New School's brand to life.

Develop a consistent naming structure for the university, divisions, and programs.

Create a clear core positioning strategy.

Develop a memorable voice.

Develop simple visual and writing guidelines.

*Bob Kerrey
President
The New School

The New School Personality
Siegel & Gale developed a set of unifying attributes that were relevant to all eight schools.

Activist
The New School has a unique history of social activism, progressive thinking, and internationalism. The New School has always strived for positive and meaningful change.

Eclectic
The New School is unconventional and different, with a constant appetite for the new and experimental.

Open
The New School is multifaceted, diverse, and international, and it appreciates the ranges of ages, origins, and cultures.

Street-Smart
The New School is not an insulated institution. It is part of New York City and the larger world. It is urban, vibrant, and dynamic.

Articulate
The New School fosters personal expression and choice, challenging students to be in active dialogue with the world around them.

Creative
The New School is made up of writers, thinkers, and artists creating their own worlds and systems of ideas.

Courageous
The New School, since its founding, has been a place where people are not afraid to take a stand on what they think is right.

THE NEW SCHOOL
A UNIVERSITY

THE NEW SCHOOL FOR GENERAL STUDIES

THE NEW SCHOOL FOR SOCIAL RESEARCH

MILANO THE NEW SCHOOL FOR MANAGEMENT AND URBAN POLICY

PARSONS THE NEW SCHOOL FOR DESIGN

EUGENE LANG COLLEGE THE NEW SCHOOL FOR LIBERAL ARTS

MANNES COLLEGE THE NEW SCHOOL FOR MUSIC

THE NEW SCHOOL FOR DRAMA

THE NEW SCHOOL FOR JAZZ AND CONTEMPORARY MUSIC

Process and strategy

Project Mirror's central goal was to provide a coherent, accurate portrayal of the university's identity. In an intensive two-year research study, Siegel & Gale interviewed a cross section from all eight schools, which included trustees, deans, faculty, administration, and other stakeholders. An invitation to participate in a web-based email survey was emailed to 1,800 students, faculty, prospects, alumni, and board members. An in-depth communications audit was conducted. The data collected was rich in narrative responses. Numerous dichotomies were identified. Although the school was known worldwide and each of the schools had significant reputations, the school's eight divisions bore no resemblance to each other or the parent. There was also no schoolwide catalog. Coherent key differentiators that were relevant to all of the schools were developed.

Creative solution

Siegel & Gale developed a new naming system for the eight schools so that the brand architecture was coherent. "No longer are we a collection of interesting schools; we are a university," remarked President Kerrey. The new visual identity is a wordmark in and out of focus; the wordmark is not fixed but has multiple states to exemplify a school that is active and alive. The design team wanted to embody the unconventional, edgy, and dynamic qualities of the school in a program that is kinetic, dynamic, and nontraditional.

Results

Every effort has been made to engage the entire community in the vision, identity, and positioning of the university. The website has the entire project dynamically presented, including the research process and findings, the strategy, and the identity examples. The transformation was well covered in the press, and new student enrollment is up 16% overall and up close to 23% at the undergraduate level.

Project Mirror is much more than a marketing effort—it not only defines our identity to the world, it helps us lay out what sets us apart from other institutions of higher education.

Bob Kerrey
President
The New School

The New School's positioning expresses what they stand for, what sets them apart, and why that's relevant to their constituencies.

Alan Siegel
President
Siegel + Gale

We eschew the cautious and predictable in favor of the courageous and bold.

Excerpt, The New School Vision

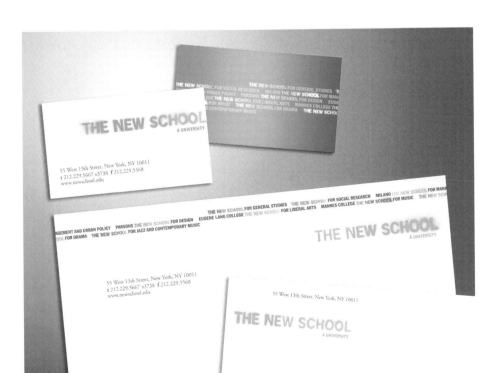

The Olympic Games are a celebration of human spirit and achievement, challenging athletes of the world to be the best they can be. The festival itself transcends the politics of a fractured world to focus on our shared humanity.

Profile : Four billion people watched the 2004 Olympics on 300 different channels. Events were simultaneously streamed into mobile phones and websites. Dormant for 1,500 years, the games were revived in 1913 by Baron Pierre de Coubertin, who designed the five colored interlocking rings Olympic trademark.

From left to right:*

Tokyo 1964:
Unknown

Mexico 1968:
Lance Wyman,
Pedro Ramirez Vásquez,
and Eduardo Terrazas

Munich 1972:
Otl Aicher

Montréal 1976:
Unknown

Moscow 1980:
Vladimir Arsentyev

Los Angeles 1984:
Deborah Sussman
and Jon Jerde

Seoul 1988:
Seung Choon Yang

Barcelona 1992:
Jose Maria Trias

Atlanta 1996:
Landor Associates

Sydney 2000:
Mark Armstrong

Athens 2004:
Wolff Olins

Beijing 2008:
Guo Chunning

*10C/Olympic Museum
Collections

Olympic Games: Baron Pierre de Coubertin

TOKYO 1964

Munich1972

GAMES OF THE XXIVTH OLYMPIAD SEOUL 1988

Barcelona'92

Atlanta 1996

Process and strategy

Olympic Games help host countries boost tourism, build new infrastructure, and display their brand globally. The host country gets special rights to use the Olympic logo owned by the International Olympic Committee. Traditionally each country designs its own proprietary trademark and mascot to garner greater attention and marketability, helping sell products and attract corporate sponsors. Some countries, such as China and Greece, held global competitions that drew thousands of entries. Experienced world-class design firms are needed to ensure that the identities can be graphically powerful and reproduced across thousands of applications. Designers are also needed to envision the look and feel of the Games, the environmental graphics, and everything from the medal design, to the sports icons, to the interactive multimedia displays.

Creative solution

The best Olympic trademarks engender pride, express a cultural difference, and look great on television and mobile phones. The challenge is to capture the spirit of the Olympics and combine it with the distinctive culture. Like other icons, the best ones have a strong central idea. The Athens 2004 emblem is an olive branch wreath, designed to express the heritage and legacy of the ancient Games in a color inspired by the Aegean sea and Greek sky. The Bejiing 2008 script is inspired by bamboo carvings from the ancient Han Dynasty.

Results

The increasing breadth and reach of the Olympic Games have made them a powerful platform for building brands for the cities and countries that host them, the corporations that fund them, and the athletes who aspire to celebrity status. The symbols of the Games are reproduced millions of times across a wide range of media and engender pride and ownership. The identities are traditionally launched in a large multimedia event.

The ever-existing challenge for each Olympics is not only to re-emphasize the original ideals, but also to be part of a process of moving them into the future.
Wolff Olins

Montréal 1976

Игры
XXII Олимпиады
Москва
1980

Games of the XXIIIrd Olympiad Los Angeles 1984

Sydney 2000

ΑΘΗΝΑ 2004

Beijing 2008

The Parkinson's Disease Foundation envisions a world without Parkinson's. Its mission is clear: to explore science, to advance treatments, and to provide information, education, and support.

Profile : The Parkinson's Disease Foundation (PDF) is a leading national authority on Parkinson's disease research, patient education, and public advocacy. PDF funds scientific research and supports the nearly one million people in the United States living with Parkinson's, their families, and their caregivers. Since its founding in 1957, PDF has awarded more than $50 million to research the causes of and cures for Parkinson's.

Project goals

Position PDF as a national leader in Parkinson's disease.

Express PDF's vision of hope through research, education, and advocacy.

Design an icon.

Create a sustainable, cohesive, economical brand identity system and toolbox.

Develop a tagline and core messages that express PDF's mission.

Parkinson's Disease Foundation

Hope through Research · Education · Advocacy

Process and strategy

PDF selected Carla Hall Design Group (CHDG) to guide a strategic and creative process that would result in a new, sustainable identity system. PDF Executive Director Robin Elliott believed that a meaningful icon would identify Parkinson's with PDF for all organizational activities: development, education, advocacy, and research. CHDG's team interviewed PDF's staff and board of directors and attended support group meetings to deepen their understanding of Parkinson's. CHDG researched the identities of peer organizations, examined their use of color and message, and developed a tagline. A communications "blueprint" and an economical, easy-to-use toolbox guided PDF and its technology, direct mail, and design partners.

Creative solution

The tulip is an internationally recognized symbol of hope for people living with Parkinson's. Parkinson's disease was first discovered by British doctor Dr. James Parkinson in 1817. A renowned Dutch horticulturist and a person with Parkinson's, J. W. S. Van der Wereld honored Dr. Parkinson by naming a tulip for him. Since no other U.S.-based Parkinson's organization had used this icon, design director Kate Dautrich chose to create a bold solitary tulip with three distinct petals, each symbolizing a core program represented in the tagline: "hope through research, education and advocacy." The symbol is geometric, objective, and clear. The bright yellow inspires optimism and differentiates PDF from the abundant red used in most disease management brands. CHDG also designed an integrated template system for the website, publications, and direct mail based on consistent placement of the signature and an imaginative use of typography and imagery.

Results

The system was launched in 2004 after a six-month collaborative process. Communicating consistently to PDF's audiences provides a distinctive visual platform for building awareness and raising funds. The guidelines facilitate the expansion of the system, align content with design, and control budgets. The commitment to adhering to the program has been made throughout the organization.

This process helped us to focus on who we are and what we do, and to determine how to clearly communicate our identity to scientists, people living with Parkinson's and their families.

Robin Elliott
Executive Director
Parkinson's Disease Foundation

Building awareness requires a disciplined and imaginative process. We have developed a communications "blueprint" to help clients identify the right marketing channels to use.

Carla Hall
Principal
Carla Hall Design Group

Core Materials and Patient Education

Logo

Stationery System

PDF Folder

PDF Newsletter

PDF Direct Mail

Web Site

Annual Report (template)

PDF Overview brochure

PDF Newsletter

Getting Involved. Newly Diagnosed, Mid-Diagnosed brochure

Q&A

Leaflets (15) Medication / Fact Sheets

These icons represent the various ways that Parkinson's Disease Foundation communicates.

The two major branches of the Presbyterian Church, separated since the Civil War, were reunited in 1983, and a seal, also referred to as a symbol, to represent this unification was needed.

Profile : The Presbyterian Church has 2.5 million members, 11,200 congregations, and 21,000 pastors in the United States. An eight-person task force comprising theologians, pastors, educators, an artist, and a musician was responsible for determining what theological ideas and images should be incorporated into the new symbol.

Project goals

Design a symbol that represents the church's mission.

Design a symbol that is emotive and evocative.

Reflect the ordered and structured nature of the church.

Suggest the vitality of the church.

Integrate theological images and ideas.

Represent the unification of two branches.

The Cross

The Pulpit

The Fish

The Fire

The Dove

The Cup

The Book

The Triangle

Process and strategy

The task force, led by John M. Muldar, Ph.D., conducted a national search for a designer and, after interviewing forty-six firms, chose Malcolm Grear Designers. The task force had extensive theological and philosophical discussions around which images should be included in the seal. Grear's studio brought in Martha Gregor Geothals, Ph.D., a historian and artist trained in theology, to give a historical perspective on the history and meaning of Christian symbols.

The primary goal was the creation of a design that would have an emotive and evocative character, suggesting the vitality of the church's mission. The design, however, needed a level of formality to reflect the ordered and structured nature of the church. The seal also needed to serve as a symbolic statement of the unification.

Creative solution

What seemed like an impossible goal for any experienced designer evolved into a design process that generated close to 4,000 sketches. Grear was obsessed with finding an answer, but initially he thought he could never develop a design that would incorporate more than three of the theological ideas.

After an exhaustive exploration, Grear was able to incorporate eight ideas in the design of the mark: the cross, the pulpit, the fish, the fire, the descending dove, the cup, the book, and the triangle. Grear's recommendation to the diverse task force received unanimous approval, but that was only the first step. The church's charter required the General Assembly, composed of 2,500 individuals, to vote on it.

Results

The General Assembly staff developed a powerful video presentation about the seal and its meaning. The assembly gave Grear and Geothals a standing ovation, and the rest is history. It represented the first unanimous vote in the history of the Presbyterian Church. The story of the process was documented in a book written by Muldar, and the church's website contains an in-depth explanation of the meaning of the elements.

The seal has been applied to an endless variety of entities, from stained-glass windows, church bulletins, and Bibles, to informational signage and clothing. More than twenty years after the initial design, the Presbyterian Church leadership returned to Malcolm Grear Designers to request a redesign of its website and the creation of branding guidelines.

I worked on possibilities all day, every day, and most of every night. I dreamed about the symbol during whatever time was left to sleep.

Malcolm Grear
CEO
Malcolm Grear Designers

The design has proved to be a simple but eloquent statement of the Presbyterian Church's heritage, identity, and mission. I have used the seal to teach people the meaning of the Presbyterian tradition, and I have been intrigued by the way the seal itself engages people's imagination–it helps them understand the content and imagery of the Bible and the abstractions of doctrine and theology.

John M. Muldar, Ph.D.

Princeton's athletic program is powerfully connected to our educational mission. The synergy between the classroom and the playing field is what differentiates Princeton athletics from most other universities.*

Profile : Princeton University was founded in 1746 and is regarded as one of the leading research universities in the world. Approximately 4,700 undergraduate students come from more than forty-five countries, and close to half of its undergraduates compete in intercollegiate varsity or club sports. Its athletic department has thirty-eight NCAA sports.

Project goals

Design a comprehensive identity program for the department of athletics.

Design a coordinated kit of visual elements for uniforms and merchandise.

Connect Princeton's athletic history with its dynamic present.

Differentiate Princeton from other universities.

*Gary D. Walters
Director of Athletics
Princeton University

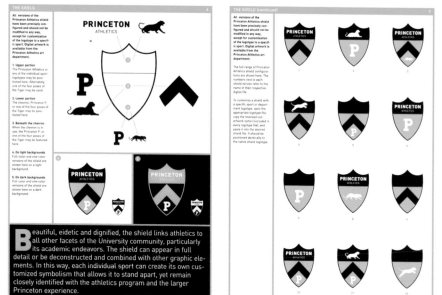

We feel that this new system reflects both Princeton's colorful athletic heritage and the extraordinary synergies between our classrooms and our playing fields.

Gary D. Walters
Director of Athletics
Princeton University

Identity program and guidelines designed by Pentagram.

Process and strategy

A university-wide steering committee was formed that included representatives of the athletics department and a cross section of university stakeholders. Michael Bierut, Pentagram partner, worked closely with Judith Friedman, director of development communications, who organized the project. Focus groups were conducted with students, alumni, faculty, coaches, and administrators. Bierut and the team reviewed Princeton's athletic history, photographs, and other memorabilia from the archive dating from the nineteenth century, and also toured the campus.

"We were struck by the consistency of all of the material, as well as the confidence and playfulness that runs through much of Princeton's visual history," remarked Friedman. "Our challenge was to tap into Princeton's complex culture in a way that would be authentic for people who know the university best," said Bierut.

Creative solution

Princeton University's distinctive new identity system will provide student-athletes, coaches, alumni, and fans with a strong and consistent look for athletic programs. The new system Pentagram designed is flexible and includes a unified family of visual elements: university shields, a new bold varsity "P," tiger silhouettes, and Princeton's core colors of orange and black. To prevent Princeton's venerable tiger from being just another cat, four distinctive elegant silhouettes of tigers were drawn, inspired by historic statuary on campus. Once Pentagram had finished the system, Friedman brought it back to all of the focus groups to build synergy and get feedback.

Results

The program was enthusiastically approved by President Shirley M. Tilghman and Gary Walters, Director of Athletics. The center spread of Princeton's newsletter, which is distributed to all alumni and friends, featured the new program, and its process, strategy, and family of elements. The new identity is evident on tickets, merchandise, and some team uniforms. The identity program will be implemented judiciously over time.

Princeton has an iconographic history but our athletic identity was not coherent. We thought that the challenge would be to design the ultimate Princeton tiger—what we found out across campus was that the shield itself had much more of an emotional connection.

John T. Miller
Director of Princetoniana and Special Projects
Princeton University

Newsletter spread designed by Ching Foster.

All of the elements in the kit of parts resonate with our history and the spirit of our University. One of the greatest things is that the new identity looks as if it had always existed.

Judith Friedman
Director of Development Communications
Princeton University

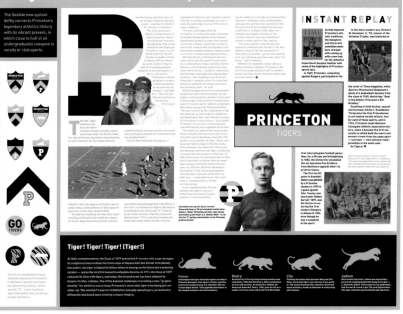

Our mission at Radio Free Europe/Radio Liberty is to promote democracy where human rights violations, regional conflicts, ethnic and religious hostilities, and controlled media are a part of every day life.*

Profile : Radio Free Europe/Radio Liberty (RFE/RL) is a private, international communications service that provides daily news, analysis, and current affairs programming to eastern and southeastern Europe, Russia, the Persian Gulf, and central and southwestern Asia. Founded in 1949, the network reaches 35 million people, is funded by the U.S. Congress, and broadcasts 1,000 hours a week to shortwave listeners across twelve time zones.

Project goals

Design an identity that embodies the ideals and values of RFE/RL.

Position RFE/RL as a global broadcast leader fostering freedom.

Create a universal image with positive connotations in eastern and western cultures.

Express a forward-looking spirit that is timeless.

Develop a brand architecture that works in twenty-eight languages.

*Thomas A. Dine
President
RadioFree Europe/Radio Liberty

**RadioFreeEurope
RadioLiberty**

Albanian
Arabic
Armenian
Avar
Azerbaijani
Belarusian
Bosnian
Chechen
Circassian
Crimean Tartar
Dari
Georgian
Kazakh
Kyrgyz
Macedonian
Pashto
Persian
Romanian
Russian
Serbian
Tajik
Tatar-Bashkir
Turkmen
Ukrainian
Uzbek

маршо радио	radio slobodna evropa	radio europa liberă
რადიო თავისუფლება	ozodlik radiosi	радио свобода
хуитьныгъэ радио	озодлик радиоси	azatlyk radiosy
radio evropa e lirë	азаттык радиосы	радио свобода
... радио	азаттык үналгысы	رادیو فردا
радио эркенлъи	радио слободна европа	رادیوی آزادی
azadliq radiosu	раднон озодй	د آزادي راديو
радыё свабода	azathq radiosi	إذاعة العراق الحر

Process and strategy

When Steff Geissbuhler was a partner at Chermayeff & Geismar,* he was given the challenge to design a logo that embodied freedom, civil society, and truth in journalism for an organization that broadcasts in twenty-eight languages.

Following an extensive briefing, the creative team immersed themselves in reading speeches, listening to web broadcasts, and reading daily "Newsline" dispatches. Since many of the newscasts are aired in largely Muslim countries, research showed that the old logo, a bell, was seen as a Christian symbol. The slogan "Illuminate Your World" became a leitmotif as the team explored images associated with freedom, leadership, communication, and broadcasting. Following several iterations, five connecting shapes that represented the five continents where RFE/RL broadcasts emerged. The image was tilted to convey action and leadership. Feedback solicited from various delegates further influenced the final design.

*In 2005 Steff Geissbuhler became a founding partner of C&G Partners.

Creative solution

The symbol, a forward-leaning torch, embodies the organization's ideals for communication and truth. The forward motion also represents leadership. The concept was introduced to the delegates through an animated sequence in which the five shapes that make up the symbol morph into flames before taking on the shape of a bird in flight. These are time-honored images of peace and freedom. Global research revealed that a warm orange was the most inviting and least controversial color across cultures. A New Year's card featuring a die-cut torch against a background of flags from the countries where RFE/RL operates was sent out worldwide to announce the new visual identity.

Results

The response by the Broadcast Board of Governors, as well as the individual service bureaus, was spontaneous and positive. The logo was modified for each language, with the new symbol appearing to either the left or the right, depending on the direction in which the alphabet flows. The logo exists in print, on the Internet, and on objects ranging from microphones to promotional items. "The new identity is forward looking and connotes action," observed Dine. "It also illuminates and that, of course, is our mission: to bring accurate and balanced news and information to people who live in restricted, even repressive societies."

RFE/RL needed a universal image that embodied its core values while remaining free of negative connotations in cultures across the globe.

Thomas A. Dine
President
RFE/RL

RFE/RL broadcasts in twenty-eight languages, including eighteen that are spoken by primarily Muslim audiences in the Balkans, the Caucasus, Russia, the Middle East, and central and southwestern Asia.

**The Superman brand goes deeper than the shield.
Authentic. Powerful. Proven. The mark of a hero.***

Project goals

Protect Superman's brand equity.

Clarify brand attributes.

Stimulate licensing opportunities with licensees, retailers, and buyers.

Preserve and grow the iconic value.

Profile : Superman, the brand, is owned and licensed by DC Comics, a subsidiary of Time Warner, and the largest English-speaking publisher of comic books in the world. Superman, the Man of Steel, a cultural icon and multimedia superhero since his 1938 debut, appears in comic strips, movies, television programs, toys, children's clothing, and thousands of other products.

*Excerpt, *Superman Brand Book*

Process and strategy

The release of the movie *Superman Returns* and the brand extensions are designed to saturate the media and the marketplace. David Erwin, Executive Creative Director of Licensing for DC Comics, wanted to ensure that their leading superhero was a well-defined brand that licensees, retailers, and buyers understood and respected. DC Comics hired Little & Company to articulate the Superman brand and stimulate licensing opportunities. The brand book needed to demonstrate that the brand was far greater than the Superman "S" logo. In order to insure a pipeline of quality products aligned with the brand's aspirational attributes, the book also needed to reverberate with quality and inspiration. The creative team included designers, writers, researchers, and archivists.

Creative solution

The Superman Brand Book is an impeccably designed and produced sixty-page hardcover book that feels like a limited edition collector's volume. Iconic imagery is juxtaposed with a strong confident voice and writing. Hold the book in your hands, and the cover reads *Indestructible* while the reader is reintroduced to Superman's inherent heroic qualities, the attributes that define the brand. Turn the book upside down, and the cover reads *Inspirational* and the book demonstrates how the brand can inspire people of all ages to be superheroes in their own lives. In a spread that features a collage of past and present Superman images, the text reads, "A hero for modern times no matter how often these times are reimagined."

Results

Five thousand copies were distributed to the employees of Warner Bros. (DC Comics licensing agent), and to targeted retailers. Bryan Singer, the director of *Superman Returns*, used the brand book to help shape his character development. The book's popularity has propelled the printing of an additional 7,500 copies. DC Comics is proceeding with a family of brand books, including Batman and Wonder Woman.

> Whether it's our internal people, our retail partners, or our licensing partners, people are starting to understand that Superman is more than just a piece of artwork.
>
> David Erwin
> Executive Creative Director
> Licensing
> DC Comics

> Our goal was to inspire marketers, designers, and licensees to incorporate the big ideas behind the Superman brand. Strength. Invincibility. Courage.
>
> Mike Schacherer
> Design Director
> Little & Company

Inspirational

Indestructible

Woven throughout the fabric of our culture.

He doesn't need his cape to fly. Only his will.

A more accessible approach to art was the vision that motivated Tate to take the institution off its pedestal and make art relevant to everyday life, reaching a larger, more diverse audience.

Profile : In the 1990s, Tate was referred to as "The Tate," implying that it had just one location. Three galleries were as architecturally diverse as their collections, which encompass international contemporary art, as well as British art from the 1500s. The opening of the fourth gallery in 2000 provided the impetus to transition Tate from an institution lead to a brand lead organization.

Project goals

Unify the brand without losing each gallery's distinctive properties.

Distinguish diverse locations for visitors.

Express the theme, "one Tate, yet many Tates."

Strengthen the institution's identity.

Articulate a forward-thinking, global, and accessible approach to art.

Position the Tate experience as culture, art, entertainment, and enjoyment.

Tate has moved from being a gallery to being a space where people can experience art, meet, think, learn and eat.

Marina Willer
Creative Director
Wolff Olins

The challenge for any museum is to find a way of combining content, building and experience to tell a coherent story.

Marina Willer
Creative Director
Wolff Olins

Process and strategy

Tate retained Wolff Olins to create a new brand to unify the collections and the four sites. Extensive interviews were conducted to clearly define Tate's opportunity and ambition. Research among visitors and nonvisitors revealed that in the United Kingdom, more people visit museums than attend football matches. Wolff Olins helped Tate discover and articulate its central brand idea.

"Look again, think again," invites visitors to reconsider the experience of a gallery. It also challenges Tate to reevaluate how it speaks to the public about art. The new brand strategy simplified the names of the four museums and dropped the definite article. What was known as the Tate Gallery or London Millbank became Tate Britain.

Creative solution

Instead of one unchanging symbol in a prescribed color consistently applied across all media, Wolff Olins created four dynamic wordmarks, each to be used interchangeably all using the name "Tate" in uppercase lettering and appearing in various degrees of visual focus. The fluidity of form reflects the essence of Tate's point of view.

Allowing flexibility within a unified identity, the design conveys transformation and nonconformity. Tate's luminous and expansive color palette is unpredictable and fresh. In addition Wolff Olins designed a custom-designed typeface called "Tate," which is used for all signatures, for the signage system, and in exhibition signage.

Results

The new brand broadened the appeal of Tate's museums, illuminated the four locations, and positioned Tate globally. In 1999 Tate galleries recorded 4 million visitors. Between 2000 and 2001 more than 7.5 million visited the newly branded Tate Britain, Tate Modern, Tate Liverpool, and Tate St. Ives.

All brand expressions reach out to a wider audience. Large billboards hang in Turbine Hall of Tate Modern advertise existing and upcoming exhibitions. Illuminated exhibition signage at Tate Modern can be read from across the Thames, and exhibition banners hang ceremoniously between the columns at Tate Britain. Wolff Olins designed an online brand toolkit, ensuring that all designers and agencies involved with Tate are in sync with the program.

Tate Museums
Tate Modern
Tate Britain
Tate Liverpool
Tate St. Ives

A successful brand is all about detail. Every facet of a brand must be apparent in an organization's communications, behavior, products, and environment.

Brian Boylan
Chairman
Wolff Olins

Tea's ancient mysterious origins and its ingredients have the power to sooth and energize. Tazo's vision is to promote tea as a blend of history and magic.

Project goals

Introduce a new product in a oversaturated marketplace.

Express the distinctive nature of the products.

Reintroduce tea to Americans.

Create a differentiated brand that reflects the nature of the product.

Position products as genuine and unique.

Develop a niche market for natural, healthy beverages.

Profile : Tazo produces and markets specialty black, green, and herbal infusions of tea in loose, bagged, and bottled packaging. Tazo teas appeared on shelves in 1995 during an explosion of new bottled teas. While tea is the most frequently consumed beverage, aside from water, in most parts of the world, its popularity and perceptions were different in the United States.

Process and strategy

Steve Sandoz, a creative director at the advertising agency Wieden & Kennedy, was retained by Tazo's co-founders. He realized that the positioning was not just about a premium product; it was about creating an aura that would make the tea "otherworldly." Sandoz then introduced the founders to Steve Sandstrom of Sandstrom Design, and the creative process for the brand identity began. Sandoz eventually came up with the made-up word "Tazo." The name seemed to be the perfect mix of the Old World—tea being the oldest beverage in the world, aside from water—and the New World—sophisticated and eclectic.

Sandoz developed a tagline that supported Smith's desire to bring about the rebirth of tea in the United States: "The Reincarnation of Tea." He avoided using generic and traditional names, opting instead to create names that evoked an emotional connection. He called English Breakfast, a caffeinated black tea, Awake, and an herbal noncaffeinated blend, Calm. Other names included Zen, Passion, and Refresh.

Creative solution

Sandstrom designed what seemed like an entire culture with its own language, artifacts, and storytelling. He created a believable antiquity while achieving a dramatic differentiation from existing established premium brands—Twinings and Celestial Seasonings among filtered tea bags, and Snapple among bottled offerings.

Sandstrom did not want to rely on an established typeface and thus developed a highly stylized rendering of the Tazo name based on Exocet, an Émigré typeface designed by Jonathan Barnbrook, that feature characters that looked both foreign (but not affiliated with a foreign country) yet recognizable.

Results

In 1999 Starbucks acquired Tazo to support its ongoing strategy to enhance the customer experience. The civilization that was created as a brand strategy now traces its roots on the website to the ancient Greeks and Babylonians, as well as several Hindi dialects. Tazo continues to create new products and spin its lore combining teas, herbs, and exotic spices with storytelling that is visual and verbal.

The beauty of Tazo is that the brand does deliver, inside and out.

Steve Sandstrom
Creative Director
Sandstrom Design

TiVo's overriding philosophy is that all people, no matter how busy, deserve the opportunity to enjoy the home entertainment of their choosing, at their convenience.*

Profile : In 1997, TiVo was founded by two Silicon Valley engineers, Mike Ramsay and Jim Barton. Now a public company, TiVo has created a seismic shift in the experience of television viewers, allowing them to record, pause, replay, and create their own playlists of their favorite shows. The technology has caused ripples in the advertising world, since it is easy for the user to fast forward through advertising right to the programmed content.

Project goals

Name a company that aspired to change the rules of home entertainment.

Design an identity that appeals to users in the digital living room.

Create an icon as recognizable as Disney's mouse ears.

Focus on the user's desire for fun, convenience, and control.

Create a name that could have brand extensions.

*Mike Ramsay
CEO and Co-Founder
TiVo

The engineering of great products is highly creative, the team was familiar with the feelings of uncertainty that exist before an answer comes and they were comfortable that we would get it right, it's one of the benefits of an "A" level team.

Michael Cronan
Principal
Cronan

TiVo meet iPod. It sounds like a marriage made in techie heaven.

money.cnn.com

Process and strategy

In 1997, Cronan was retained to create a new name and identity for a confidential Silicon Valley project with the code name Teleworld. Michael Cronan, Principal, began by immersion into the new product: understanding its genesis, using it, watching others use it, and framing its cultural context. "Once I began to understand that it could essentially change behavior, I began to ask 'what would the next TV be like?'," said Cronan. Although his team generated over 1,600 names, once Cronan started to envision the next generation of television, he instinctively knew that the name needed to include the T and V. He looked at the visual forms of the letters, integrated an "i" and "o", symbolic of the in and out engineering acronym, and created the fabricated name, TiVo.

Creative solution

Designing the identity was simultaneous with creating brand extensions and a new TiVo culture. Cronan aspired to design an icon "as recognizable as the mouse ears are to Disney." His early sketches were stick figure drawings with television bodies and rabbit ears. An early morning bumpersticker sighting of a Darwinian fish with human legs made Cronan realize the icon needed legs. "Everyone started nodding, and we started thinking about the TiVo identity as a mascot," said Cronan. Explorations into the look and feel of TiVo generated color palettes and other graphic elements. Once there was agreement about the name and the character, an animation team began the work of breathing life into the mascot.

Results

TiVo has become the most popular DVR in the U.S., and cites that its technology fueled "one of the most rapid and enthusiastic adoption rates in the history of consumer electronics." Consumer research has revealed that subscribers fall in love with TiVo, and would sooner disconnect their cell phone than unplug their TiVo. TiVo has recently formed an alliance with Apple and Sony to download television content to mobile devices. Although the business category is being saturated by bigger players, TiVo will always have the first mover advantage.

The first time I used TiVo in my own home, I clicked the button to pause live TV when Karin walked in with the kids. I began to feel, like most TiVo users do, that I wish I could use TiVo's feature set in life outside the box.

Michael Cronan
Principal
Cronan

Unilever's brand is a powerful symbol of our Vitality mission, demonstrating that we stand accountable for the difference we make on a daily basis to our consumers, our employees and the communities and environment in which we operate.*

Profile : Unilever sells 400 food, home care, and personal care products, many of them local brands that can be found only in specific countries. Unilever's portfolio of familiar brands includes Birds Eye, Dove, Hellmann's, Knorr, Lipton, and Ben & Jerry's.

Project goals

Work with leadership to articulate what "One Unilever" stands for.

Identify a core brand idea for a diverse business model.

Design a brand identity aligned with the vision.

Engage the employees, customers, and other stakeholders.

Build an online brand center to tell the story.

*Anthony Burgmans
Niall FitzGerald
Chairmen
Unilever

Vitality brings the opportunity to build a great company: one that seizes the most exciting opportunities, leads on important issues and succeeds as a result.

Patrick Cescau
CEO
Unilever

Process and strategy

While the conglomerate reduced its brand portfolio from 1,600 to 400 brands in 1999, it has remained a vast organization. Unilever, the brand behind the brands, was largely invisible to consumers, known primarily to the investment community. Wolff Olins began working early in 2002 to articulate what the business stood for and to identify an anchor and touchstone for the future. "Through a process of workshops and discussions with the leadership team, the concept of 'vitality' emerged as the idea to build the Unilever brand on," said Ian Stephens, Wolff Olins. It has been captured in the new Unilever mission: "Adding Vitality to Life." The company identified vitality as a consumer motivation for buying Unilever products that help them feel good, look good, and get more out of life. Vitality symbolizes Unilever's commitment to social and environmental responsibility, recognizing that today's consumer examines the behavior of the company behind the brand.

Creative solution

Wolff Olin's creative team designed a new U symbol, composed of twenty-five individual marks, which embodies the vitality theme on many levels. The fish represents products like fish fingers, as well as Unilever's sustainable fish policies. Bees create honey, an ingredient in many food products, and symbolize nature and the environment. Wolff Olins consulted many experts as the brand developed. Religious experts advised changing what was a six-pointed star into the seven-pointed star. Cultural advisors suggested clarifying the hand next to the flower so it could not be mistaken for the sole of a foot, which would cause offense in Thailand. The team checked to see that even seen upside down or reflected in a mirror, none of the icons could be misread as offensive in any language or culture. They worked to obtain the buy-in of hundreds of stakeholders: business leaders worldwide, employees, external opinion makers, investors, and consumers.

Results

The vitality mission and the new identity were launched simultaneously at an annual shareholder meeting, followed by leadership forums around the world. An eighteen-month plan was developed to put the Unilever name and logo on products in supermarkets from Shanghai to Seattle. An online brand center, which told the vitality story and provided identity information, received 100,000 visits within months of its launch.

If Unilever is truly to stand for vitality and if Unilever's employees are truly to embrace the new mission, then the idea has to weave its way into everything that Unilever does: the decisions people make, the new ideas they create, and the future commitments they make.

Unilever has 240,000 employees.

Workplace

Packaging

Training Center

Vanguard's stay-the-course approach to investing adheres to the disciplined, timeless principles of balance, diversification, and a long-term focus, in all market conditions.

Profile : Vanguard, one of the world's largest investment management companies, oversees nearly $900 billion in U.S. mutual fund assets (2005). Its 18 million accounts are established by individual investors, institutions, and financial professionals. Vanguard offers investment products and services, including more than 130 funds, to U.S. investors and 40 additional funds in foreign markets. The company introduced the first index mutual fund for individual investors in 1976.

Project goals

Articulate brand positioning to provide the foundation for strategic marketing communications.

Recommend processes to ensure consistency of brand expressions across business lines and media.

Develop a communications system that integrates design and message.

The value of Vanguard consists almost entirely of an intangible asset—our reputation. We have to be far more conscious about managing the brand than we have been in the past.

Jack Brennan
CEO
Vanguard

The new signature was displayed on every print and digital communication.

Process and strategy

Vanguard needed an enterprise-wide system to develop marketing communications that ensured a consistent brand experience across business lines and media. A multidisciplinary team was formed, representing marketing, research, editorial, design, web, public relations, and legal. Carla Hall Design Group brought an external perspective to the initiative. Documenting the brand was the critical first step. The CEO and eight managing directors created a brand brief to succinctly communicate what the brand stood for, to be applied across business lines, products, and services. The brand consistency team used Vanguard's Six Sigma DMAIC (define, manage, analyze, improve, control) methodology to develop a disciplined approach and benchmark measures for the initiative. A large-scale audit of marketing communications was conducted, measuring the degree of variation around key brand attributes. The team also examined workflows from conception to delivery. The team identified five guiding principles, the foundation for all future marketing communications.

Creative solution

The internal design and editorial team collaborated to develop an integrated, differentiated framework aligned with the new guiding principles. After examining numerous directions, the creative team presented a single strategy to the CEO and managing directors. "Stay the Course," the new creative direction, expressed a consistent and strategic approach to content, design, and architecture across business lines and marketing channels, from the website and advertising, to educational materials. The team recommended using the communicative name "Vanguard" in the refined corporate signature. It also recommended a grid system for print and online materials, key message blocks, color palettes, typographic guidelines, and an approach for imagery. After unanimous approval by senior management, the team began to refine and build the system, the guidelines, and an online branding site.

Results

As a result of Vanguard's brand consistency initiative, the development cycle of marketing programs has been streamlined, integration within and across campaigns has been enhanced, and variation in brand expression has decreased significantly. A function that uses an audit to measure Sigma on every marketing communication has been instituted to oversee the consistency of the brand experience. Processes have been instituted to position the company's programs, products, and services. An online branding site has been launched, and design and message guidelines are available to internal and external creative teams.

There's a perception that Six Sigma is focused solely on eliminating non-value-added steps within a process to help drive costs down. Vanguard took a slightly different view. The team identified value-added steps that were missing from our processes that would help us stay on the mark with consistent expressions.

William McNabb
Managing Director
Vanguard

Company-wide road shows were delivered to build awareness and momentum.

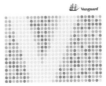

Velfina is dedicated to developing the most innovative solutions in the field of medical products and to responding to the most exacting demands of our clients.*

Profile : Velfina, a Romanian medical company previously known as Actimed Emergency Systems, provides both branded and private label medical products to European and international markets. Its products are used in the treatment and prevention of wounds.

Project goals

Create a brand that supports company growth.

Conduct consumer and competitive research.

Create a new name, brand identity system, and architecture.

Target a new global market.

Perform ongoing brand management activities.

*Costi Braga
CEO
Velfina

It is extraordinary to work with a client that never takes a step without asking what the impact on the brand would be. And, therefore, it is as extraordinary to watch the brand value and the client business grow.

Marius Ursache
Chief Creative Officer
Grapefruit

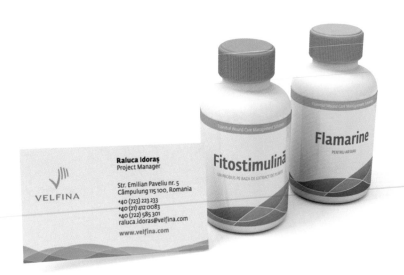

Process and strategy

Grapefruit, a branding firm in Romania, was hired to help Actimed Emergency Systems revitalize its brand to support the growth of the company in new markets. Grapefruit assessed the existing brand and identified opportunities and risks inherent in a launch into the European market. Working closely with the CEO, Grapefruit identified a new set of key values for the brand: innovation, efficiency, and fast response. Following a brand audit and preliminary legal research, Grapefruit discovered that Actimed was already a registered trademark in most of the European Union member states, as well as in the United States, mandating a name change. Grapefruit proposed a name that would communicate the key features of the brand: gentleness and superior care. Following linguistic, cultural, and legal research, Grapefruit suggested more than 150 names that were ultimately short-listed to fit the strategic needs of the brand. Since the target market was multilingual, the final choice needed to be easy to pronounce in a range of languages. Velfina, a fabricated name, is inspired by "velum" meaning veil, or bandage, and "fine," which stands for the ultimate ideal of quality and excellence.

Grapefruit identified the phrase "Professional Wound Care Management" as Velfina's core competency. Communicating a clearly defined niche market helps the company differentiate itself from competitors. Articulating this specialization enabled Velfina to meet demanding market expectations.

Creative solution

Velfina's new logo is the result of extensive creative exploration of symbols in medical research. The chosen symbol represents the brand's niche in wound care management: the caring hand with the veil-like fabric used to make bandages. Grapefruit chose shades of teal and orange to differentiate the brand from Velfina's competitors, which used shades of cool whites. The firm developed Velfina's brand architecture, as well as created a new name (Flamarine), for a subbrand that is an innovative burn-care product. After designing a series of applications, including stationery and marketing collateral, Grapefruit began to design a packaging system. The repetitive pattern on the packaging communicates a young, cutting-edge, and optimistic positioning dramatically different from the competition. The packaging also makes the products look proprietary and not generic.

Results

Although the program is relatively new, the client is tracking income and monitoring the sales of Velfina-branded versus private label sales. Since early 2004 when the new brand was introduced, Velfina's turnover has experienced a 250% yearly growth rate to $2 million in 2004 and an estimated $5 million in 2005 from around $0.8 million in 2003.

Grapefruit is one of the top branding firms in Romania. It founded Wireality (www.wireality.com), an online international forum on branding and identity, and also publishes a weekly blast email called *The Weekly Wire*, featuring the latest news, articles, and trends in branding worldwide.

The Wild Center is alive. As the Natural History Museum of the Adirondacks, it is a basecamp for exploring a 6 million acre collection. It is not 40,000 objects in storage; its living collection is the Adirondacks themselves.

Profile : Situated on a 31-acre campus in Tupper Lake, New York, the museum's main exhibit will follow a river to the summit of a snowcapped mountain and will include waterfalls, a lake exhibit, forests, and streams. Two hundred live animal species will inhabit this living museum. The museum's Great Hall is dominated by a towering ice wall, and its core contains a forest populated with high-definition interactive media.

Project goals

Work collaboratively to define the museum's vision, brand and voice.

Determine positioning and naming strategy.

Design the brand identity.

Write the mission, master plan and exhibit text.

THE W!LD CENTER

Our mission is to inspire a broad public understanding of the natural systems that shape and sustain life in the Adirondacks.

The Adirondacks are unique in the world. Surrounded by people, they house great expanses of nature interspersed with small towns and communities. They can be a model for a future where man and the rest of the natural world find better ways to coexist.

Donald K. Clifford, Jr.
President
The Natural History Museum of the Adirondacks

The museum team included:

Museum project manager and staff

Board of Trustees

HOK, a global architectural practice that specializes in innovation in the built environment, designs museums, wayfinding, and exhibits

Chedd-Angier-Lewis, museum media design and production

ConsultEcon, economic research and management consultants

Points North, communications and branding firm

Process and strategy

Points North Communications worked closely with the project manager, museum staff, Board of Trustees, the architectural and exhibit design team, and the market research group. Points North interviewed board members, scientists, experts on the Adirondacks, and museum staff, and examined the successes and failures of similar institutions. In addition to looking at natural history subjects and Adirondacks-related material, the Points North team interviewed tourism leaders and read their research. The team traveled repeatedly to the Adirondacks to hike and boat—to see what the museum would cover. The team also sat in on every meeting the architects had with the Board to shape the vision of the museum.

Points North was engaged to write the master plan and the mission, and to direct the visual identity program and the naming. The firm subsequently was hired to do all marketing and communications, and to write the text for all of the museum's exhibits. "The exhibit work gives us a chance to speak to the visitor inside the Center, and the marketing work gives us the chance to speak to them before they step inside," said President Howard Fish.

Creative solution

The dynamic symbol design embodies the fundamental essence of nature always changing. The museum logo, drawn by WoodPile Studios, is a fish changing into an otter, to suggest part of life's endless process. In nature, when the otter dies, it will feed the river, which illustrates the connection between the land and the water.

The symbol captured the spirit of the museum and was subsequently used as a guide in the naming process. Originally named the Natural History Museum of the Adirondacks, the team felt that the words "museum" and "history" misrepresented the engaging experience. The New York State Constitution created the forest with a commitment to being "forever wild." The team wanted a name that could be easily said and remembered by visitors who travel from around the world. The Wild Center would be distinguished from other national and world museums and institutions.

Results

The crowd for the groundbreaking ceremony in 2004 was bigger than the crowds for the 1980 Lake Placid Winter Olympics groundbreaking. The museum has exceeded all fund raising targets. Initial surveys reveal that The Wild Center will become the most recognizable brand in the Adirondacks. It is the most successful nonprofit start-up in the history of the Adirondacks.

We were defining the brand while it was still evolving. We had to come up with a solution that would clearly define the museum but not constrict it in the future.

Howard Fish
President
Points North Communications

The symbol also mirrors an aerial view of the museum's location on an oxbow on the Raquette River. The color of the symbol will change with the seasons.

At Zoom®, kids are the stars, the originators, and the authors, in an environment free of adults and commercials. Since Zoom's founding, its driving force has been "by kids, for kids.™"

Profile : Zoom encourages kids to "ask questions, create, experiment and have fun." Zoom is a platform for kids to share their creativity, their ideas, and their opinions, and to take action in their community as volunteers. The website that started as a companion to the television experience keeps Zoom in the lives of kids even though production for the show has ended. An average of 45,000 kids visit the website every day, 15,000 votes are cast each week, and in 2005 it received its 5 millionth submission.

Project goals

Strengthen the "By Kids, for Kids™" message.

Create a more vibrant kids' space for playing, learning, exploring, and talking.

Simplify and unify navigation.

Make the website more current, dynamic, and expandable.

Build on viewer feedback.

Dear Zoom

I think your shows are awesome. Your website came in handy when my cousins came over to visit. Especially when I have 6 of them! Your web site helped me plan my day! Our day was a blast...

Heather, age 11, from North Carolina

We at the Boys and Girls Club of Yellowstone County, in Billings, MT watched your video of you building the Super Golf Tower. In it you built your tower reaching a total of 132 cm. You challenged the viewers to beat that and we accomplished it.

If you could ask your pet anything, what would it be?

I would ask my pet how he is doing up in heaven and what it is like.
Dakota from Chicago

I would ask my pet fish 'How's it going in there?'
Olivia, age 8, Spanish Fork

How come when Dad throws the ball you look the other way?
Rose, age 7, Williamstown

The new 1,000-plus-page website has seventy areas that are updated continually with kids' submissions.

Process and strategy

In 2003 an internal team of interactive media producers, content developers, designers, and technologists developed user profiles based on the results of user testing, online surveys, and kids' feedback since 1999. In the years since it was first designed, there has been a growing desire by kids to do community-oriented things online, and to interact and share with each other through the website. The wealth of viewer feedback revealed that Zoomers (the kids) want the website to be even more engaging, funny, and cool, with more games and information about the cast members. Content developers worked collaboratively with the design team to amplify Zoom's wacky essence and to make the interface more compelling. Outdated technical aspects of the site were re-engineered.

Zoom Website User Types

Show activity seeker

Send it to ZOOM/join-in kid

Interested in cast kid

Game player

Interested in behind the scenes kid

Grab and go kid/offline activity seeker

Creative solution

The "By Kids, for Kids" message was strengthened by bringing up kids' voices and covering the site with bolder, specific calls to action. There were more features about the cast, taking users behind the scenes of the show to learn about their role models. The site was restructured into nine main content areas based on the user expectations outlined in each of the user profiles. The playful feeling was enhanced with a simpler and more exuberant color palette. Rotating highlights and small animations make the site feel more current and dynamic. New games, gizmos and downloads were developed: 3 Puck Chuck teaches kids about Newton's law of motion and physics; Kitchen Chemistry teaches about acids and bases; and Goldberger to Go teaches about the design process of mechanical engineering.

Results

The new 1,000-plus-page website has seventy areas that are updated regularly with submissions from kids. Web traffic continues to grow exponentially, with kids returning to the site independent of any experience with the television show. WGBH continues to create measurable change in viewers' science process skills and understanding. Beyond the website Zoom encourages kids to participate by distributing its Zoom Into Action Family Guide to Volunteering and Zoom Into Action Conservation Guide through museums, after-school programs, and Boys and Girls Clubs nationwide.

The website is every kid's own ZOOM studio space where they can create, play, and share with each other. We're just here to do the equivalent of effective parenting—to give kids a safe and monitored environment that not only allows but directly asks them to take the lead in their own learning and growing.

Meredith Nierman
Producer
WGBH Interactive

ZOOM is its audience—the kids—and our design goals needed to reflect that.

Katie Caldwell
Designer
WGBH Interactive

Advertising + branding

1890: Henry John Heinz markets a line of foods and uses the number 57 as a symbol for his company's variety of products.

1893: Aunt Jemima character is created.

1893: Coca-Cola trademark is registered.

1898: Bibendum, the Michelin Man, is designed.

1898: N. W. Ayer & Son is the first ad agency to create an in-house design department.

1904: Shell Transport and Trading Company (Shell Oil) selects a scallop shell as its trademark.

1911: Morton Salt Girl trademark is introduced.

1911: Procter & Gamble becomes the first company to pay an external agency, J. Walter Thompson, to launch the shortening Crisco.

1916: J. Walter Thompson coins the phrase "It pays to advertise."

1917: BMW logo is designed.

1921: General Mills introduces Betty Crocker in its ad campaigns. Her character becomes the company's trademark in 1947.

1921: J. Walter Thompson hires eminent behavioral psychologist John B. Watson to help with consumer research. He subsequently develops the blindfold testing for advertising.

1930: *Advertising Age* magazine is launched in Chicago.

1931: Brand manager system is developed within Procter & Gamble.

1941: Landor Associates is founded and becomes one of the leading graphic identity firms in the United States.

1949: Bill Bernbach and Ned Doyle establish the advertising agency Doyle Dane Bernbach in New York and devise the concept and creation of "creative teams" that include copywriters and art directors.

1951: CBS "eye" is designed by William Golden.

1954: CBS becomes the largest medium for advertising in the world.

1959: NASA logo is designed by James Modarelli.

Events that shaped the evolution of brand, design, brand identity, advertising, packaging, and technology

1890 → **1910** → **1930** →

Media + technology

1890 Ty Tolbert Lanston invents the Monotype typesetting machine.

1923 Arthur Nielson, Sr. creates innovations in performance measurement and media research.

1932 The *Chase & Sanborn Hour* premieres on the radio in a variety/comedy format.

1938 Chester Carlson invents xerography.

1947 *Meet the Press* premieres on NBC's local Washington station and goes network within several weeks.

1948 A poll shows that 68 percent of television viewers remember the names of the programs' sponsors.

1957 *Hidden Persuaders* written by Vance Packard.

BIBLIOGRAPHY

Heller, Steven, and Elinor Pettit. *Graphic Design Time Line: A Century of Design Milestones.* New York: Allworth Press, 2000.

"Graphic Design and Advertising Timeline," *Communication Arts* 41, 1 (1999): 80–95.

1960: International Paper logo designed by Lester Beall.

1961: United Parcel Service (UPS) logo designed by Paul Rand.

1963: American Broadcast Company (ABC) logo designed by Paul Rand.

1964: Mobil Corporation corporate ID program designed by Chermayeff & Geismar.

1965: Exxon oil company logo designed by Raymond Loewy.

1965: Wolff Olins, a British identity firm, is founded in London.

1965: The Pillsbury doughboy trademark is created by Leo Burnett Company.

1967: Levi's logo is designed by Landor and Associates.

1971: Nike swoosh logo is designed by a student, Carol Davidson.

1972: Paul Rand adds stripes to the IBM logotype.

1975: I LOVE NY designed by Milton Glaser.

1975: Thomas J. Watson Jr., president of IBM, delivers the speech "Good Design Is Good Business" at the Wharton School of Business.

1976: Architect and designer Richard Saul Wurman coins "information architecture."

1977: Apple Computer logo is designed by Rob Janoff.

1985: Bass & Associates designs AT&T logo.

1995: TAZO tea line is designed by Sandstrom Design.

1995: David Aaker wrote *Building Strong Brands*.

1999: *The Experience Economy* written by B. Joseph Pine II and James H. Gilmore.

2000: BP designed by Landor Associates.

2001: Tom Peters wrote *Brand You*.

2001: VSA Partners names Cingular and designs identity.

2002: *The Tipping Point* written by Malcolm Gladwell.

2003: *The Brand Gap* written by Marty Neumeier.

2003: Target redefines big box stores.

2004: *Dictionary of Brand* published by AIGA and edited by Marty Neumeier.

1960	1970	1980	1990	2005

1963 Digital Equipment Corporation unveils the first "mini-computer."

1965 International Business Machines (IBM) develops a method for digitally storing type.

1970 The first digitized photographs are introduced.

1971 Intel Corporation develops the microprocessor.

1972 Texas Instruments develops the pocket calculator.

1973 The first fax machines are introduced for commercial use.

1973 The Internet is developed for use by the U.S. Department of Defense.

1977 Apple Computer introduces the Apple II, the first personal computer with color graphics capabilities.

1977 Hewlett-Packard introduces a portable mini-computer.

1980 The compact disc is introduced by Philips Electronics.

1981 Bitstream, the first digital type foundry, is established by Matthew Carter and Mike Parker.

1981 IBM introduces the first personal computer (PC).

1981 Computerized page layout programs are developed.

1982 Apple Computer introduces "Lisa," the first personal computer with a graphical user interface (GUI).

1984 First one-megabyte memory chip is introduced.

1984 Apple Computer unveils the Macintosh, the mouse-driven computer with a graphical user interface.

1985 Adobe Systems introduces PostScript, the programming language that describes the appearance of the printed page.

1986 Adobe Systems releases its drawing program, Illustrator.

1988 The Canon color laser copier is introduced.

1990 Adobe Systems introduces its electronic imaging program, PhotoShop.

1995 Netscape (formerly Mosaic Communications Corporation) goes public.

1998 Apple Computer introduces the iMac.

1998 Joan Blades and Wes Boyd launch MoveOn.org.

1999 Personal computers are owned by nearly half of all U.S. households.

2001 Paul Saffo, director Institute of the Future, names this "the decade of remote sensing."

2003 Mobile phones become marketing channels.

2004 Cheskin develops digital ethnography.

2005 iPods become the necessary lifestyle accessorty.

2005 Blogs become mainstream.

Aaker, David A., and Erich Joachimsthaler. *Brand Leadership*. New York: The Free Press, 2000.

Aaker, David. *Brand Portfolio Strategy*. New York: The Free Press, 2004.

AdamsMorioka. *Logo Design Workbook: A Hands- On Guide to Creating Logos*. Gloucester: Rockport, 2004.

"A Discussion with Chris Hacker," *Enlightened Brand Journal*, www.enlightenedbrand.com.

Advertising Metrics, www.marketingterms.com.

AIArchitect, "Best Practices, Center for Health Design Releases Findings on How Design Can Improve the Standard of Care in Health-Care Facilities," February 2005.

Baker, Stephen, "Looking for a Blog in a Haystack," *BusinessWeek*, July 25, 2005.

Beckwith, Harry. *Selling the Invisible*. New York: Warner Books, 1997.

Blake, George Burroughs, and Nancy Blake-Bohne. *Crafting the Perfect Name: The Art and Science of Naming a Company or Product*. Chicago: Probus Publishing Company, 1991.

Bruce-Mitford, Miranda. *The Illustrated Book of Signs & Symbols*. New York: DK Publishing, Inc., 1996.

Buell, Barbara, "Can a Global Brand Speak Different Languages?," *Stanford Business*, August 2000.

Business attitudes to design. www.design-council.org.uk.

Calver, Giles. *What Is Packaging Design?* Switzerland: RotoVision, 2004.

Carlzon, Jan. *Moments of Truth*. New York: Harper Collins, 1987.

Carter, David E. *Branding: The Power of Market Identity*. New York: Hearst Books International, 1999.

Carter, Rob, Ben Day, and Philip Meggs. *Typographic Design: Form and Communication*. New York: John Wiley & Sons, Inc., 1993.

Chermayeff, Ivan, Tom Geismar, and Steff Geissbuhler. *Trademarks Designed by Chermayeff & Geismar*. Basel, Switzerland: Lars Muller Publishers, 2000.

Conway, Lloyd Morgan. *Logo, Identity, Brand, Culture*. Crans-Pres-Celigny, Switzerland: RotoVision SA, 1999.

"Crowned at Last: A Survey of Consumer Power." *The Economist*, April 2, 2005.

DeNeve, Rose. *The Designer's Guide to Creating Corporate I.D. Systems*. Cincinnati, OH: North Light Books, 1992.

Duffy, Joe. *Brand Apart*. New York: One Club Publishing, 2005.

Ehrbar, Al. "Breakaway Brands," *Fortune*, October 31, 2005.

Eiber, Rick, ed. *World Trademarks: 100 Years*, Volumes I and II. New York: Graphis U.S., Inc., 1996.

"Fighting Dragons and Lightening Skin; Two Companies Go to Asia," Minnesota Public Radio, May 16, 2005.

Gardner, Bill, and Fishel, Cathy. *Logo Lounge: 2000 Identities by Leading Designers*. Gloucester: Rockport, 2003.

Gladwell, Malcolm. *The Tipping Point: How Little Things Can Make a Big Difference*. New York: Little, Brown and Company, 2000.

Glaser, Milton. *Art Is Work*. Woodstock, NY: The Overlook Press, 2000.

Godin, Seth. *Purple Cow: Transforming Your Business By Being Remarkable*. New York: Portfolio, 2003.

Gobe, Marc. *Emotional Branding, The New Paradigm for Connecting Brands to People*. New York: Allworth Press, 2001.

Grant, John. *The New Marketing Manifesto: The 12 Rules for Building Successful Brands in the 21st Century*. London: Texere Publishing Limited, 2000.

"Graphic Design and Advertising Timeline," *Communication Arts* 41, 1 (1999): 80–95.

Heller, Steven. *Paul Rand*. London: Phaidon Press Limited, 1999.

Hart, Susannah and John Murphy, eds. *Brands: The New Wealth Creators*. New York: Palgrave, 1998.

Heller, Steven, and Elinor Pettit. *Graphic Design Time Line: A Century of Design Milestones*. New York: Allworth Press, 2000.

Hill, Sam, and Chris Lederer. *The Infinite Asset: Managing Brands to Build New Value*. Boston: Harvard Business School Press, 2001.

Hine, Thomas. *The Total Package: The Evolution and Secret Meanings of Boxes, Bottles, Cans, and Tubes*. Boston: Little, Brown and Company, 1995.

The History of Printmaking. New York: Scholastic Inc., 1995.

Holtzschue, Linda. *Understanding Color: An Introduction for Designers*. New York: John Wiley & Sons, Inc., 2002.

Javed, Naseem. *Naming for Power: Creating Successful Names for the Business World*. New York: Linkbridge Publishing, 1993.

Joachimsthaler, Erich, David A. Aaker, John Quelch, David Kenny, Vijay Vishwanath, and Mark Jonathan. *Harvard Business Review on Brand Management*. Boston: Harvard Business School Press, 1999.

Klein, Naomi. *No Logo*. New York: Picador, 2002.

Kerzner, Harold. *Project Management: A Systems Approach to Planning, Scheduling, and Controlling*. New York: Van Nostrand Reinhold, 1989.

Landa, Robin. *Designing Brand Experiences: Creating Powerful Integrated Brand Solutions*. Clifton Park: Thomson Delmar Learning, 2005

Lippincott Mercer. *Sense: The Art and Science of Creating Lasting Brands*. Gloucester: Rockport, 2004.

Lipton, Ronnie. *Designing Across Cultures*. New York: How Design Books, 2002.

Lubliner, Murray J. *Global Corporate Identity: The Cross-Border Marketing Challenge*. Rockport, MA: Rockport Publishers, Inc., 1994.

Man, John. *Alpha Beta: How Our Alphabet Shaped the Western World*. London: Headline Book Publishing, 2000.

Meggs, Philip B. *A History of Graphic Design*. New York: John Wiley & Sons, Inc., 1998.

Mok, Clement. *Designing Business: Multiple Media, Multiple Disciplines*. San Jose, CA: Macmillan computer publishing USA, 1996.

Mollerup, Per. *Marks of Excellence: The History and Taxonomy of Trademarks*. London: Phaidon Press Limited, 1997.

Napoles, Veronica. *Corporate Identity Design*. New York: John Wiley & Sons, Inc., 1988.

Neumeier, Marty. *The Dictionary of Brand*. New York: The AIGA Press, 2004.

Neumeier, Marty. *Brand Gap: How to Bridge the Distance between Business Strategy and Design*. Berkeley: New Riders, 2003.

Newark, Quentin. *What Is Graphic Design*? Switzerland: RotoVision, 2002.

Ogilvy, David. *Ogilvy on Advertising*. New York: Crown Publishers, 1983.

Olins, Wally. *Corporate Identity: Making Business Strategy Visible Through Design*. Boston: Harvard Business School Press, 1989.

Olins, Wally. *On Brand*. New York: Thames & Hudson, 2003.

Paos, ed. *New Decomas: Design Conscious Management Strategy*. Seoul: Design House Inc., 1994.

Pavitt, Jane, ed. *Brand New*. London: V&A Publications, 2000.

Pentagram. *Pentagram Book Five*. New York: Monacelli Press, 1999.

Perry, Alicia with David Wisnom III. *Before the Brand: Creating the Unique DNA of an Enduring Brand Identity*. New York: The McGraw-Hill Companies, 2003.

Peters, Tom. *Reinventing Work: The Brand You 50*. New York: Alfred A. Knopf, Inc, 1999.

Phillips, Peter L. *Creating the Perfect Design Brief*. New York: Allworth Press, 2004.

Pine II, B. Joseph and James H. Gilmore. *The Experience Economy*. Boston: Harvard Business School Press, 1999.

Remington, R. Roger. *Lester Beall: Trailblazer of American Graphic Design*. New York: W. W. Norton & Company, 1996.

Ries, Al, and Laura Ries. *The 22 Immutable Laws of Branding*. London: Harper Collins Business, 2000.

Ries, Al, and Jack Trout. *Positioning: The Battle for Your Mind*. New York: Warner Books, Inc., 1986.

Rogener, Stefan, Albert-Jan Pool, and Ursula Packhauser. *Branding with Type: How Type Sells*. Mountain View, CA: Adobe Press, 1995.

Roush, Wade. "Social Machines," *MIT's Magazine of Innovation, Technology Review*, August 2005.

Scher, Paula. *Make It Bigger*. New York: Princeton Architectural Press, 2002.

Schmitt, Bernd. *Customer Experience Management*. New York: John Wiley & Sons, Inc., 2003.

Schmitt, Bernd, and Alex Simnoson. *Marketing Aesthetics: The Strategic Management of Brands, Identity, and Image*. New York: Free Press, 1997.

Sharp, Harold S. *Advertising Slogans of America*. Metuchen, NJ: The Scarecrow Press, 1984.

Spiekerman, Erik, and E. M. Ginger. *Stop Stealing Sheep & Find Out How Type Works*. Mountain View, CA: Adobe Press, 1993.

Sweet, Fay. *MetaDesign: Design from the World Up*. New York: Watson-Guptill Publications, 1999.

Traverso, Debra Koontz. *Outsmarting Goliath: How to Achieve Equal Footing with Companies That are Bigger, Richer, Older, and Better Known*. Princeton, NJ: Bloomberg Press, 2000.

Vogelstein Fred, "Yahoo's Brilliant Solution," *Fortune*, August 8, 2005.

Williams, Gareth. *Branded? Products and Their Personalities*. London: V&A Publications, 2000.

Yamashita, Keith, and Sandra Spataro. *Unstuck*. Portfolio, 2004.

Miscellaneous Credits

Motorola RAZR and Motorola logo are reproduced with permission from Motorola, Inc. ©2005 Motorola, Inc.

Alina Wheeler: designer, consultant, speaker

Alina Wheeler applies a dynamic process to help enterprises express their brands. Her clients include entrepreneurial companies and foundations whose leaders embrace the future. Wheeler collaborates with strategists, designers, and managers, seizing every opportunity to build brands and provide compelling customer experiences.

Wheeler speaks frequently to management and creative teams in companies, as well as to business and design students at universities. She introduces branding fundamentals, identifies brand trends, and connects their relationship to innovation and business.

For speaking inquiries, please email:
speaker@alinawheeler.com

To provide feedback on the book, please email:
author@alinawheeler.com

Wheeler is currently working on her new book, *Managing Perception or Why the King Wore Turquoise.*

My business is managing perception. My service is strategic imagination. My passion is brand identity.

Alina Wheeler